# Organizational Self-Assessment

# Organizational Self-Assessment

**Tito Conti**

TQM
Ivrea, Italy

**CHAPMAN & HALL**

London · Weinheim · New York · Tokyo · Melbourne · Madras

**Published by**
**Chapman & Hall, 2–6 Boundary Row, London SE1 8HN, UK**

Chapman & Hall, 2–6 Boundary Row, London SE1 8HN, UK

Chapman & Hall GmbH, Pappelallee 3, 69469 Weinheim, Germany

Chapman & Hall USA, 115 Fifth Avenue, New York, NY 10003, USA

Chapman & Hall Japan, ITP-Japan, Kyowa Building, 3F, 2-2-1 Hirakawacho, Chiyoda-ku, Tokyo 102, Japan

Chapman & Hall Australia, 102 Dodds Street, South Melbourne, Victoria 3205, Australia

Chapman & Hall India, R. Seshadri, 32 Second Main Road, CIT East, Madras 600 035, India

First edition 1997

© 1997 Tito Conti

Typeset in 10/12 pt Times by Cambrian Typesetters, Frimley, Surrey

Printed in Great Britain by Hartnolls Ltd, Bodmin, Cornwall

ISBN 0 412 78880 2

A catalogue record for this book is available from the British Library

Library of Congress catalog card number 96–71791

∞ Printed on acid-free text paper, manufactured in accordance with ANSI/NISO Z39.48-1984 and ANSI/NISO Z39.48-1992 (Permanence of Paper).

# Contents

# Foreword

During the 1980s, companies in the United States were strongly and often successfully challenged by foreign competition. In order to respond to this challenge and recognizing the crucial role of quality in obtaining a competitive edge, the Malcolm Baldrige National Quality Award was established in 1988. The underlying criteria can be used by any organization that wishes to evaluate its quality improvement efforts with a view to increasing its productivity and competitiveness.

Around this time, Europe also came under pressure from mostly Asian competitors who, in contrast with previous years, now offered top quality goods at aggressive prices. Seeking to meet this challenge, 14 leading European companies took the initiative to form the European Foundation for Quality Management (EFQM), recognizing the potential of the Total Quality concept for regaining their competitive advantage. As a founding member of the EFQM board I strongly supported the aim of the foundation to create a model of business excellence tailor-made to the European entrepreneurial spirit: the European Model for Total Quality Management, against which companies could assess their performance, identify their strengths and weaknesses, and take measures to improve their results. The elements 'Impact on Society' and 'Business Results' were given a prominent place in the European model because we believe that a company has to satisfy the expectations of all stakeholders, making sure that, at the same time, superior business result and a lasting competitive edge are achieved.

Tito Conti was a key contributor to this model, both with his keen analytical abilities and his creative ideas, backed by an immense practical and research experience. In the present book, Conti undertakes to achieve several objectives:

- to explain the role of self-assessments as a diagnostic tool covering the whole organization and involving all stakeholders
- to explain the self-diagnosis process and how the results should be interpreted

- to demonstrate the value of cross-diagnosis as a key element
- to develop a methodology of introducing self-assessments in an organization and integrating it into the company's planning cycle.

The most important objective, however, is to examine to what extent the European TQM model as it exists today meets the new needs as they have emerged over the years and to suggest appropriate modifications.

He succeeds brilliantly in achieving these challenging objectives, thanks to his extensive knowledge and experience of the subject of Total Quality, and through his clear hands-on explanations supported by detailed figures.

We have all observed and even personally felt the changes taking place during this last part of the 20th century. What bothers many of us is the perceived complexity of these changes coupled with the unprecedented speed of change – what recently has been called: 'The speeding up of history'! We are all conscious of the fact that we are clearly in a transition 'away from something' but it is not so evident what we are moving *towards*. It is the responsibility of leaders in business to try to imagine the scenarios of the future and then to adapt current strategies to ensure profitable survival in a new environment. In this endeavour it is important that we work with instruments that are geared to the latest changes: we cannot assess the performance of a business at the end of the 1990s with a reference model dating from the late 1980s.

Dr Tito Conti succeeds admirably in showing where the European TQM model needs adaptation to take account of recent developments if it is to continue playing a useful role in the future. I can highly recommend his book to all managers who wish to use the self-assessment process as a powerful tool to improve the competitiveness and ensure the future success of their businesses.

Heini Lippuner
Former President and Chief Operating Officer of Ciba-Geigy
Member of the board of Novartis

# Introduction

Organizations can be assessed from different points of view, in relation to a wide variety of characteristics and objectives. In this book, assessment involves an analysis of the organization's ability to achieve its missions and goals, in particular its ability to maintain and improve competitiveness in a changing scenario. A systematic process, which is conducted at set intervals, assessment aims to identify the weaknesses – in processes as well as in systemic factors – that can stunt the company's competitive growth, so that improvements in critical capabilities can be planned concurrently with improvements in performance goals. The terms 'self-assessment' and 'self-diagnosis' do not mean that the company performs the assessment entirely with its own resources – indeed, organizations are rarely able to identify their weaknesses on their own – they indicate that the company is the active subject of the assessment; it will employ all the external and internal resources it considers necessary, but will not outsource responsibility for a process that is so closely linked to its key strategic decisions. This point needs to be clarified, since it continues to cause confusion. The view that third-party assessments, such as quality award assessments, are more reliable than self-assessments because the company is scrutinized by an independent observer is true only if the self-assessment is poorly planned, or if management is unwilling to listen to the findings of consultants it has paid to investigate the true state of the company. If anything, the opposite is true: in self-assessment, management can employ the services of external resources whose expertise is far greater than that generally available for the award assessments; and it can retain these resources for as long as it takes to collect, analyse and interpret information (reading a report and conducting a three- or four-day site visit may be a sufficient assessment for an award, but it will certainly not provide a reliable *diagnostic* picture of the company's weaknesses). Naturally, to ensure reliability, management must allow the self-assessment to be conducted in a fully independent manner. As the book observes, the main role of management is to 'listen': to its customers and stakeholders, to its processes and to the people who work in the organization, at every level.

The process described here transcends the quality assessment from which it was originally derived to embrace the full range of company goals and the entire company system. It is neither a 'certification' nor an assessment of the type used by the quality awards, because it serves an entirely different purpose. Today, there is a growing tendency to adopt the assessment approach used by the awards for self-assessment, so it should be pointed out straightaway that the approach described here is quite different. It has been conceived and developed for the sole purpose of enabling the company to identify its weaknesses – and strengths – in relation to its goals; to plan the necessary improvements/renewal in its capabilities; to integrate assessment into the corporate strategic and operating planning process. In other words, it is not a by-product of tools that have been designed for other purposes. The approach depends on the objective. If the objective is an award, or even just a comparison with other companies, the approach will inevitably focus on scoring and neglect diagnostic considerations (my long years of experience confirm this: once management has paid the necessary lip service to self-assessment, its main interest will be the numbers game).

This then is the main reason for this book: to present an assessment approach that has been specifically designed as a diagnostic tool and is closely related to company planning. It does not, of course, presume to offer a definitive solution to the problem. This is *one* solution, and may lead to others. Hopefully, the book will stimulate debate, research and experimentation on an issue of vital importance to the business community. It moves out of the mainstream, which still pays little attention to self-assessment and always presents it as a by-product of the awards. The book will have achieved its goal if it helps to establish self-assessment as an important management tool in its own right and encourages research and experimentation.

The above remarks explain what this book sets out to achieve and the need it fills. But perhaps a few more comments are necessary to demonstrate why a new approach to self-assessment is so essential. Consider what has happened with ISO 9000 certification and risks happening with the quality awards. Some of the very same people and organizations who used to extol certification as a magic formula to improve efficiency and competitiveness, in a dogmatic fashion that brooked no criticism, now evangelize TQM, the awards and related self-assessment (or vice versa, as is happening in the USA). These 'infatuations' probably stem from an incurable tendency to give image and form priority over substance. They are fuelled by a coalescence of different interests: the interests of those managers who put their faith in these miracle cures and fail to make the effort to see what lies beneath the external image; the interests of the standards bodies or the award organizers or the quality associations, who inevitably wish to maintain a key role; the interests of consultants, who have to keep up with the latest trends and the new business opportunities they bring. The results that have been achieved should lead us to ask who is looking after the interests of our companies. In the case of certification, the risk of throwing the baby out with the bathwater is only too real: some of the new 'TQM extremists' (the most dangerous enemies of TQM) apparently want to get rid of quality assurance together with certification (not realizing that quality assurance is a fundamental element of TQM). These swings are the typical products of extremism with no cultural moorings (where are all the learning organizations?) and of fashion (I refer to the fanatics and not, of course, to the many professionals around the world who have made serious attempts to understand and implement the extremely positive concepts of Total Quality Management). Current events suggest that, unless we adjust our course, TQM and the awards will soon lose their appeal. And not because of any intrinsic failings, but because of the relentless determination to pursue 'all that glitters', to serve vested interests and obtain rapid (but often equally ephemeral) returns in terms of image.

Many companies compete for a quality award, others plan to do so in the future, still others accept what they are told, that they can measure themselves reliably using the assessment criteria adopted by the awards. They should, however, be aware of the risks, in order to avoid them and to ensure that the awards retain the role and prestige that they merit. We have already mentioned the first risk – a real risk in my opinion – which is the obsession with numbers: my company's score compared with the best-in-class; the score of one corporate division compared with another. Many companies become hopelessly addicted to the numbers game. Somewhat provocatively, perhaps, my model does not weight the various categories, although it discusses weighting and provides an example in Section 3.4. The second risk is that companies competing for an award may make special cosmetic adjustments to meet the requirements of the model, rather than introduce long-term measures of real substance. The book reflects my firm belief that self-assessment can be an extremely important tool to improve company performance; that the risks of the latest fashionable trends should be made clear; that companies should be offered the most effective tools possible.

The model used by the self-assessment approach described here could be defined as a *third-generation* model, as distinct from the TQM models developed in the 1980s, which can be regarded as *first-generation* models, and the TQM models of the awards, typically the Malcolm Baldrige National Quality Award (MBNQA) and the European Quality Award (EQA), which are *second-generation* models. The latter are still TQM models rather than fully fledged 'business models' designed to express the dynamics of the organization. The EQA model, with its 'enablers' and 'results' structure, is a link between the second and third generations, but in my opinion further adjustments are needed to complete the transition: the right side of the model should be reviewed in terms of 'missions/goals', a separate central processes block is required, and further additions should be made to the left-hand systemic factors block. But the main feature that distinguishes my proposal from current practice is its strongly diagnostic ('right–left') approach.

The book is divided into two parts: the actual text, in seven chapters, and two appendices. The first appendix is almost a second book: a step-by-step practical guide to the self-assessment approach described in the first seven chapters. The second appendix, a revised version of a paper I presented at the EOQ Congress in Lausanne in 1995, is a detailed discussion of the logical development of the model. Readers interested in this aspect may wish to begin by reading this appendix. It has not been included in the main text, since many readers will want to get straight down to the central theme and then perhaps return for a more detailed discussion at a later stage. This leads me to suggest a first-time reading order, for people who simply wish to understand the main concepts: Chapters 1 and 2; Chapter 3, omitting Sections 3.4 and 3.5.3; the introduction to Chapter 4; Chapters 6 and 7. Readers involved in company assessment should find Appendix A particularly useful, because it describes the self-assessment path in full detail, and also notes similarities and differences with the EQA and MBNQA approaches. The methodologies described to assess, first, results and, second, processes are particularly important and quite innovative. Furthermore, the criteria suggested for assessment of 'leadership' and the company organization category (whose name, 'organizational architectures', underlines the fact that the assessment looks at the fundamental organizational decisions that have a decisive impact on efficiency and effectiveness, not at organization charts) offer significant added value in relation to traditional assessment approaches.

Finally, I should like to express my gratitude to Bernardo de Sousa, Franco Raiteri and Luciano Rattin, with whom I have frequently discussed these themes, for generously offering to read the manuscript and providing me with their perceptive comments and advice. I am especially grateful to Heini Lippuner, for agreeing to write the foreword to the book. A former President and Chief Operating Officer of Ciba-Geigy, champion of Total Quality Management in Europe and promoter of the European Quality Award, Mr Lippuner is a successful and enlightened European executive who closely follows corporate competitiveness issues. My warmest thanks for his words, which accurately interpret the purpose of my book.

# From quality audits to self-assessment/self-diagnosis in relation to the company's missions

## 1

Organizations decide to assess themselves, or have themselves assessed, for a variety of reasons. Traditionally, most corporate assessments stem from the concept of the audit: the organization has introduced a set of rules to enable it to achieve certain goals and wishes to make sure, through a specific audit, that those rules are correctly applied. The audit originated in the financial field: *Webster's New World Dictionary* defines it as 'A regular examination and checking of accounts or financial records; a settlement or adjustment of accounts; or a final statement of accounts'. Its use subsequently spread to other fields such as quality and the environment. The main features of the audit are reference to set rules or performance standards; application of set assessment or measurement criteria; implementation by a third party; inference of conclusions about all the activities being audited from statistical samples [1]. The audit can therefore be extended to all corporate activities that are governed by set rules, such as personnel management or logistics; indeed, most large companies have a corporate audit function, which is responsible for guaranteeing correct operation in all fields the company considers to be of critical importance.

As the concept of quality assurance [2] has developed, the importance of quality audits has grown. Quality audits can be sub-divided into product audits, process audits and system audits. In the last 30 years or so, system audits in particular have been widely used in the quality-assurance field, especially since the appearance of the ISO 9000 standards in 1987. This book looks at assessments that originated from quality audits but later developed separately, with their own distinguishing characteristics, as general self-assessments or self-diagnoses covering the whole company and involving all its employees. This type of self-assessment/self-diagnosis is designed to describe the company's situation and potential – its capabilities – in relation to its missions. It therefore has a far broader scope than the conventional quality assessment. The ultimate goal is to identify weaknesses and strengths so that action can be planned to bring the company's capabilities into line with its missions and goals.

Since audits check compliance with pre-specified rules and performance standards in well-regulated areas of the company, they are usually concerned with tangible characteristics, which can be measured or otherwise assessed with a fair degree of objectivity. The situation is different with the self-assessment/self-diagnosis processes examined in this book, which aspire to cover the entire corporate system. Achieving this level of coverage clearly involves conceptual difficulties of a much more complex nature, due both to the dimensions of the object being assessed and, above all, to the fact that self-assessment/self-diagnosis brings into play many *intangible* characteristics, which are extraordinarily difficult to measure or even just to assess. The management and human resources sub-systems are typical examples of areas where intangible factors prevail. On the other hand, the differences between excellent companies and the rest are largely based on intangibles; thus any attempt at global assessment must necessarily take such intangibles into account.

All assessments have to refer to models. The main challenge raised by the global approach to company assessment is to define an appropriate model. The assessment will be significant only if the model is significant. Flexibility is the guiding principle here. The model must be an interpretation of reality, a 'working hypothesis' to be used until a better interpretation is found. Consistency with results must be checked daily. The current tendency to 'freeze' assessment models is therefore more than a little alarming. If a TQM model is incorporated in an international standard, it does not matter how non-prescriptive that standard is declared to be: the model will be interpreted in a rigid, dogmatic fashion by the numerous ranks of those whose main concern is to avoid the risks associated with change. And it will be frozen for years. Although the models used by the quality awards are less rigid than standards, they too may fail to keep in step with self-assessment needs, partly because companies tend to apply them as they stand, without making allowances for their particular situation, and partly because the award bodies are, naturally, more sensitive to the requirements of the awards than to the complexities and dynamic nature of self-assessment.

This book looks at global corporate assessment for the purposes of improvement. Since the company itself performs the assessment, the process is known as *self-assessment*. Since the goal is improvement planning, the approach is highly diagnostic; thus the term *self-diagnosis* may also be used. In order to clarify the basic concepts of self-assessment, this first chapter offers a critical historical analysis of the evolution from the quality audit to global corporate self-assessment.

## 1.1 THE EVOLUTION OF QUALITY: THE SYSTEMIC VIEW OF ACTIVITIES IN THE PRODUCT LIFE CYCLE

A fundamental advance in the evolution of quality was the introduction of the concept of the product life cycle. This generated a systemic view of the various activities relating to the product: development, production engineering and management, marketing, support, phase-out; that is, all the activities that begin with the idea for a product and market research and end with the withdrawal of the product and subsequent supply of support for a guaranteed number of years. Today, in order to limit negative impact on the environment, this systemic view also tends to include product-component recyclability. Dr Juran must be given much of the credit for the realization that the quality of results can only be guaranteed through a systemic view, where the interrelations among the various processes are of paramount importance (under the holistic system concept, a system is more than the sum of its parts: the interrelations among those parts may, and usually do, characterize the system even more than its constituent parts). The 'Juran spiral' [2] highlights the close links between the various phases in the product life cycle: prevention in fact means coordinating the whole set of activities in order to ensure the quality of the end result and overall efficiency; specifically, it means doing everything necessary at each phase – or process – to meet the requirements of the subsequent phases and of the end user.

In recent years, management theory has moved away from the idea of sequential activities towards the idea of concurrent engineering: as far as possible, engineering activities are carried out in parallel, in order to maximize interactivity and thus improve the quality of the result and reduce development time. This is a demonstration of how a simple modification of the interrelations among processes – an organizational, systemic idea – can bring a dramatic change in results. The importance of concurrent engineering lies not in the changes made in the various processes, but in their mutual interaction. An important point is that in corporate organizations, process changes are usually governed by those directly involved in the relevant sub-system, while systemic changes are governed by top management. The latter have the greatest impact. Significant changes in time-to-market (concurrent engineering, see above) can be made only through modifications in the organization of the development cycle, not through modifications to individual processes in the cycle – and only through the intervention of top management, not from inside the system.

In the last few years, particularly with the growing use of TQM models stemming from the awards, there has been something of a regression from the systemic view of the organization. The system – the organization – has disappeared from the models, leaving only processes. The reason may be the importance attached to processes, which, given the need to move away from the 'vertical' view of the company, is more than justified. But, as often happens, a good idea has been taken to extremes, creating other problems. The 'horizontal', process-based view of the organization is fundamental, but it must be part of a systemic approach that highlights process interrelations.

In the 1950s and 1960s, the product life cycle concept provided a rational foundation for product quality assurance. By highlighting the processes involved in the various phases of product life, it constituted a basis on which to develop a quality-assurance policy for results (not just for the main result of the life cycle, i.e., the product, but also for the results of the various phases of the cycle: development, purchasing, production and maintenance). The key to this strategy is that it takes a holistic, systemic view of the organization, its resources and processes. This makes it possible to *plan* what should be done to achieve quality objectives and subsequently to *control* the variability that inevitably causes results to diverge from objectives. Quality management in the product life cycle is the means by which the organization assures the quality of results. If, as has happened in the last 20 years, the quality requirements of results rise, the current system can be improved by action to minimize process variability, promote teamwork and improve supplier quality. But when the company wants to make further progress in quality and simultaneously reduce costs and shorten cycles, then deeper, systemic changes are needed, in the organization of people, resources and processes (concurrent engineering is an example, as is research in the field of high-performance work systems). But this is all recent history; the origins and early development of quality assurance followed the traditional sequential approach to the product life cycle.

## 1.2 FROM QUALITY AUDITS TO QUALITY SYSTEM CERTIFICATION [3]

A quality system of this type (which, with the advent of TQM, would later be defined as a 'sub-system', since it was only a part of the entire corporate quality system) obviously needed to be submitted to periodic checks, to verify both alignment with company standards and effectiveness, that is, the system's real ability to generate the planned results. So the *quality system audit* was born. Generally speaking, responsibility for conducting, or organizing, these audits on behalf of top management was assigned to a quality function (this type of audit is a *first-party* audit, because it is performed by the company on itself). It was not long, however, before many large organizations that depended heavily on their suppliers – mainly organizations working in critical areas such as defence, aerospace, nuclear development or energy in general – decided to extend these quality-assurance and management procedures to their suppliers, whose own quality systems were required to comply with the standards of the customer company. Conformity was checked through what came to be known as *second-party* audits, since they were performed by the customer on the supplier. *External* quality assurance is the goal of second-party audits, which give the customer confidence in the supplier's ability to meet the quality goals set by the customer. External quality-assurance and second-party audits spread extensively in the 1960s and 1970s. At first, standards multiplied, creating enormous problems for suppliers, who had to comply with a different set of standards for each customer, and for purchasing companies, too, who had to extend their quality systems to all their suppliers and then audit them. As it became clear that this diversity was an uneconomic proposition for all concerned, a move to establish uniform external quality-assurance standards began, at first in like technological areas and later at a global level. The result, in 1987, was the development of the ISO 9000 international standards, which, by creating uniform criteria, made a sharp reduction in the number of audits possible. This in turn has led to the *third-party* audit, or certification, conducted by organizations that specialize in assessing the compliance of corporate quality systems with the ISO 9000 standards. As a result, quality certification is valid universally, or, at the very least, among mutually recognized systems. The standards governing certification bodies and procedures, and national and international certification systems (the European system, for instance) are all designed to foster the widest possible use and mutual recognition of certifications.

The ISO 9000 standards meet the need for external quality assurance; however, they also include a *guide* to quality system construction, ISO 9004, which can be used as an internal tool for the development, auditing and improvement of the corporate quality system. In addition to the ISO 9004, companies wishing to perform internal audits have another major resource at their disposal: results. And results, as we shall see, are what make the difference.

Since the ISO 9000 standards were designed for the purposes of external quality assurance, they investigate whether the company is able to produce good results, by assessing the conformity of its quality system with a model. The focus is not on the end results perceived by the customer, but on the company's quality system and processes. This deductive rather than inductive approach is geared to preventive assessment, when results may not be available or easily verifiable. It is reasonable to assume that reliable assessments of a company's ability to generate quality can be deduced from an audit of the system, because nothing is more tangible in a company than its product-related quality system, particularly if it is a manufacturing company. The findings of the experts, who take the standard as their guideline to analyse in depth the company's organizational structure, programmes, flows, process capabilities, standards, procedures and documentation – and who talk to the company's employees – will, of course, provide reliable forecasts of the organization's ability to achieve satisfactory quality results. But forecasts need to be confirmed by results. The judicious company will require supplier certification (or at least a guarantee that the supplier has a good quality-assurance system) as a condition of entry, but it will reserve final judgement until results can be assessed (vendor rating).

Unfortunately, over-emphasis on the ISO 9000 standards and certification has created widespread confusion in the last few years. Too often, ISO 9000 certification has been mistakenly regarded as a guarantee of results. The firearms licence has been confused with the ability to score a bulls-eye. Certification has come to be regarded as an end in itself. In practice, the road from certification to a good competitive quality position may not be short. To begin with, the quality of the certification itself can vary: a certified system is not necessarily a good quality system. Moreover, even a good quality system is not a sufficient guarantee of competitiveness.

## 1.3 INTRODUCING RESULTS INTO ASSESSMENTS

Second-party audits or quality system certifications are significant factors if they are regarded simply as the minimum preliminary requirement, the condition for entry (like a firearms licence or driving licence). We said above that the customer may require this together with other references, before adding a new company to its group of suppliers. Generally speaking, however, the new company will be admitted on a trial basis. Only when the condition for entry has been confirmed by good results and satisfactory supplies will it be elevated to the ranks of the organization's approved suppliers. Results, therefore, are the real test of audits, which will always have a certain margin of uncertainty, because they are based on conformity with a model and on the auditors' judgement.

Leaving aside second- and third-party assessments to return to first-party assessments – those the company performs on itself to measure the effectiveness of its quality system – there is absolutely no reason why the company should not extend the assessment to all available results, which should be more complete than those on which individual customers could have visibility. But although internal quality system audits are frequent, complete assessments that include results – real results as perceived or assessed by customers – are not so common. This situation is beginning to change as companies realize that the ultimate goal can only be customer satisfaction (or, better, *to be chosen* by the customer).

Nevertheless, if we look at the companies with the greatest interest in ISO 9000 certification, those that supply other, usually larger, organizations, as yet only a small number ask their customers to perform periodic assessments in order to rate their performances against competitors. Comparison is vital: the customer satisfaction results used in the assessment must always be compared with the corresponding results of reference competitors. Either the company itself conducts satisfaction surveys among its own and its competitors' customers (the solution normally chosen by companies that sell directly to the market), or it asks its main customers for their vendor rating results, which *compare* its performance with the performance of its competitors.

Figure 1.1 highlights the substantial difference between conventional quality-assurance-oriented audits and customer-satisfaction-oriented assessments.

The former are system audits (they include processes, but do not place specific emphasis on them), and are designed to provide guarantees for management (part (a) of Fig. 1.1) or to create customer confidence (part (b)). In both cases, these audits are *assessments of conformity*: the result is positive if the system conforms with the reference standard. Customer-satisfaction-oriented assessments (part (c) of Fig. 1.1) combine an examination of customer satisfaction results with the system audit (in fact, they take customer satisfaction results as the starting point for the assessment of the system), and their goal is *improvement* of customer satisfaction (they are therefore improvement-oriented assessments). They have a much greater diagnostic content than system audits and necessarily place specific emphasis on processes, since processes are the elements that generate the results being examined. Moreover, the systemic breadth of these assessments is naturally wider. The move from product conformity to customer satisfaction inevitably pinpoints causes of non-satisfaction outside the scope of the product sub-system: administration, personal relationships, pre-sales support, etc. It is not surprising that growing awareness that the company's mission is to satisfy its customers has fuelled the idea of total quality: the voice of the customer shows that many if not all of the company's employees can make a contribution to customer satisfaction.

Regular assessment of customer satisfaction results in relation to expectations fosters a customer-based corporate culture. The organization becomes more sensitive to the need for action when results fall short of goals, taking a more serious approach to the problem of how defects perceived by the customer can be rapidly corrected. At the same time, it

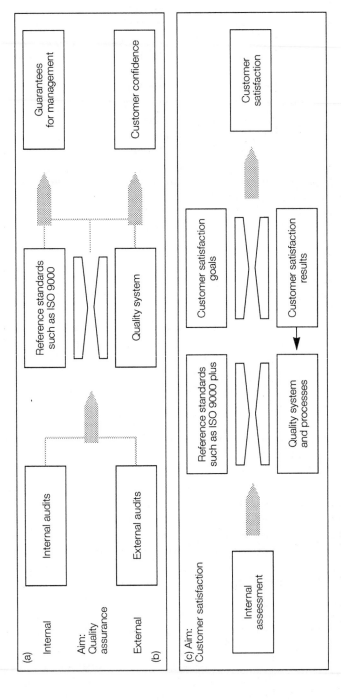

**Fig. 1.1** Different types of assessment:
(a) Internal quality assurance: quality system audit with reference to standards.
(b) External quality assurance: quality system audit with reference to standards.
(c) Customer satisfaction: assessment of discrepancies between results and goals and consequent assessment of processes and quality system.

develops a greater understanding of its processes and company system; as it learns where to intervene for corrective purposes, it also learns where to intervene to improve its goals: in other words, to plan performance improvements. Thus the company moves towards self-assessment geared to competitive customer satisfaction. As a result, its reference quality-system model is enhanced compared with the traditional quality-assurance sub-system. This is why the expression 'ISO 9000 plus' is used in Fig. 1.1. The expression is explained in Fig. 1.2, which illustrates the main additions that should be made to the ISO 9000 standards to progress from 'quality assurance' to 'customer satisfaction'. Many companies have evolved naturally from the ISO 9000 level to higher levels of the type illustrated in Fig. 1.2 in pursuing the goal of competitive customer satisfaction.

## 1.4 EXTENDING ASSESSMENT TO THE ENTIRE COMPANY SYSTEM

The next step is to extend the approach used to assess customer satisfaction to all company goals. This is examined in detail in the next chapter. Here, it is considered as the next phase in the evolution of the concept of assessment. If the company broadens its horizons from winning customers and ensuring customer loyalty to competitiveness in general, the breadth of the assessment also widens, from providing input in order to improve customer satisfaction to providing input in order to improve performance in every area (Fig. 1.3).

At this point, two observations must be made. The first is that the assessment represented in Fig. 1.3 is no longer a quality assessment if the term 'quality' has the conventional meaning of attribute of products and services and of the system that generates them, of the factors that affect customer satisfaction. It is a quality assessment if the concept of quality is extended to all the company's results and to the company itself (TQM).

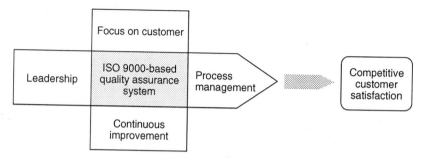

**Fig. 1.2** Expansion of the reference model with the move from quality assurance (central component) to customer satisfaction.

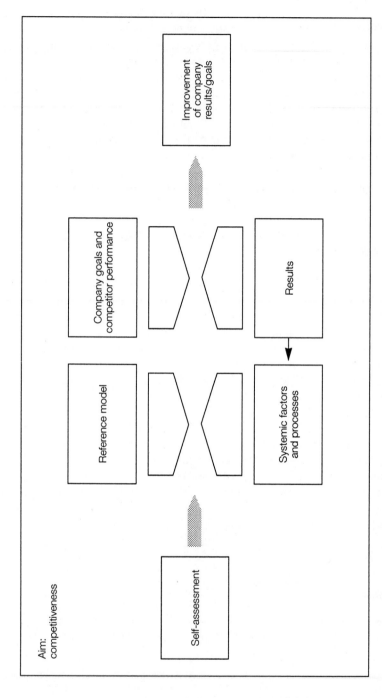

**Fig. 1.3** Self-assment extended to all company goals.

The second observation is that, even at this level, assessments may be assessments of *conformity* with the model, and therefore similar to audits, or *diagnostic* assessments, or a combination of the two.

The nature of the assessment depends on the needs of the company. If the company's main aim is to identify weaknesses in order to improve performance, then the assessment should be strongly diagnostic. It will be an 'improvement-oriented assessment' as illustrated in Fig 1.3 (the evolution of Fig. 1.1(c)). This assessment begins with results and then extends to processes and the company system (as described in full detail in the following chapters). If, on the other hand, the company wishes to verify the degree of conformity with a model and with reference standards, then the conformity assessment is appropriate. If, however, the audit concept is extended from sub-systems such as the product sub-system to the entire company system, reliability will drop sharply if the company attempts to extract other information beyond simple formal conformity with the chosen reference model.

This argument may sound theoretical, because neither the awards nor the self-assessments based on them adopt a TQM assessment approach that reproduces the conformity audit model. Nevertheless, the usual mix seems to have more in common with conformity assessments than with improvement-oriented assessments. As far as the award assessments are concerned, the diagnostic element is superfluous, because the purpose of these assessments is to judge excellence by identifying strengths (which must be many) and weaknesses (which must be few), not the underlying causes. Pinpointing causes is the job of the company. But if the company

**Table 1.1**

| Area | Type of assessment | What is assessed | Purpose of assessment |
|------|--------------------|--------------------|------------------------|
| Q U A L I T Y | First-party audit | QSS | Internal Q. assurance |
| | Second-party audit | QSS | External Q. assurance |
| | Third-party audit | QSS | Certification |
| | Management quality audit | QSS + P + R | Ensure that QSS is geared to product/service goals |
| T Q M | Management TQM audit | QS + P + R | ensure that QS is aligned with planned corporate goals |
| | Total Quality Award | QS + P + R | Demonstration of excellence |
| | Diagnostic self-assessment | QS + P + R | Improvement planning |

uses the approach adopted by the awards for its self-assessments, the diagnostic element will tend not to emerge. These questions will be examined in greater depth in the following chapters. Here, the reader's attention is drawn to *improvement-oriented self-assessment*. This is the state of the art of company assessment today and the basis for a new, much wider approach, which considers the company as a whole in relation to its full set of missions and to the general goal of continuous improvement of performance. Diagnostic self-assessment for the purposes of improvement and the role of self-assessment in the company's strategic and operating planning processes are the main themes of this book, although, for reasons of contiguity, reference will at times be made to the quality awards.

Table 1.1 summarizes the various types of assessment (QS = company quality system, QSS = products/services quality sub-system, P = processes, R = results).

# The model: an integrated view of the company and its missions

## 2

A serious approach to company assessment must always take full account of the difficulties and risks involved. The probability of superficiality and error is high, and directly proportionate to the size and complexity of the company. So the casual attitude frequently adopted towards these risks is a cause of some concern, especially as regards self-assessment. Fewer problems arise with the awards, provided that results (those measured by end users, not by the company) are given a high weighting; the European Award has always done this and the Malcolm Baldrige Award is gradually increasing the weighting it attributes to results. In this way, the proven ability to satisfy customers, shareholders and the other stakeholders identified by the award model becomes a preliminary requirement. The main risk is that the award may be given not to a company that produces good results thanks to substantial, instinctive but as yet unstructured, non-formalized quality, but to a company whose real quality, capabilities and competitive potential are inferior, but whose formal presentation skills, which will impress the examiners, are better. The reverse and more dangerous possibility, of the award going to a formally perfect quality system that dazzles the examiners, while the company's customers are less dazzled by its results, is more remote. The reason is that when customer results have a 50% weighting (e.g., the European Award), they must be very good before the company can move up to the competitive level; second, although the good examiner will take account of the possible time lag between systemic factors and results, he or she will never give factors a high score if they do not produce good results. In short, with the awards, even procedures that offer no high intrinsic guarantee of the reliability of their assessment of systemic factors will work if a condition for entry is that the company must already have achieved excellent results. Ultimately, of course, the award is not a matter of vital significance to the company; it is an examination, with all the accompanying risks and powers of discretion, which those applying for the award must accept.

The situation of improvement-oriented self-assessment is different. Here, the goal is not to give a score but to identify the factors and processes that require action in order to improve the company's performance and boost competitiveness. In this case, results are not a discriminating factor as they are with the awards: the mechanism must work just as well, if not better, for companies with very poor results. In these companies, clear identification of the causes of bad results is vital. The assessment model and procedures must therefore be as reliable as possible when measuring systemic factors – tangible and intangible – and identifying the cause–effect links between weaknesses in results and the company's systemic factors and processes. While the role of the model in the case of quality awards is to highlight excellence and to discriminate correctly at the more advanced level, in the case of self-assessment its purpose is to help the company grow and continuously improve performance. Consequently, the self-assessment model requires particularly careful analysis. This is what this and the next chapter set out to provide.

Assessment procedures, too, need to be distinguished from those used by the awards in order to guarantee the diagnostic content and reliability of the self-assessment. Methodology in fact is another area where self-assessment differs substantially from award assessments. Award assessments are necessarily performed rapidly, keeping costs as low as possible, while self-assessment can take all the time that is necessary and use the skills of expert consultants, especially when assessing intangibles and top management processes. The company that decides to perform a serious, thorough self-diagnosis will invest the necessary resources, making use of the requisite expertise and continuing for as long as the assessment takes. Clearly, then, self-assessment can achieve levels of effectiveness and reliability far beyond the reach of award assessments (which is why the author has argued for years that award assessments would be more reliable if they considered the company's self-assessments and consequent improvement plans over a period of at least three years, together with results achieved which, obviously, must be excellent). Self-assessment methodologies are the subject of the next chapter.

## 2.1 REVIEWING THE COMPANY IN RELATION TO ITS MISSIONS

A point already touched on above is that the self-assessment model should not be a model of excellence. This can be left to the awards, granted, for the sake of argument, that the ingredients of excellence can be incorporated in a model. The aim of self-assessment – or at least of the type of self-assessment considered here – is to provide input for improvement planning in order to bring the company's capabilities into line with its current goals and its mid-term goals and strategies. The model therefore needs to be useful for the purposes of improvement, with a high diagnostic potential. It should help the company pinpoint weaknesses (and strengths) in relation to its business goals, plan improvement and check the results achieved.

An assessment model cannot be formulated until the company has defined its missions. It is in relation to these missions and related strategic goals that the company and its capabilities have to be assessed. What else is a self-assessment if not a verification of the company's capabilities in relation to its missions, its fundamental goals? Without prior definition of missions, any assessment model will be general, if not arbitrary. So the company must begin by asking itself what its purpose – its mission – is. Each company will have its own answers, but a general framework of possible answers can be drawn up; within this framework – or guided by it – each organization will be able to personalize its answers to match its specific situation.

No-one would dispute that the fundamental mission of the business corporation is to remunerate the risk capital invested in it. In the past, more often than not, this was considered the company's only purpose. Today, shareholders are no longer regarded as the sole beneficiaries of the company's results. This view would be counter-productive: *exclusive* focus on profits and dividends puts exaggerated emphasis on short-term business and financial results, to the detriment of other important factors such as customer and employee satisfaction and the need for growth; over time, this would inevitably impair the company's profit-making ability. Awareness that other missions exist besides capital remuneration has spread in the last few years.

The first reason is the realization that other, previously neglected factors have an increasingly significant influence on long-term business/financial results. In a market where demand is low and needs are rising, the ability to make profits on a consistent basis is linked more and more to customer satisfaction and customer loyalty. A shift in focus from dividends to enhancing the company's value and its ability continuously to generate profits over the long term is today a condition for survival. Customer satisfaction and attainment of business goals clearly depend on employee empowerment and satisfaction. Respect for the social and physical environment is now considered mandatory.

The second reason is that, increasingly, the company is perceived as a social entity, which has other ends besides the purely economic one; obviously these objectives are not counter to profit-making, since this is the condition for survival. In fact, if the other objectives are correctly analysed and carefully balanced, they will contribute to, rather than conflict with, the company's primary mission of economic/business health and growth. Employee well-being, growth and involvement is an example. This objective or mission stems from the consideration that the company is made up of people whose potential is often not fully realized and whose involvement is not only vital to the company's success but also a means to self-realization – increasingly important in socially advanced societies. Together with economic rewards and the social and physical environment, self-realization contributes to employee satisfaction. For a company with an eye to the future, being a place where people realize themselves through their work could become a distinguishing characteristic as well as a factor in success.

Companies with some form of TQM strategy will have considered the problem of customer and employee satisfaction and sometimes also the question of impact on society, but all too often they lack a global, systemic vision. Many companies adopt the award models, which are acceptable starting points. The award models, however, are essentially assessment models, designed to assess the existing situation and correct the main imbalances rather than to review and if necessary reformulate the company's missions. Moreover, awareness of the importance of customer satisfaction frequently leads to the blind extrapolation of this concept to the category of stakeholders. A contract often exists between the company and the various stakeholders – and in the proactive, cooperative approach favoured by this book, a pact always exists, a mutual commitment that has no legal force but is more binding than a contract – whereby each partner undertakes to satisfy the needs of the other to the best of their ability. The relationship between the company and the customer, on the other hand, is more labile: the company, the party with the greater interest in maintaining the tie, will try unilaterally to prolong the relationship (continue to be chosen) for as long as possible, by increasing customer satisfaction. Customer loyalty certainly generates supplier satisfaction, but is not the result of a mutual commitment. This shows that certain automatic extrapolations should be avoided and that the model should be based on a thorough critical analysis.

Customer satisfaction, achieved through continuous competition with other players, is therefore the goal in relation to some recipients of the company's results (typically customers). In relation to others, the problem is to build a real partnership based on an extended vision of the 'company system', whereby benefits are shared out to each partner in relation to the contribution provided. Planning initiatives to consolidate the partnership with stakeholders will therefore be a less complex affair than planning action to improve the ability to keep current customers and win new ones.

At this point, we can briefly examine how perception of the company in relation to its missions has changed.

Figure 2.1(a) represents the 'paleo-industrial' view of the company's missions; in Fig. 2.1(b) customer satisfaction has been elevated to the level of primary mission together with shareholder satisfaction. The next step is the realization that the company's success in fulfilling its primary mission (attaining its business goals) depends on contributions from and satisfaction of the expectations of a wide range of stakeholders, whose roles differ, but who all play an important part in the 'company system'.

An explanation of the concept of the stakeholder is called for here. A stakeholder is anyone who has a relationship of mutual give and take with the company. The stakeholder contributes to the attainment of the company's goals through his or her labour (employee), venture capital (shareholder), services of various kinds (partners), the socio-physical environment (society), and expects benefits in return. For its part, the company is founded on risk capital and labour, receives the cooperation of

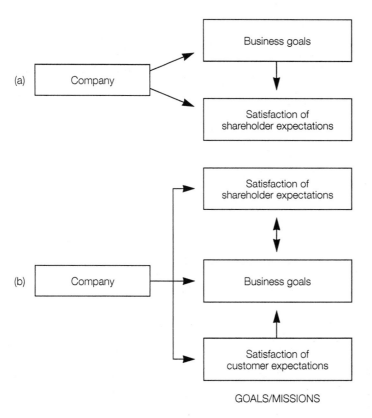

GOALS/MISSIONS

**Fig. 2.1** The first steps in the evolution of perception of the company's missions: recognition of customer satisfaction as a primary mission.

other organizations, chooses environments in which to locate its operations and it must adequately recompense the contributions it receives.

Obviously, one of the main groups of stakeholders are the company' owners, referred to here for simplicity as the 'shareholders'. This term refers chiefly to controlling shareholders, those with the power to appoin top management and plan or approve the company's long-term pro grammes. These shareholders have a special interest in the company' fortunes, unlike the speculator, who has no ties with the company and wil withdraw his capital if other investments offer better potential returns Naturally, the company will also consider the satisfaction of speculators but at times its long-term interests may mean not satisfying and therefor not attracting this type of investor.

Figure 2.2 represents the fundamental missions of the company in thei most succinct conceptual form.

It shows that the company's mission is to attain its short- and long-term business and image goals (the term 'image' covers all aspects of the company's identity – how it is and how it wishes to be perceived), and tha it does so with contributions from a variety of stakeholders, who, in return expect satisfaction of their own legitimate expectations: not just economi expectations, but also, for example, self-realization for employees beginning with management; transparent relationships for business part ners; respect for the environment and contributions to the social growth o the community and its governing bodies. The figure also shows tha

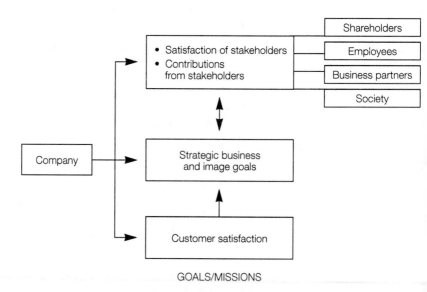

GOALS/MISSIONS

**Fig. 2.2** A modern view of the company's mission.

customer satisfaction is a fundamental mission if the company is to achieve its business and image goals.

With so many missions, the company has to make choices; it has to decide which is the best way to distribute its efforts and management time among its missions. Similarly, it must also decide how to share out the value it creates among the company itself (investments), customers (best value/price relationship) and stakeholders. The most difficult decisions will be those regarding stakeholders: how to share out benefits – not just profits, but also items that affect operating results – among shareholders, employees, business partners, society. In the absence of a declared benefit distribution policy, the company's efforts, by default, are likely to concentrate solely on the attainment of short-term business goals and, consequently, on the satisfaction of shareholders' short-term expectations. Organizations that pursue this goal alone may look efficient and effective on paper, but they probably live in a constant state of crisis, beset by chronic problems, probably wondering why they cannot achieve results consistent with their plans and formal organization. On the other hand, companies that pursue the goal of maximum customer and employee satisfaction without paying sufficient attention to business goals are probably pleasant places to work in, but they will not survive for long. The challenge for management is to achieve a balance among the various missions that optimizes overall results for the company and its stakeholders.

## 2.2 PROCESSES AND SYSTEMIC FACTORS

The right side of the model represents the missions on which the company's strategic goals are based. The left side, consisting so far of the general term 'company', must be expanded to indicate the ways the company can reach those goals.

All results are achieved through *processes*, as Fig. 2.3 shows.

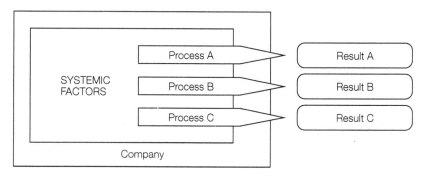

**Fig. 2.3** The relationship between systemic factors, processes and results.

The effectiveness, efficiency and flexibility of processes in achieving goals depend on a wide range of factors, which make up the company system. Adopting an extension of quality assurance terminology – and of ISO 9000 terminology in particular – the author has in the past referred to these factors as the 'quality system' [3]; in this book, they are called 'systemic factors'. A detailed analysis is not called for here, but Fig. 2.4 shows the 'systemic factors' of critical importance to the attainment of the missions and related goals on the right side of the model (or to the improvement of results, when goals are not reached or need to be improved).

In Fig. 2.4, the systemic factors of critical importance to the attainment of the company's missions are: leadership, the motor that propels the organization; strategies and plans; human resources; technical, financial and information resources; organizational architectures. These factors correspond to a series of sub-systems into which, in a systemic approach, the company can be sub-divided: the managerial sub-system, the values and goals sub-system, the human/social sub-system, the technical sub-system and the structural sub-system [4]. The 'organizational architectures' category requires some explanation to avoid confusion and because the European and Malcolm Baldrige award models do not include an organizational category. The term 'organizational structure' might be clearer, but it could be confused with the formal structural sub-division of powers and responsibilities represented by organization charts. What is meant here are *the ways* in which the company uses its resources to achieve its missions: not just its business missions, but customer and stakeholder satisfaction, too. The choice of the expression 'organizational architectures' underlines the fact that the view of the organization assumed here is very similar to that described by D. A. Nadler, M. S. Gerstein and R. B. Shaw in their book *Organizational Architectures* [5]. For Nadler *et al.* the term 'organizational architectures' denotes *how* the company organizes its efforts: the concept embraces the formal structure, definition of working practices, informal organization and the methods and styles of management used to run the organization as a social body, as a set of people united by common missions. This is a systemic view of the organization, where the system is a dynamic, socio-technical system which interacts with the environment in which it operates (see also [4]). In this system, the interrelations among people, organizational sub-systems and processes are of absolute prime importance (holistic system). This is a contingent (non-universal) vision of the organization, which emphasizes the company's specific features as shaped by the market, technology, the company history and the company employees. Above all, it is an 'adaptive' view, which aims to help the company detect even the weakest internal and external signals in order to adjust rapidly to change. In this vision, the design of the company, its construction, administration, improvement and continuous

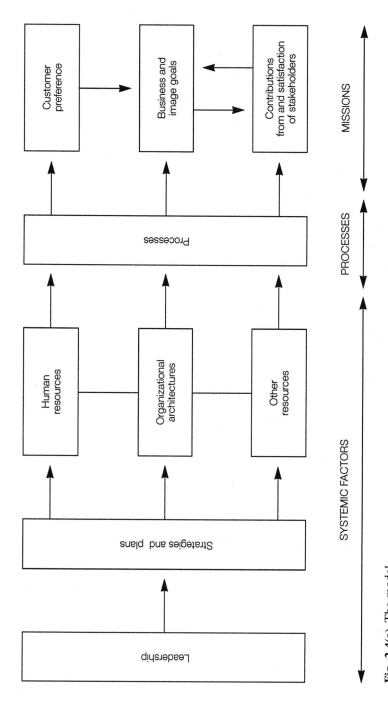

**Fig. 2.4(a)** The model.

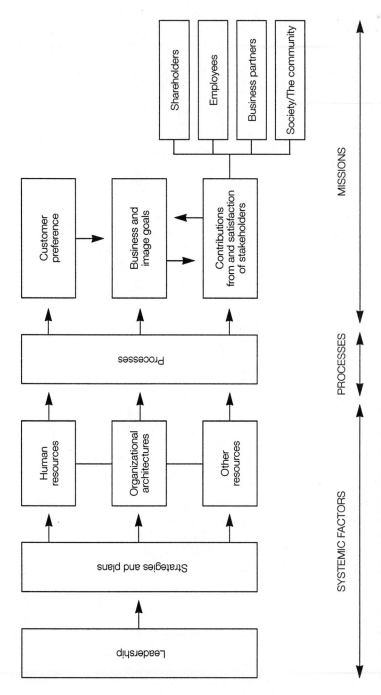

**Fig. 2.4(b)** The model, with stakeholders displayed.

adjustment are primarily the responsibility of management, led by top management. The ability to adapt is directly linked to a dynamic corporate culture and a capacity for continuous learning. The organization must be able to perceive and transmit upwards ideas and suggestions from anywhere in the company, in particular from the front end. In turn, top management must adopt an open-minded attitude, encouraging internal debate and utilizing the output as the basis for a dynamic review of company strategy; at the same time, it must develop the organizational solutions needed to make such reviews possible.

## 2.3 CHARACTERISTICS OF THE MODEL

The introduction of an 'organizational architectures' category is one of the main differences between the model described here and the European Quality Award model (Fig. 2.7 illustrates the European model as of 1995). The Deming Application Prize includes an organization category, but the US Malcolm Baldrige Award does not. The two western awards cover various aspects of the organization in other categories – for example, the human resources category – but do not count the organization as a critical success factor.

The absence of an organization category in the TQM models of two of the major awards probably reflects recent scepticism about the role of organization as a critical competitive factor. The real problem stems from a bureaucratic–structural interpretation, which associates the concept of organization with the distribution of power and organization charts. This is a pity because it has come at a time when new organizational forms are needed and when company managers themselves should become the new architects of their corporate organizations.

A significant indication of the difficulties inherent in the European model due to the absence of an organization category emerged when the model was extended to small/medium enterprises. For these companies, the first positive contact with quality is usually the assimilation of the product life cycle concept and the organization of that cycle to ensure product/service quality at minimum cost (Quality Management and Assurance and Quality System). Although the ISO 9000 standards are often misinterpreted and poorly applied, they provide the basic ingredients the company needs to organize the product life cycle so as to control variability and attain its product quality goals (although, as noted in the previous chapter, if those goals are extended to competition at the level of customer satisfaction, costs and time-to-market, the ISO 9000 organizational approach is no longer sufficient). To maintain the focus on organization adopted by so many small/medium enterprises as a result of the rapid spread of the ISO 9000 standards since 1987, especially in

Europe, a number of adjustments have had to be made in the assessment model of the European Quality Award (EQA). The prevailing view was that the model should retain its nine-category structure, so a new 'quality system' category was not added (the term used by the ISO standards for the systemic and structural organization factors that affect quality); instead, the 'processes' block was turned into a 'quality system and processes' block. This is a satisfactory solution as far as the award is concerned, but it is far from ideal as far as self-assessment is concerned.

This example illustrates an observation made at the beginning of this chapter: that the awards have their own logic. This makes them somewhat rigid, tending to turn them into de facto TQM national/regional standards. If self-assessment is subordinated to the awards, it will inevitably be hampered by a lack of flexibility. The full benefits of self-assessment will emerge only if the company has complete freedom to adapt the model (and the approach) to match its specific needs and to achieve the main objective of self-assessment, which is improvement. In the example mentioned above, the problem arose with small/medium enterprises, because of the need for consistency with the ISO 9000 standards, but evidently it also applies – on an even wider scale – to large companies.

Clearly, solutions can be found to make up for the absence of an organization category, at least as regards award assessments. Organizational themes can be incorporated in other categories: leadership, human resources, strategies and plans, processes. Alternatively, systemic factors can be examined together with results, although this produces hybrid assessments, where causes are mixed with effects, and undermines the significance of comparative analysis. Since the Malcolm Baldrige Award does not distinguish between systemic factors and results, it is particularly prone to this mixing. But problems arise with the EQA model, too. Take the example of people. The EQA model has a people assessment category on the left side, among the enablers, and one on the right side, among results. So people-related organization issues can be – and normally are – assessed when the left-hand category is examined. Now consider customers, or impact on society: there is no category on the left for the relevant organization factors: *how* the company organizes itself to compete at the level of customer satisfaction; *how* it organizes itself to minimize negative impact on society and build up a positive relationship with the community. The usual practice is to combine assessment of these factors (enablers) with assessment of results and produce a single judgement. To sum up: for the purposes of self-assessment, an organization category is essential, and the bigger the company the more important it is. It is no coincidence that one of the answers to the problems of non-efficiency and non-effectiveness in large organizations is the lean organization.

A second feature that distinguishes the model proposed here from the award models, including the EQA model, concerns the 'processes' block.

This is kept separate from systemic factors (enablers in the EQA model) and thus constitutes the third basic component of the model, together with factors and missions [3]. The 'processes' block does not include development of a process-based organization, which comes under the 'organizational architectures' category. It focuses on the specific processes that contribute to the attainment of the goals on the right side of the model.

Processes should be placed at the centre of the model between systemic factors and results, especially for self-assessment. Obviously, the company will not assess all of its processes. It will choose those with the greatest impact on achievement of its missions and list them in this central block. Then it will collect all the information and indicators needed to assess the state of control and performance of these processes and to compare the final measurements with customer/stakeholder results (this information is described in detail later). The central position of processes also highlights the cause–effect links among the three components of the model (Fig. 2.5), which are of fundamental importance in diagnostic assessments.

The main characteristics of the right side of the model – illustrated in Fig. 2.4 at a general level (a) and in detail (b) – have already been described. But given the model's conceptual affinity with the EQA model, it is useful to pinpoint and explain the differences. It will become clear that the model proposed here is a conceptual evolution of the European model; it is not based on a different approach, nor is it a criticism of the EQA model (hardly surprising, given the author's role in defining the conceptual basis of the EQA, and his continued support of it). Compared with the EQA model, it places the business goals category at the centre of the block of the company's strategic goals. This makes it clear that business results too are the product of specific processes, as well as of 'customer preference' and 'contribution of stakeholders'. In turn, attainment of business goals is crucial for 'stakeholder satisfaction'; the relationship between the two categories is therefore two-way. Image has been included among the company's business goals. This is an important 'product', which addresses a multiplicity of customers, including many key customers. Image is a channel through which the company can enhance its business results and its results in general, and communicate its distinguishing

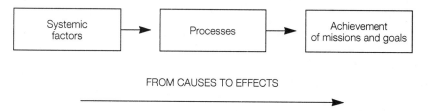

Fig. 2.5 The cause–effect links among the three main components of the model.

characteristics. Furthermore, a clear distinction is made between the business goals category and the shareholder satisfaction category: these are two different concepts, which cannot be combined. Business goals are objectives for which management is responsible and which produce benefits for *all* stakeholders. Shareholder satisfaction is a consequence of the achievement of business targets; conceptually, therefore, it is one of the components of the general 'satisfaction of stakeholders' category.

The model's business targets make no explicit reference to management. This is because management expectations are linked to achievement of all the goals on the right side of the model, in particular business targets. Consequently, 'satisfaction of management', too, is a consequence of the achievement of goals in general and business targets in particular. Of course, personal satisfaction, arising from the benefits produced by work well done, is also a factor, but it appears as a special item inside the 'satisfaction of employees' category. To sum up, management is present, if invisible, in all systemic factors, especially leadership, and throughout the right side of the model, especially in business targets and business results. Figure 2.4(b) shows all the stakeholders: this model has a larger number of stakeholders than the EQA model: *shareholders*, but also the company's *business partners*, in particular its suppliers and distributors, and everyone else who is involved in the corporate value chains.

## 2.4 THE MODEL AS AN EXPRESSION OF THE ORGANIZATION'S FOCUS ON ITS MISSIONS

As Fig. 2.4 shows, the model clearly reflects the company's focus on its fundamental missions and the relevant corporate mechanisms. Figures of this type help to make concepts clear, so, at the risk of seeming redundant, an even more concise representation is offered in Fig. 2.6.

This figure shows that leadership is the 'propellant' that steers systemic factors, via processes, towards missions, whose central component, on

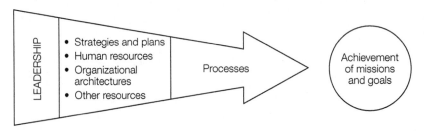

**Fig. 2.6** The company system, represented by the model in terms of systemic factors and processes, is designed to attain the organization's missions.

which all the other missions depend, but to which they also contribute, is business goals. Leadership should therefore be regarded as the 'motor' of the model. The definition of the company's 'vision' and related 'missions' (right side of the model) and the formalization of its key 'values' depend on the leadership provided by top management. The definition of strategies and plans consistent with this vision and these missions depends on leadership. The ability to organize people and resources and to govern processes solely for the purpose of generating value for customers, the company and stakeholders (and therefore to combat the widespread tendency to squander value in internal relations between people and departments, in red tape, in power struggles) depends on leadership. The ability to involve and motivate people and groups, to transmit the meaning of the company's missions and to foster a sense of belonging depends on leadership.

The 'strategies and plans' category has been placed next to leadership, to emphasize its strategic importance and omni-comprehensive nature. Fuelled mainly by the right side of the model, but guided and supported by leadership, 'strategies and plans' translates general missions into goals, strategies, plans, which are subsequently implemented with resources, organization and processes. The 'quality of goals' [3], which, together with the quality of realization, determines the quality of results, depends mainly on this phase.

'Resources' are the raw materials with which the company pursues its missions. Of these, people are by far the most important. The company's missions and values will provide the guidelines for recruitment (focusing, for example, on corporate goal sharing, an aptitude for teamwork, empathy with the customer), training and internal social organization. Considering that in most companies, people realize only a small part of their potential, organizations that discover ways of freeing that potential will open up huge competitive spaces for themselves. Financial, technological, material and IT resources also need to be thoroughly reviewed in relation to the company's missions and continuous improvement of performance. IT resources, for example, can play a significant role in creating a mission-focused, process-based organization.

The goals of the 'organizational architectures' category have been described. But how do they relate to the 'leadership' category? Leadership must create a lean, flexible, adaptable learning organization; it must ensure that the organization is committed to its goals and capable of adapting to and, if possible, anticipating change.

As far as the relationship between 'organizational architectures' and the two resource categories is concerned, if the organization mobilizes resources to attain the company's goals, through processes, resources in turn contribute to the construction and continuous renewal of the organization. This applies first of all to human resources: the degree to

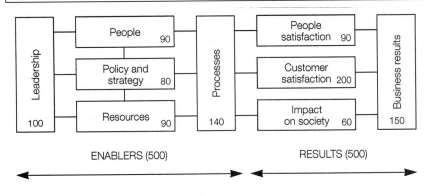

**Fig. 2.7** The European Quality Award model (1995).

which people offer suggestions and support organizational change will depend on the level of individual and group empowerment and on the company's ability to be a learning organization. But it also applies to IT resources, which can be important 'building blocks' [5] in new organizational architectures.

As we have seen, the 'processes' category consists of specific activities or value chains, whose outputs are the results corresponding to the missions and goals shown on the right. Processes are the area in which activities and the gradual results of those activities can be measured. Since the company can measure itself only via its processes (and possibly via products, the result of those processes), process measurements are essential to predict the quality of results and avoid customer and stakeholder dissatisfaction. It is worth repeating that the alignment of process measurements with results is an absolute priority.

The model shown in Fig. 2.4 is the model referred to in this book. It is more complex than the EQA model (Fig. 2.7) because it takes account of all self-assessment requirements, at least as they are perceived today by the author. The model can obviously be simplified for award assessments, just as it can be simplified – or made more complex – when it is adopted within a specific corporate environment.

So far, we have looked at the model's conceptual framework. But greater details are needed if the model is to be fully understood and applied. When each category is described, and the categories are sub-divided into sub-categories, the model assumes a precise physiognomy, which can be adapted to meet the specific characteristics of the individual company. From a strictly scientific point of view, such a description should be provided in this chapter, which looks at the model; the reader, however, is referred to Chapter 3, which examines the self-assessment process. A detailed description of the model will be necessary when discussing the assessment criteria for the various categories. So, to avoid repetitions and since self-assessment is the purpose of this book rather than theoretical discussions of the model, this description is provided later. Readers wishing for even greater detail are referred to Appendix A.

## 2.5 THE MODEL IN THE VARIOUS PHASES OF CORPORATE ACTIVITY

### 2.5.1 Planning

Planning is the phase during which general missions are translated into strategic and operating plans. It is based on the following input:

- the company's expectations in terms of development of market share and image;
- the contributions the company expects from the various stakeholders and the benefits stakeholders expect in return;
- the expectations of the market, in particular customer satisfaction needs in relation to market share goals and known and predictable competitor behaviour;
- past performance, at the level of results, processes and systemic factors;
- the company's capabilities – human, financial and technological resources, etc., organization and processes – assessed in relation to missions and strategies and to foreseeable changes in external scenarios.

For input one and two, expectations are defined by management. The third input is provided by the various sensors and methodologies used by the company to sound out and interpret the market. Self-assessment is a perfect opportunity for an annual review of the last two inputs, but ideally they should be available on a continuous basis or whenever needed, provided this is economically feasible. Figure 2.8 shows the use of the model during planning.

In this phase, top management involvement is considerable. Leadership is exercised through direct participation in strategy planning and definition. The innovation presented by this model is that strategic planning is extended from the business and market areas to all the company's stakeholders. This is extremely important: the company's *real* policy, as opposed to its stated policy, is reflected in the way strategies and plans treat stakeholders, as regards both cooperation in attainment of goals and distribution of financial and other benefits (output).

### 2.5.2 Implementation

During the implementation phase, results are present. One of the problems companies face is a lack of up-to-date information on their

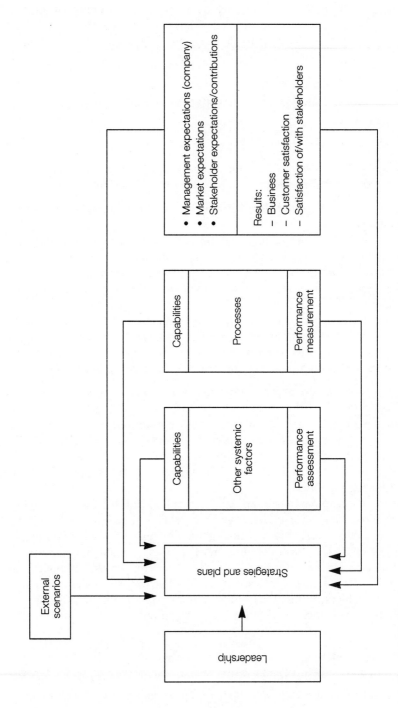

**Fig. 2.8** Planning.

performance. This may be caused by a lack of data, but at times the reason is an inability to extract *reliable, up-to-date* information from data. An abundance of data is not synonymous with exhaustive information; indeed, at times it means the opposite. In practice, managers frequently base decisions on unverified information, instinct, experience (which can help, but can also create dangerous assumptions), or on the opinion of the most influential people in the company, rather than on information extracted correctly from reliable data. 'If you can't measure it, you can't improve it' is a maxim that every manager should keep in mind; together with a dose of common sense, however.

In the quality age, many companies are obsessed with measurements, departments compete with one another for the greatest number of indicators, putting sensors everywhere. Then they wear themselves out analysing mountains of data and forget about the customer. Eventually, they realize that a great deal of data is difficult to interpret or is insignificant, and exhaustion or scepticism take over. Every indicator, every sensor has to be monitored and this requires time and effort. First of all, therefore, sensors and indicators must be introduced only where they are needed. Generally speaking, critical areas in results lead the company to look for an internal indicator that will highlight the risk in advance; better still, analysis of processes identifies the main variables and warning sensors are placed on them. The second objective is to extract the necessary information, or indicators, from the data provided by the sensors. Data in its pure state may provide the information expected; but usually it will need to be processed. A process variable that is about to overstep the tolerance limit is a case in point: intelligent processing of the trend, rather than absolute figures, will highlight the danger. Companies therefore need to construct the right indicators, those that convey the information needed. In all cases, sensors, data and indicators must be tested. Only when tests confirm that the indicator can provide a meaningful warning about what will happen later, at the level of results (usually when it is too late) can that indicator be included as one of the measurements that are indispensable for improvement.

In the last few years, growing familiarity with process control has led to a strong increase in the use of indicators, even in fields that were not previously considered measurable. Today, indicators are used frequently in service processes, sales and marketing processes, administrative processes, and in other areas too. Clearly, excessive measurement must be avoided: only areas of significance for control and improvement should be measured. But the thesis of this book is that if the area is significant it must be measured, even if at first sight this may seem difficult, if not impossible. As mentioned above, where no measurements are taken, no control or improvement is possible. In cases where the particular characteristic apparently cannot be measured (or the company does not know how to measure it), a 1–5 assessment scale can be used, where 1 represents the lowest value and 5 the highest; the assessment will be performed by a panel of experts.

Figure 2.9 illustrates the model during implementation. The right side is now labelled 'results'. In the middle, the processes block is the main focus of attention as far as measurement is concerned. The company that is not familiar with process control methodologies will find itself somewhat at a disadvantage here. But as it acquires experience, processes will become the crucial area, the area in which the concepts of TQM and, above all, continuous improvement, take on the greatest meaning. If the 'processes' block occupies a central position in the model, it is with good reason.

In addition to process measurements, during this phase the company also needs reliable, up-to-date information on its results (right side of the model). Companies are accustomed to collecting and providing management with up-to-date information on business results. Many companies systematically monitor customer satisfaction levels and gather objective data on product defect rates, complaints and so on. Systematic monitoring of direct or indirect personnel satisfaction indicators is more rare, as is monitoring of the satisfaction of other stakeholders.

Many indicators on the right side of the model do not need to be monitored continuously. Personnel satisfaction surveys, for instance, are usually carried out on an annual basis. Normal customer satisfaction indicators, too, do not usually require continuous monitoring, whereas other less common indicators, such as lost customer indicators, require real-time monitoring and immediate processing and circulation. The right side will be examined in greater detail in the next section, which deals with self-assessment.

Systematic measurement of the left side of the model – systemic factors – is not usual during implementation. This side, as we shall now see, is the main object of scrutiny of the self-assessment phase.

### 2.5.3 Self-assessment

If management had a control panel with a full set of instruments to monitor results, processes and systemic factors on a continuous basis – and if staff were trained to conduct systematic diagnostic analyses of the causes of differences between results and goals – then perhaps a special self-assessment/self-diagnosis session would not be needed every year. Or perhaps it would be needed, but at a later stage in the development of the corporate TQM culture, when the concept of improvement is extended from results that fall short of expectations to planning of goals beyond current expectations or current capabilities. As we saw in Chapter 1, self-assessment can be used to check whether the company performs as expected, in accordance with a model or a set of rules (conformity-oriented self-assessment, or audit); or it can be a tool for improvement. Here, we

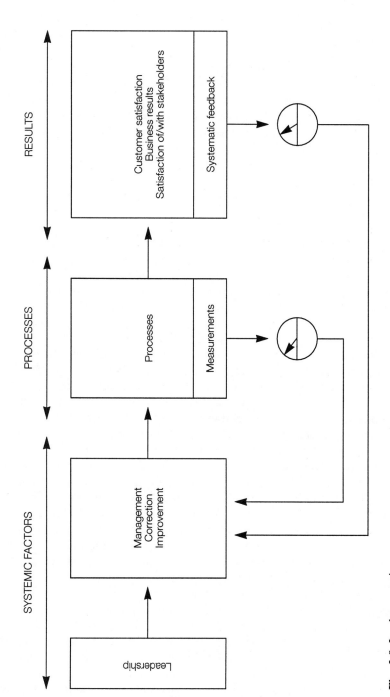

**Fig. 2.9** Implementation.

consider the second type of self-assessment, which is strongly diagnostic. For improvement-oriented self-assessment, the model assumes the form shown in Fig. 2.10.

A new instrument has been added to the control panel, a device that 'measures' systemic factors (for simplicity, a single instrument is shown in the figure, but clearly it represents a set of instruments). The verb 'measure' is in inverted commas because the measurements it refers to are *sui generis*, based on the 1–5 scale suggested above or an equivalent. In other words, these 'measurements' are assessments, judgements made by experts, the findings of interviews or questionnaires, and relate to criteria or behaviour models that must be defined as clearly as possible. Providing management with a complete control panel that permits measurement of the left side of the model is one of the main purposes of self-assessment. The left side comprises many factors that elude normal measurement systems; some are intangible, like leadership, values and culture, personnel motivation and involvement. But it is usually these 'soft' characteristics that make the difference between the excellent organization and the rest. If management is sensitive to improvement, it will insist on 'measuring' these characteristics, given that 'you can only improve it if you can measure it'.

Why is this new instrument introduced during self-assessment and not during routine implementation? Partly because reliable assessment of systemic factors is an expense that companies usually cannot afford more than once a year; but also because of the delicate nature of some of the procedures involved (questionnaires and interviews, for example): if these were performed with greater frequency, they could cause disruption or annoyance and reduce the reliability of the assessment. Of course, if the self-assessment helps the company identify characteristics that can be monitored with routine indicators, so much the better. This usually happens with the more tangible characteristics such as resource management and organization, and less with intangibles like leadership and strategic personnel management. Assessment of systemic factors will be examined in greater detail later, when the self-assessment process is analysed. The point stressed here is the fundamental importance of providing management with a complete control panel to guide the company towards improvement, and the indispensable role of self-assessment. Too often, self-assessment is presented as a sub-product of the awards and the procedure itself as a score-attribution exercise delegated to a special self-assessment team. The assessment team usually adopts a stereotype model, which management has neither conceived nor validated as a representation of the company system and its missions and goals. Thus, self-assessment is unable to achieve its fundamental purpose: to provide a model and a panel of instruments to help management effectively guide the company towards continuous improvement.

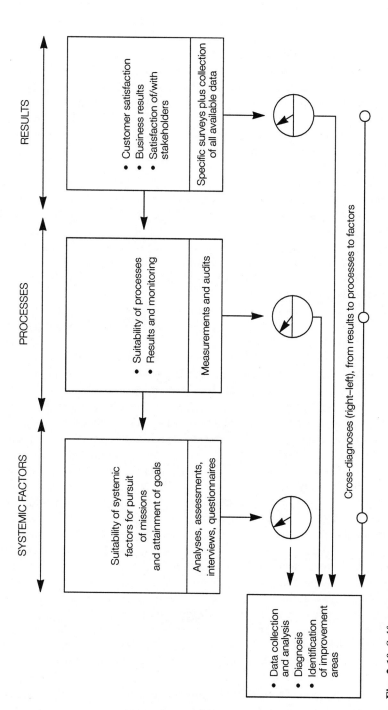

**Fig. 2.10** Self-assessment.

The control panel plays an important role in the continuous learning process. The great value of the model and of self-assessment is that they highlight the cause–effect chains linking the three areas: systemic factors, processes, results. Through right–left cross-diagnosis (which is a specific part of self-assessment, but can also be performed at any time during implementation), the company learns to recognize the chains that have a critical impact on results. This knowledge will be used during the subsequent planning and implementation phases, to activate the levers that should produce the desired improvement in results (in a PDCA approach, Section 3.3).

Self-assessment not only completes the control panel, by providing the third set of instruments, it also extends and improves the tools used to measure results and processes. First, because when a procedure is performed on an annual basis, it makes practical and economic sense to execute surveys and measurements that are important but could not be conducted on a routine basis. Second, because wide-ranging in-depth surveys of the kind described above often suggest ways to improve routine measurements.

Now we can consider a few examples of the more detailed level of measurement required by self-assessment, with reference to the right side of the model – results. Self-assessment of the 'customer satisfaction' category generally involves wider ranging surveys in order to ensure complete coverage of the various market segments and of the competition. As far as stakeholders are concerned, annual surveys to measure the satisfaction of stakeholders with their relationship with the company – and vice versa, the company's satisfaction with the relationship – are a reasonable proposition, and self-assessment provides a suitable opportunity for such surveys to be performed.

Business results are an interesting case. Usually, the company monitors business results continuously and in detail; in theory, therefore, self-assessment should be simply a question of collecting and consolidating information that is already available. In practice, certain business measurements will not be available (e.g., efficiency improvements, market share variations) or will not be of great significance (e.g., variations in market share are measured, but variations in the value of the customer base due to customers lost and customers gained are not measured). Moreover, if the company regards self-assessment as a diagnostic procedure, a critical review of its visions, missions and long-term strategies, then it will find it necessary to have other instruments available, related to the future rather than to the present. If, for example, the company's long-term strategies require gradual development of new capabilities (technological, commercial, etc.), then management will need specific measuring tools to monitor their growth. In most cases, the actual results have little intrinsic value: they are significant when compared with competitors' results (where this is possible, and always in relation to customer satisfaction) and with the results of previous years, because the improvement rate is one of the most important yardsticks of the company's vitality and competitiveness.

With regard to processes, a general assessment of the way the company controls and manages its processes is conducted at systemic factor level, during assessment of 'organizational architectures'. As we noted earlier, the central block of the model, 'processes', is the main source of measurements. If the company has good process management, these measurements will always be available. The specific purpose of self-assessment is to identify key processes in relation to the priorities on the right side of the model (the process–result correspondence shown in Fig. 2.3); and then assemble all available data on these processes and make any missing measurements. If process management is inadequate, special steps must be taken to collect the required data; above all, this inadequacy will be recorded as one of the most serious shortcomings found by the self-assessment, for which remedial action must immediately be taken. To avoid complicating matters, it is best to begin with a small number of fundamental processes in the first year of self-assessment (e.g., the main processes that affect customer satisfaction and business results, typically five and never more than ten). Subsequently, year after year, as process control expertise grows, other processes can be included, although Pareto's Law should not be forgotten (consider the few that have a significant impact on results and ignore the many of little importance). Once the main processes have been selected, the company will assess the measurements provided by the most meaningful indicators, in particular final indicators, which should be closely correlated with results (measured on the right side of the model). The alignment of process measurements with result measurements (business results, customer satisfaction, etc.) is one of the main process assessment criteria. As we saw earlier, process measurements are used by management to control the implementation phase and, if necessary, to take real-time action to modify the course of events. If these measurements fail to match the measurements obtained from results, the corrective action taken by management will be ineffectual or counter-productive. The company must ensure that its internal indicators are reliable, the level of reliability being reflected in the degree of alignment between process and result measurements. In addition to routine process measurements, which self-assessment can help to improve, the self-assessment usually involves audits of the selected processes in order to verify their state of control. These audits, which are described in greater detail in the next chapter, are normally based on a 'process management model' [3] and produce a score on a pre-specified scale.

Besides the three measuring instruments described above, Fig. 2.10 also includes a 'right–left cross-diagnosis' path (lower part of the figure). This will also be described in greater detail in a later chapter. It is mentioned here for the sake of completeness, because, together with the management 'control panel', it constitutes one of the most original and interesting aspects of the assessment approach described in this book. If self-assessment is to be diagnostic, the three types of measurement must be integrated with one another, not kept separate. Integration is achieved first of all through the right–left sequence adopted by self-assessment (see next chapter); above all, it is achieved through methodical cross-diagnosis of the most critical results. Cross-diagnosis is related to the cause–effect logic illustrated in Fig. 2.5. If a result falls short of target, the reason must be sought initially in the company's processes, then in its systemic factors. A diagnostic path always begins with effects and moves back through the possible causes until it finds the right one, or ones. In addition to measurements, therefore, self-assessment should generate a series of 'diagnostic paths', which begin with results that are below expectations – or that the company wishes to improve – and move back through the processes that produce those results until, if necessary, they reach systemic factors; and in any case until the causes of the results have been identified, so that improvement can be planned.

## 2.6  A BUSINESS MODEL GEARED TO IMPROVEMENT

Since this chapter introduces the main concepts underlying the model in a gradual progression, the reader may have found it difficult to understand their full significance and incorporate them into a unified whole. This section summarizes and where necessary expands on these concepts.

● The model is not a quality model or a TQM model, but a *business model*. The company's missions and goals are the focal point of the model, which then highlights the processes and systemic factors (critical success factors) that are believed to play a decisive role in the attainment of those goals. In this book, the model is used for the purposes of self-assessment and improvement planning, but it can be applied to all the other phases in the company cycle (examples are provided).
● The model is sub-divided into three blocks:
  – *missions and goals*: identification of missions and goals is essential when the self-assessment is being organized, to establish a reference framework for assessment of results; it is also important as a way of focusing everyone's attention on the company's missions.
  – *processes*: that is, the value chains by means of which the company achieves its missions and goals. Until a few years ago, the organizational importance of processes was overshadowed by the bureaucratic/ function-based organization approach, but now it is re-emerging. Unified organizational monitoring of processes, and process management that optimizes effectiveness (results consistent with goals) and

efficiency (minimum costs and time) are vital for competitiveness. It is a pity that the EQA model continues to include processes under systemic factors (enablers); over the years, the Malcolm Baldrige Award model has clearly moved towards a separate category for processes, even though to date (1996) it still does not create groupings among and within the categories that distinguish clearly among systemic factors, processes and results (not internal results, which are a logical part of processes, but end results as perceived by the users of those results). The grouping of processes into one of the three basic components of the model is consistent with a process-based approach to company organization.

— *systemic factors*: that is, the factors that characterize the company as a system and steer it towards its missions and goals (and for the latter reason can therefore also be referred to as 'critical success factors'). Although the TQM approaches on which the main awards are based do not always attribute sufficient importance to processes, paradoxically they tend to view organization simply in terms of processes, and fail to view it as a system. The process-based approach is fundamental, but processes should be seen as part of a systemic environment (Fig. 2.3), in which the relations among processes and between each process and systemic factors are vital elements (holistic approaches to systems typically place great importance on interrelations). It is misleading to consider the organization simply as the sum of processes. Business process re-engineering approaches that regard breakthroughs in the engineering of new processes as miracle cures capable of producing dramatic improvements in performance are very likely to have disappointing results. In the same way, benchmarking theories based on the assumption that excellence can be achieved by cloning (difficult in itself) the processes of the best-in-class will prove highly frustrating. The systemic environment in which processes operate is fundamental. But it is particularly difficult to decipher and interpret, since its key factors are often intangible (e.g., management style, quality and involvement of human resources). The corporate organization could also be said to have a *metaprocess* dimension, which exists beyond processes, but permeates the entire environment in which processes develop; this is the dimension referred to here as the systemic factors area. These factors are more than enablers, or critical factors for successful attainment of missions and goals; they are the attributes that define the physiognomy of the 'system'.

• The model's three components are linked by cause–effect relationships, as shown in Fig. 2.5. Links between results and processes are direct, those between results and systemic factors, where they exist, are indirect, through the medium of processes. This explains the diagnostic use of the model. The continuous search for causes fuels a diagnostic culture, which gradually increases people's ability to understand the links between systemic factors, processes and results. This enables them to identify the systemic and process levers that can be activated to steer the company towards its missions and goals and if necessary adjust its course. This is the essential purpose of the model: to become a *continuous learning tool* to help the people in the company improve their understanding of the cause–effect relationships between systemic factors, processes and goals/results. As the company expands its understanding of these links, it will be able to personalize and fine-tune the model (which initially will be a general model), allowing it gradually to evolve as the company and its needs change.

- In order to identify the correlations between the three areas, the company must develop its measuring abilities. This brings us to another important concept concerning the model and its application in implementation and, above all, self-assessment: the management 'control panel' illustrated in Fig. 2.10 (and referred to in Chapter 3, Figs 3.2 and 3.3). Management should improve its understanding of the model by studying ways of measuring results, processes and systemic factors. We shall come back to measurement methods in Chapters 3, 4 and 5. The introduction of the control panel as a way to keep the three areas of the model and their correlations under quantitative control is one of the fundamental concepts of this book.

# The self-assessment/ self-diagnosis process

## 3.1 CHARACTERISTICS

The distinguishing features of the self-assessment approach discussed in this book are described below.

1. The approach is based on a model that considers *all* the company's missions, not just that of providing customers with good products and services; it therefore extends beyond the traditional sphere of quality assessments to cover every aspect of the company and its business. The models used by the quality awards, in particular the EQA model, all aim to move beyond the traditional confines of quality, but this can only be achieved by adopting a different type of conceptual approach: an approach that begins with a critical analysis of the company's purposes and therefore forces management to define those purposes if they are not sufficiently well stated (Chapter 4 and Appendix B). The business model should focus on missions and strategic goals, in order to help the company define those missions and goals and gear its processes and systemic factors to them. Then it will also be a useful tool for self-assessment, and at this point it will incorporate results. The model is sufficiently general to be used as a basis for assessment of any type of organization, including non-profit-making organizations, in which case the 'business goals' category can be replaced with a category that considers the body's specific missions.

2. The approach is geared to improvement. All the current self-assessment models claim this characteristic. In practice, however, the relationship of these models to the awards and the desire to measure performance with a score mean that companies tend to concentrate on identifying strengths rather than weaknesses (euphemistically referred to as 'improvement opportunities'). The approach described here is based on a precise reading of self-assessment (defined as 'improvement-oriented self-assessment'); identification of weaknesses and their underlying causes is the main objective. Consequently, weights have deliberately

not been given to the various categories of the model (this will surprise readers who are familiar with the awards), since weights and global scores (not category scores, which *are* used here) distract attention away from the real purpose of the exercise. Moreover, if the ultimate aim is self-assessment, then each company will have to allocate its own weights; if it is comparison with other companies, then a standard model and standard weights must be adopted. The characteristics described below in (3) and (4) – an approach based on results, a diagnostic approach – confirm the model's unequivocal focus on improvement. At this point, however, a fundamental clarification is needed as regards the term 'improvement'. Here, improvement has two distinct meanings (given the lack of two distinct terms). The first is the traditional meaning: the action taken when performance fails to meet goals or expectations, in order to reach the required level. The second meaning is setting higher goals – often significantly higher goals – for specific performance areas: goals that have never been reached before, that sometimes require substantial improvements in certain capabilities. Expanding the concept of improvement to include this second meaning is essential to move beyond the limited vision of TQM as incremental improvement (according to which business process re-engineering, for example, would be extraneous to TQM). Self-assessment, together with benchmarking, helps companies identify the causes of the limitations in current performance and plan action to improve current processes/ factors or re-engineer them, as the case may be.

3. The approach is based on results. The difference between results and goals (or expectations) or the difference between the company's intended future performance and its current performance is the main motor of improvement and therefore of improvement-oriented self-assessment. This characteristic distinguishes the approach described here from the award models, which inevitably produce improvements based more on the actual models than on results. With the award models, the assessment process is conducted criterion by criterion; in evaluating systemic factors, it considers the company's approach and deployment; in evaluating results, it considers actual positioning in relation to goals and to competitors, as well as result trends. Naturally, the assessor attempts to establish correlations among the model's various assessment categories (or criteria), in particular among factors (enablers) and results, but since this method proceeds on a criterion basis, it is structurally fragmented. Moreover, although the award models are not prescriptive, they are the starting point and frame of reference for the identification of weaknesses and therefore for improvement planning. The risk is that the weaknesses identified in relation to the model may not be the real cause of the weaknesses in the company's results; consequently, those real causes may remain hidden.

4. A diagnostic, process-based approach. This key characteristic is the culmination of the previous three and the feature that makes this approach so totally different from those of the awards and the current methods derived from them. The diagnostic approach begins with results and looks for the relative causes. Figure 2.5 showed the model in terms of cause–effect relationships; Fig. 3.1 amplifies this, representing the tree of causes with reference to a specific result (for example, an unsatisfactory market share, non-competitive operating margins, customer dissatisfaction).

In the figure, the result is generated by two processes (a complex result is usually the outcome of a number of processes, but those whose effect is negligible will be excluded during the preliminary analysis). The main branches of the tree are the processes, the second-level branches are the five systemic factors categories (which in turn expand into the third-level branches of individual factors). If a result falls short

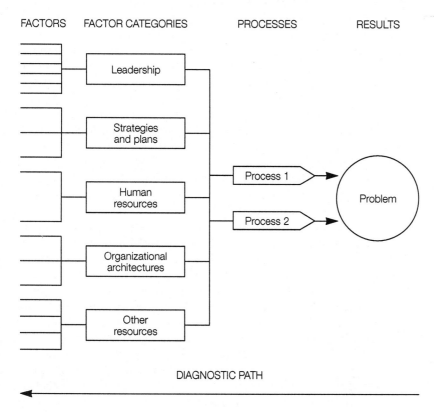

**Fig. 3.1** The tree of causes: the diagnostic path begins with a problem in results (effect) and moves back along the tree until it identifies the root causes.

of the goal, the underlying root causes can be found in the relative processes or among systemic factors, that is, those factors that affect the process but come before it and are therefore extremely likely to affect all processes. For example, if the company's leadership is inadequate, the most immediate causes of the problems can be identified in the processes being examined, but the remote cause, or root, lies in the system; similarly, if the organization adopts a functional structure, the most immediate cause can be found in the management of the process concerned, but the remote cause lies in the system.

The diagnostic approach always begins with symptoms (results) and moves back along the tree of causes to find the underlying causes. Every time the branch splits, the company must decide which sub-branch to follow, devising specific tests if it is unable to make a decision. The self-assessment approach proposed here is diagnostic because its basis is a 'cross-diagnosis', which begins with results, moves back along processes and, if necessary, reaches systemic factors. This approach can also be described as a 'right–left self-assessment' [6], to indicate the direction followed by the tree of causes and create a distinction with the 'left–right' procedure typically adopted by approaches that begin with the model (in particular, systemic factors) and attempt to extrapolate conclusions regarding results (intermediate or final) based on the effectiveness of the specific implementation of the model. Clearly, left–right extrapolations tend to have a low success rate, unless the cause–effect chains are evident, which is unlikely, especially in the area of 'soft' characteristics. For example, if the organization is not process-oriented (a fairly tangible characteristic), it will be easy to predict specific dysfunctions, although it will be difficult to quantify them in terms of results; if leadership (a typical soft characteristic) is defective, it will only be possible to make general predictions as regards negative impact on results as a whole.

The award assessments cannot have a high diagnostic content. Diagnoses are expensive because they take time and require specific skills. This is an investment decision that can be taken only by the company determined to identify the causes of its current weaknesses or analyse the obstacles that could prevent it from attaining higher levels of performance in the future. The award organizers can do no more than examine application reports and conduct site visits. The reliability of award assessments would certainly improve if reports had to be based on a sufficient number of annual cycles comprising diagnostic self-assessment – improvement planning – improvement implementation – results analysis [7]. This can be justified at several levels: first, because a true improvement process is impossible without systematic diagnostic self-assessment; second, because presentation of at least three annual PDCA cycles (Plan–Do–Check–Act, Section 3.3) [8] is a film of the company in action, the best demonstration of its real capacity for improvement; third, because it would remove many of the current problems with award examiners, whose numbers, diverse backgrounds and limited training make it difficult to guarantee the level of experience and uniformity needed for a reliable assessment (for instance, the enormous complexities involved in assessing intangibles).

Clearly, the approach described above is a reversal of the current situation. Today, self-assessment is usually based on the award models. This book recommends the diagnostic approach to self-assessment and suggests that award assessments be based on diagnostic self-assessments conducted independently by the applicant company. The awards apart, however, if self-assessment is to be an effective tool for improvement – improvement based on results – it must lose the connotation of compliance with a model in favour of a diagnostic approach.

## 3.2 THE CONCEPTUAL FRAMEWORK

Figure 2.10 showed the model in terms of self-assessment. The key concept was that management could be provided with a complete set of instruments – a control panel – to measure results, processes and systemic factors. Figure 3.2 illustrates the characteristic measurements and operations of the self-assessment phase in greater detail.

The instruments in the top row take current measurements, typically of processes and results. During self-assessment, this data is consolidated and recorded. The second row represents assessments, surveys, interviews, specific self-assessment measurements. The lower half of the figure illustrates the typical analyses and processing operations of diagnostic self-assessment, which can be sub-divided into two categories: those performed mainly within each of the three areas of the model and those designed to highlight the cause–effect links between the three areas, of which cross-diagnosis is a typical example.

The control panel concept and the use in the figures of measuring devices to represent measurements and assessments stress the point that all the characteristics the company wishes to monitor and therefore improve must be measured in some way. Nevertheless, it is important to remember that most assessments are subjective by nature. Therefore it is essential that they be made by the right subjects. Results are a case in point: in the past, companies tended to use internal measurements to assess perform-ance; today, no-one disputes the fact that the key factor is the perception of the customer, whose opinion takes account of the presence on the market of a whole range of different competitors and offers. Once stakeholders are included too, it follows that measurement of their perceptions, from which their attitudes stem, should come directly from

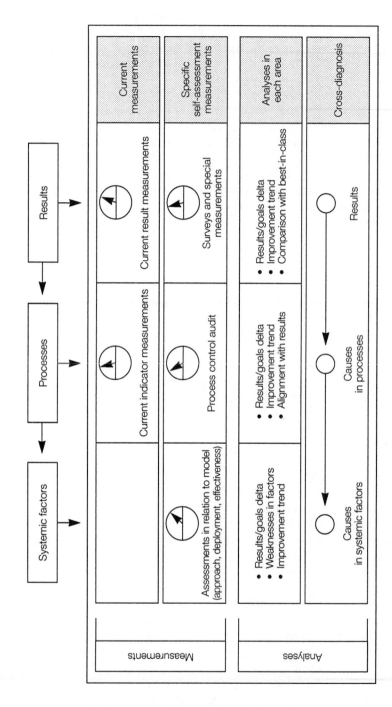

**Fig. 3.2** Typical self-assessment measurements, surveys and analyses.

them. In other words, assessment of stakeholder satisfaction will reflect the voice of the stakeholders and will not be subject to interpretation by management (management is responsible for assessing the company's satisfaction in relation to its expectation of stakeholder contributions).

So, identifying and listening to the voice of the appropriate subjects is vital to obtain the correct measurements; but not only with regard to results. This principle is of fundamental importance in the area of systemic factors too, especially intangible factors. Consider leadership. If the 'recipients' of leadership – managers, office staff, factory staff – have no perception of leadership, then the assessment must be negative, whatever the opinion of those responsible for exercising leadership. In this case – and for all systemic factors in general – the corporate reality being assessed is highly complex; the assessment should therefore listen to the voices of everyone who works in the company and at the same time collect the greatest possible quantity of objective data.

This highlights the need for a representation emphasizing that management, which is responsible for self-assessment, must avoid the risk of an incomplete 'reading' of the company's situation; that the role of management is to *listen*: to listen to the voices of the 'recipients' of results and of everyone in the company who strives to gear systemic factors to results. Obviously, this also includes the assessments performed by management. These points are represented in Fig. 3.3, where, by analogy, the voices of the recipients of results and the company employees are flanked by a 'voice of the processes' [3].

At first sight, this appears to be a purely formal addition, since processes are expected to provide hard measurements, not voices. But in fact a good reason exists: all too often, companies have 'experts' who claim to know everything about their processes and interpret results without reference to measurements, which are the only accurate representation of the true situation. These experts talk about processes without letting the processes talk. And processes can be extremely eloquent, via the appropriate indicators. The extension to processes of the term 'voice' is a reminder that processes should be allowed to talk.

Figure 3.3 also makes specific reference to an input whose presence was implicit in the previous figures, in particular Fig. 3.2, with regard to the 'delta' (gap) between results and goals. This is the 'goals of current plan' block.

## 3.3 SELF-ASSESSMENT AS PART OF A PDCA CYCLE

Diagnostic self-assessment can and must become an integral part of the annual planning cycle, interacting both with strategic planning and annual updates and with operational planning (Chapter 7). When this happens,

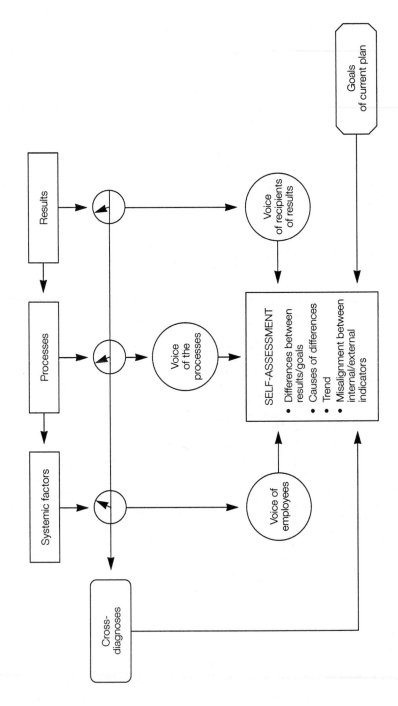

**Fig. 3.3** Inputs for self-assessment.

self-assessment becomes the 'Check' phase in the Plan–Do–Check–Act (PDCA) cycle (Fig. 3.4), which begins with the annual improvement planning session (an integral part of the company's business plan) and continues through the year with the 'Do' phase, when the planned improvements are implemented. The managerial 'Act' phase begins by examining the output of the self-assessment and ends with the relevant decisions. Its purpose is to record, consolidate and extend progress; and, at the same time, to redefine goals and strategies to provide input for the next planning phase.

Apart from the first year, when data from a previous Plan phase will not be available, the Check phase will normally refer to the improvement goals set during the previous Plan stage as the various categories of the model are assessed. It should also refer to the strengths and weaknesses identified in the previous year's self-assessment report (in other words, the situation that emerged during the previous Check). This is to ensure that no lapses have occurred in the areas where no improvement goals were set during the Plan stage.

As far as the awards are concerned, assessment of whether the company – or unit – has achieved or beaten its improvement goals, or not achieved them, will have a significant impact on the final score. As far as self-assessment is concerned, since improvement is the sole purpose of the exercise, the comparison of results with goals will serve above all as an assessment of the company's real capabilities. In particular, the company should identify the reasons for any differences – negative and positive – between results and goals. Non-attainment of goals, for example, may be due to shortcomings in the self-assessment process, in planning or in implementation. It is important to understand the reasons for any differences if the new improvement planning stage is to be more reliable than the old one. In other words, a static appraisal is not sufficient as each category is assessed; a dynamic approach must be adopted, linking the

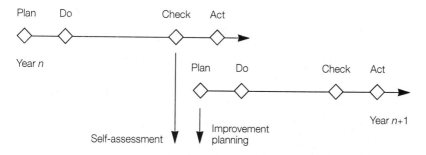

**Fig. 3.4** The improvement planning PDCA cycle incorporating self-assessment.

current situation with the past (previous PDCA cycle) and with the future (capabilities, improvement potential).

## 3.4 WEIGHTS AND SCORING

Anyone who is familiar with the self-assessment models used by the awards will be surprised that Chapter 2 and Chapter 3 discuss this model without reference to weights. How can a self-assessment be performed without weighting the various items in the systemic factors, processes and results categories? The fact is that the emphasis on weights stems from the use of models for comparative purposes: to create a scoreboard or to compare a company with other companies. Weights could be eliminated altogether in improvement-oriented self-assessment, although in some ways they can be useful, if approached with caution. Self-assessment sets out to discover the *causes* of the weaknesses revealed by results, by analysing processes and systemic factors. Its main purpose is to identify inadequate capabilities and the necessary improving action. Where possible, however, the company should try to make an overall quantitative assessment of each category – give it a score, in other words. This is useful for an overall appraisal of each category, and essential if the categories are to be combined taking their relative importance into account. It is also useful as a general indication when the company is considering benchmarking with other organizations. The score for the systemic factors block and for the processes block will be based on an individual assessment of each category and on the cross-diagnoses.

In order to give a score, a scale must be set for each category, preferably from 0 to 100. For example, in the case of leadership, the company will define a 'behaviour model': if its performance matches the model in full, the leadership category will be given a score of 100%; otherwise, intermediate grades – 25, 50, 75% – will be given. Obviously, this is not the most accurate way to measure a 'soft' characteristic like leadership. But if the company avoids mechanistic approaches, if the assessors have sufficient expertise to penetrate to the heart of the corporate climate and interpersonal relations and, above all, if the voice of the people who work in the company is taken into account, then it will be possible to make a reliable judgement based on the reference model. Now an example from the 'results' area: customer satisfaction. In this case, 100% can be positioned on the best-in-class and 50 on the average (obviously, the company will consider a number of different market sectors and competitors).

To sum up, a reference scale will be set for each category, together with criteria determining how scores should be allotted. In this way, two groups of information will be available once the assessment has been completed: the first and more important of the two will be a list of weaknesses (and strengths) in the company's systemic factors and processes, linked, where possible, to weaknesses in results; the second will be a score – between 0 and 100 – for each category (Fig. 3.5, which gives an example of the average scores of the three areas as well as the individual scores of each category).

At this point, weights can be introduced, but they must be introduced gradually. Assuming that the model is being used for internal purposes, and not for comparative reasons or to compete for an award (in which case the model and weights of the award will be used), the company will find it useful to weight its 'missions', that is, the categories on the right side of the model. This will make explicit its scale of values as regards: corporate targets for the future; customer retention and winning new customers; satisfaction of the various stakeholder groups. Weighting is particularly useful to establish the company's priorities with regard to improvement. Assuming a final total of 1, each of the six right-hand categories (a specific weight should be assigned to each stakeholder group) will be assigned a fractional value that reflects its relative importance in the company's policy (example on the right side of Fig. 3.6). Each fraction, or weight, can then be multiplied by the percentage score given to the relative category during the assessment. The example moves from the scores in Fig. 3.5 to the weights in Fig. 3.6, and from there to the weighted scores in Fig. 3.7. The sum of these weighted scores will provide a conventional score for the 'results' area. As in the case of any average, weighted or not, the number obtained loses the analytical and diagnostic significance of the individual percentage scores of each category, but it will be useful for global assessments and comparisons, as long as the same weighting system is adopted throughout.

Weighting the systemic factors – the five categories in the left-hand block – requires greater thought on the part of management. Unlike the weighting procedure for the right-hand categories, it cannot be based directly on company policy. On the one hand, it has to consider the competitive scenario in which the company operates, on the other it has to take account of strengths and weaknesses. For example, if the company operates in a fiercely competitive high technology field, priority should be given to the 'leadership' and 'human resources' categories by giving them a higher weight than would be allocated by a company in a more mature, less aggressive area. If strategic planning or productivity of financial resources are weaknesses, the company may wish to adopt a tactical approach and give a high weight to 'strategies and plans' and 'resources' respectively. Once weights have been allocated (fractions of a unit that produce a total of 1, see example on the left side of Fig. 3.6), then, as with 'results', weighted scores can be obtained for each systemic factor category, together with a conventional global score for the 'systemic factors' area as a whole (the left-hand sides of Figs 3.5 and 3.7 illustrate

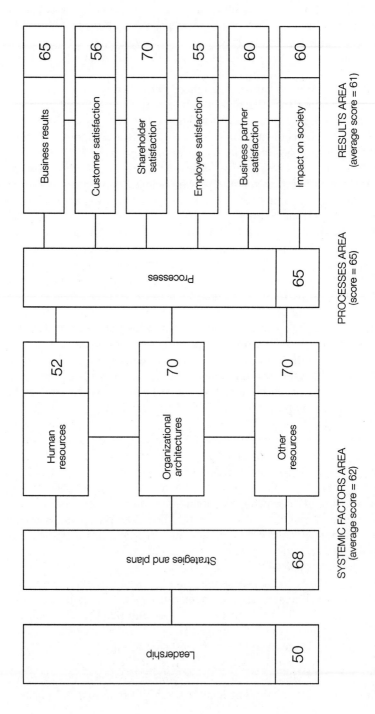

**Fig. 3.5** Possible set of percentage scores for all categories in the model. The numbers in each of the 12 categories are arbitrary. The arithmetic averages of the three areas have been calculated with these numbers.

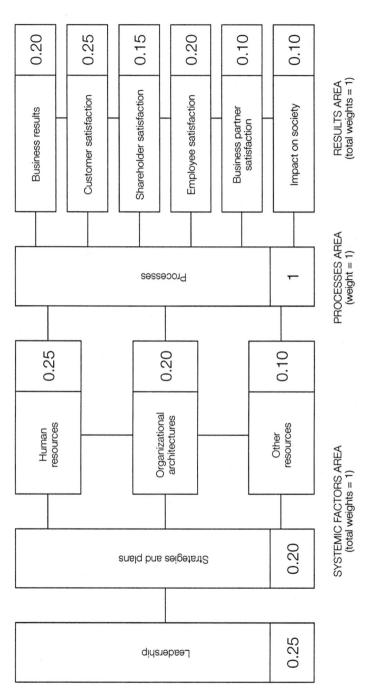

**Fig. 3.6** Example of weighting in each of the three areas of the model.

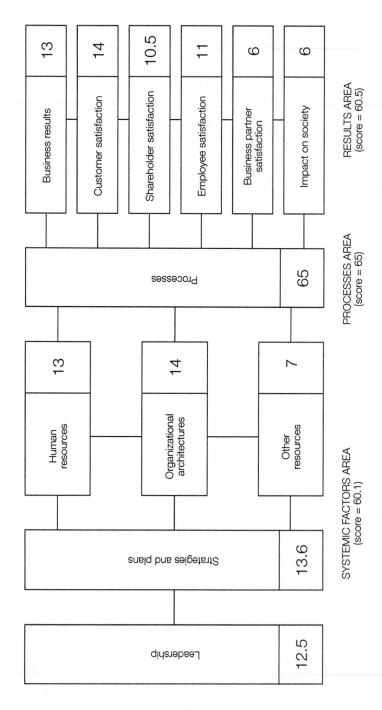

**Fig. 3.7** Weighted scores for the categories and total scores for the three areas, based on Figs 3.5 and 3.6.

scoring of systemic factors respectively before and after weighting with the coefficients of Fig. 3.6). Since 'processes' – the model's central block – has only one category, the problem of weights only arises inside the block. Therefore, the assessment score for the area as a whole is not weighted.

On completion of the weighting procedures described above, the results of the self-assessment are condensed into three numbers, one for each area (lower part of Fig. 3.7). Where required, the next step in the weighting procedure is to produce a single figure, a global score for the entire company (or corporate business unit). Here, the conventions are even more arbitrary and the distinction between self-assessment and awards more important than ever. Since the awards have to reach an overall score, they must necessarily establish a conventional frame of reference and, in so doing, can acquire specific characteristics. The European Award, for example, assigns a 50% weighting to results and therefore is clearly intended as a recognition of companies that are already well regarded on the market and that satisfy stakeholder requirements; although it also requires proof that results stem from excellent enablers (the remaining 50%). As far as self-assessment is concerned, the previous stage in the weighting procedure, where a percentage is obtained for each of the three areas, factors, processes and results, is the last significant level of aggregation. Correct self-assessment should produce a situation of equilibrium among the three areas and therefore three fairly similar figures. Strong differences indicate that the assessment is incorrect. Some degree of variation is possible, but the company should understand the underlying reasons. Exogenous factors may produce positive or negative imbalances in short-term results; changes in leadership (which may be positive or negative) that will produce significant changes in mid-term results may not be reflected as yet in the self-assessment. Figures 3.5, 3.6 and 3.7, to which reference has already been made above, illustrate the various stages in the scoring and weighting procedure.

Figure 3.5 shows a possible set of self-assessment scores. The company appears to be relatively strong in planning, organizational architectures and resource management, and weak in leadership and human resource management. This situation is reflected in the right-hand categories, with relative strength in business results and shareholder satisfaction, and weakness in customer satisfaction and employee satisfaction. The scores suggest that the company is run well, but along traditional lines, with management concentrating on products and business results and paying little attention to human resources and customers. The divergence between customer satisfaction and business results, and, even more, between customer satisfaction and shareholder satisfaction could suggest good products (confirmed by the high processes score) which sell well, combined with low attention to service and customer relations. But the real reasons will be discovered by analysing the results of the self-assessment in greater detail; as noted earlier, aggregate figures tend to mask the findings of the self-assessment, and are useful only as a basis for global conclusions and comparisons. The three averages are fairly similar, indicating that the assessment has been performed correctly.

In Fig. 3.6, the weighting of the various categories could reflect a desire on the part of the company to remedy the situation that emerged in the assessment by giving a higher weight, in the systemic factors block, to leadership and human resources and, in the results block, to customer satisfaction and employee satisfaction as well as to business results. The variations produced in the average score of each area by the introduction of weighting – Fig. 3.7 – are significant but not dramatic (systemic factors fall from 62 to 60.1, results from 61 to 60.5). The key role of the weights is to establish the company's priorities as regards action and investments.

We noted above that the final level of aggregation, which produces a weighted average of the scores of the three blocks, is significant only for the awards (where scores are expressed in thousandths) or when the company wishes to conduct a comparative assessment (although in this case it would be much more useful to make separate comparisons of the scores of each of the three areas). Results are certainly the most important area as far as the awards are concerned (the company must already perform at a level of excellence), followed by the ways these results are achieved. For self-assessment, however, results or, better, performance gaps are simply the starting point for diagnostic paths that *must* identify processes and factors on which action must be taken in order to improve performance. There is therefore no point in combining three totally disparate elements. The last level of aggregation at which useful information can be obtained are the scores of the three areas: results, processes, systemic factors.

## 3.5 ASSESSMENT CRITERIA FOR THE THREE BLOCKS IN THE MODEL

This section looks at the conceptual criteria used to assess the 'results' and the 'systemic factors' areas. The specific criteria used to assess the individual categories in these two areas are illustrated in Chapter 4. The reader is also referred to Chapter 4 for a discussion of the assessment criteria for the 'processes' area, since this area is composed of only one category. Appendix A examines assessment in full detail, with the use of examples.

### 3.5.1 Assessment criteria for 'results'

We have already stressed the fact that correct identification of the company's missions and official goals in relation to the various categories on the right side of the model is the indispensable first step for a successful self-assessment. It is not worth spending money on self-assessment (which in relative terms is always expensive) unless missions and goals have been identified, because this is the only way to ensure that self-assessment refers not to 'quality' but to the company's 'business'. This concept is examined in greater detail at the beginning of Chapter 4.

Once the company has identified its missions and goals, the starting point for the self-assessment/self-diagnosis is the results that correspond to those goals. Some goals will as yet have no corresponding results, but since they are of strategic importance they must be considered (Chapter 4). They are not discussed in this section, which covers assessment criteria for results. By measuring results, the company will be able to assess the deltas – or gaps – in relation to goals, and also in relation to the expectations of the 'recipients' of results and to competitors (the self-assessment should not simply consider results in relation to goals, it should also identify any inconsistencies in goals). The self-assessment should also highlight trends for key parameters. Action can then be taken to correct deltas and trends in order to improve the company's competitive position. This correction is achieved indirectly, as a result of action taken on processes and systemic factors.

Two types of criteria are used to assess results: objective criteria, which apply mainly to business results; and criteria obtained through perception surveys or direct interviews, used to measure customer satisfaction and stakeholder satisfaction.

The self-assessment focuses mainly on critical results, that is, results that present particularly large deltas and/or negative or not sufficiently positive trends. The company's specific results are what count, therefore, and they must be recorded in the self-assessment, when possible with charts that link importance with criticality (Chapter 4). Each critical set of data provides the starting point for a diagnostic path. However, the company should not overlook the secondary purpose of the assessment, which is to give a percentage score to each of the six categories in the results area. Different methods can be used depending on the particular characteristics of each category, but at a conceptual level the approach is broadly similar. The customer satisfaction category can be used to exemplify scoring. Customer satisfaction is measured through questionnaires where the respondent is asked to reply to questions covering the various branches of customer satisfaction [3], on a 1–5 scale: 1 = totally dissatisfied; 2 = dissatisfied; 3 = equal balance between reasons for dissatisfaction and satisfaction; 4 = satisfied; 5 = very satisfied. The percentage of answers in groups 4 and 5 (satisfied and very satisfied) is assumed as the percentage measurement of customer satisfaction. Today, this rather imprecise approach is often substituted with methods that distinguish different levels of satisfaction/dissatisfaction with greater accuracy, but these methods need not be discussed here. The measurement obtained is already a percentage and could be used as such. In practice, the company will probably operate on a number of different market sectors, with different product/service offers. It will therefore have a customer satisfaction percentage for each sector. Depending on the weights assigned to the sectors (Chapter 4), a weighted average percentage can be calculated for the entire customer satisfaction category.

The disadvantage with this simple system is that it does not take account of the competition. This is a significant drawback, since the company's goal is 'to be chosen' and the end customer's purchase decision is always based on a comparison of the value for money offered by the various suppliers. A better scoring method is to set the best-in-class at 100; alternatively – and this solution is particularly suitable for companies applying for an award or comparing themselves with competitors on the basis of the award criteria – the best competitor can be set at the maximum score given to the winners of the awards (around 80%, taking the 1995 EQA as a guideline). The method recommended here is to set the best-in-class at 100 and the average value of all competitors considered (including the company) at 50. In this way, the score obtained will have an immediate comparative significance. For example, let us assume that the satisfaction of the company's own customers is 80%, the satisfaction of the customers of the best-in-class is 90% and the average value of the entire sector is 70%. Therefore, 100 on the scale corresponds to 90% customer satisfaction and 50 on the scale to 70% customer satisfaction. Consequently, zero on the scale will correspond to 50% customer satisfaction and the company will have a score of 75, an immediate indication that the company is halfway between the average for the sector and the best-in-class (Fig. 3.8).

Similar procedures will be applied to the other results categories, although in some cases it will be extremely difficult to make comparisons with competitors or best-in-class. The greatest effort must be made, however, to benchmark results, since this provides the basis for subsequent benchmarking of processes, where possible. Within each category, it will always be possible to benchmark results over time, and this should be done as a matter of course.

### 3.5.2 Assessment criteria for 'systemic factors'

The following sections provide guidelines for assessment of the 'systemic factors' area. Each systemic factors 'category' is sub-divided into a certain number of 'factors', which are sub-divided in turn into 'elements' (Fig. 3.9). When the model is used for self-assessment, the elements are called 'assessment elements'.

Factors can have the same or different weights, but it is best if all the assessment elements of a particular factor have the same weight. The

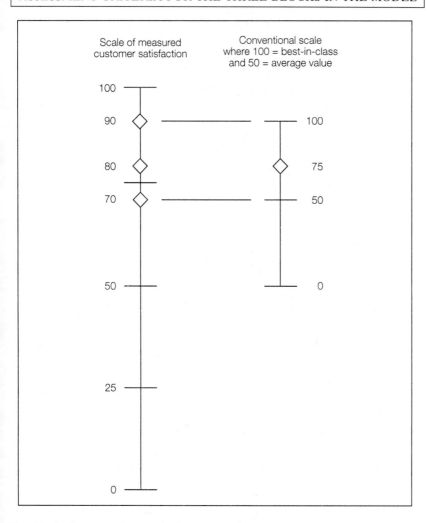

**Fig. 3.8** Scale conversion to obtain comparative score.

assessment is performed element by element and an average is calculated at factor level; then a weighted average is calculated for the category from the averages of the various factors. The process can be simplified by conducting the assessment at factor level, applying the criteria described below for assessment of elements.

Factors and elements should obviously be identified before the assessment begins and described in a special 'guide' (Section 6.5). Appendix A provides examples of factors and elements in the section entitled 'Area 3: systemic factors'. The following sections introduce criteria for assessment

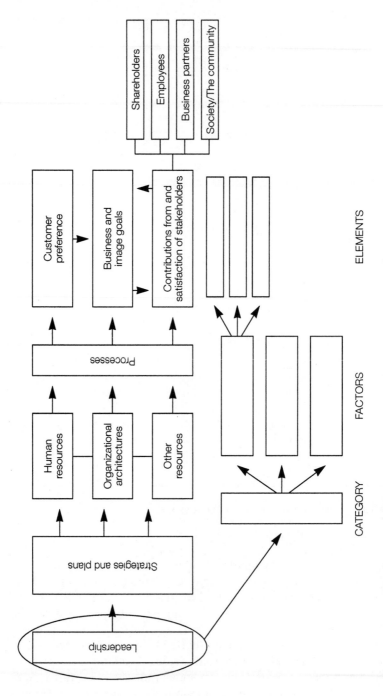

**Fig. 3.9** Each 'category' subdivides into 'factors' and these in turn into 'elements'.

of elements (which are combined to obtain an assessment for the relevant factor) or for direct assessment of factors, together with explanations regarding scoring.

### 3.5.3 Assessment of elements

Each element is assessed in relation to three criteria: *approach, deployment* and *effectiveness*. This is a major difference compared with the method used by the awards and award-based self-assessments, which consider only approach and deployment. The reason for the inclusion of 'effectiveness' is explained below. The second major difference is that while the awards add the approach and the deployment scores (both of which are expressed as percentages) in order to obtain an average score for the element, the method used here multiplies the percentage score for approach by the deployment value, which is expressed on a scale ranging from zero (no deployment) to one (deployment throughout the unit being assessed). Again, the reason for this will be made clear as the discussion proceeds.

### 3.5.3.1 Approach

The approach criterion evaluates 'how' the unit achieves the element concerned. For example, if the element is 'attention of staff', the 'how' will be the organizational and behavioural approach adopted to ensure attention. Assessment of approach will normally be based on reports and personal and group interviews with the unit's senior and junior managers, whose first-hand knowledge enables them to provide significant information, especially as regards 'how things should be'. Personal interviews will be conducted with senior managers, while focus group interviews will be organized with middle management (Chapter 6). During the interviews, assessors will record strengths and weaknesses and assess approach, in percentage terms, from three different points of view (the three sub-criteria illustrated below). They can make an overall assessment of the approaches adopted by the unit as a whole; or they can assess each approach separately and then calculate the overall average. This second method may appear to be more precise, but the attention to detail may lead the assessors to lose sight of the element as a whole. The less detailed first method is preferable when the assessor has sufficient expertise to make an overall appraisal of the average value of the positive approaches to a specific element, linking this value with the corresponding deployment value, as explained in the next section. Since approach and deployment are closely related, the section on deployment must be read for a complete understanding of the approach criterion. So we shall return to this point shortly. The value assumed as the approach score is 'the average approach for the quota of the unit to which deployment refers'. As far as scoring is concerned, only those approaches whose score – taking account of all three sub-criteria described below – is more than 25% (significance threshold) are considered.

The three sub-criteria for assessment of approach are:

1. the *intrinsic value* of the approach or set of approaches adopted by the unit (Fig. 3.10, first vertical axis). A series of approaches will usually be involved. As noted above, the assessor will decide whether to assess the *average intrinsic value* of the whole set of approaches (Fig. 3.10, left-hand graph) or to perform a detailed assessment, approach by approach (Fig. 3.10, right-hand graph). The term 'intrinsic value' signifies the *potential effectiveness* of the approach or set of approaches, in other words, the answer to the question: 'if these approaches are correctly and systematically applied, how effective will they be in achieving the element concerned?';

2. *systematicness*. A systematic approach is a non-episodic approach based on a precise strategy or plan, rather than an approach dependent on the efforts of certain individuals. If the assessment element is a tangible characteristic (e.g., personnel recruitment methods, training, planning), evidence of systematicness will usually be provided by documented procedures. If the element is an intangible characteristic such as leadership, systematicness has to be looked for in established behaviour patterns, which reflect the underlying corporate culture and values that permanently shape organizational behaviour. It should be noted here that self-assessment of intangibles often adopts the easiest approach, and considers 'what' is done rather than 'how' things are done. Impressive lists of initiatives are provided: these may be the result of behavioural changes, but they may also be 'soulless' initiatives that disappear as quickly as they were set up. As we shall see, the third assessment criterion used here – 'effectiveness' – permits a more reliable reading of the state of intangibles.

   In the graphs in Fig. 3.10, systematicness is shown on the second vertical axis; on the right, as an average value for an assessment that looks at approaches one by one, on the left, as an overall value for approaches as a whole.

3. *feedback and control*. Companies tend to plan and launch initiatives without providing adequate checks; they expect things to go as planned, but this is often not the case. The initiative itself is then implicitly taken to be the cause of this partial or total failure, and a new initiative is planned and launched, which suffers a similar fate. During self-assessment, especially self-assessment for awards, management's emotional involvement is often high: the managers responsible for launching a particular initiative will declare its absolute effectiveness

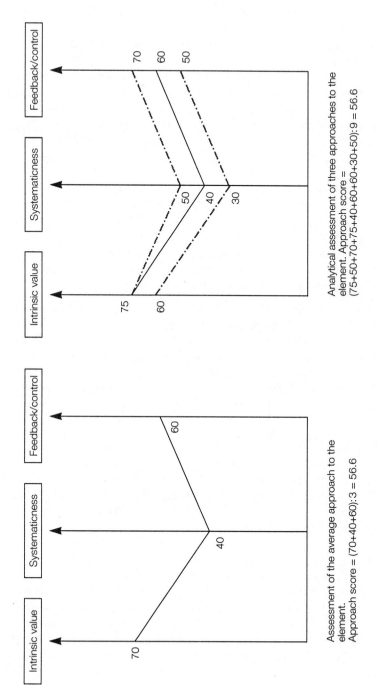

Assessment of the average approach to the element.
Approach score = (70+40+60):3 = 56.6

Analytical assessment of three approaches to the element. Approach score =
(75+50+70+75+40+60+60+30+50):9 = 56.6

**Fig. 3.10** Assessment of approach in relation to three sub-criteria: intrinsic value, systematicness, feedback/control.

with the utmost conviction. When the recipients of the initiative are subsequently questioned (Section 3.5.3.3), effectiveness often turns out to be flawed, a fact of which management is unaware.

The feedback and control sub-criterion examines the extent to which positive approaches incorporate feedback, control and review mechanisms that enable the company to check effectiveness and, if necessary, adjust the approach. Providing every initiative with a control mechanism is one of the most significant ways in which the systemic vision and quality concepts that have been so valuable in improving industrial processes can be transferred to the company's business in general. No initiative is perfect, but it can achieve its goal if it incorporates a self-correction system (which also provides a basis for continuous improvement). This third sub-criterion therefore assesses whether the approach has been designed – and is implemented – in such a way as to check effectiveness, monitor variations, make adjustments and therefore operate in the interests of continuous improvement. It is shown on the third axis in the graphs in Fig. 3.10, again as an overall judgement on the left, as an analytical judgement on the right.

The final approach score will be obtained from a graph similar to those shown in Fig. 3.10, as the average of the percentage scores of the three sub-criteria described above. If the company has made a global assessment of its approach to the specific element, the average will be obtained from a single curve; if has used the analytical method, it will be obtained from a series of curves. In either case, the result will be a number between 0 and 100 representing the average value of positive approaches.

### 3.5.3.2 Deployment

This criterion estimates the deployment of significant approaches within the unit. Since the conventional significance threshold is 25% (everything beneath this value is automatically treated as zero), the deployment criterion is applied only to approaches that are found to have a value of 25 or more when assessed as described above.

Deployment is a somewhat ambiguous concept if it is not related closely to approach. It can be taken as the answer to the question: to what portion of the unit being assessed is the approach score applicable? In practice, however, when the approach of a complex organizational unit is assessed, sector by sector, a series of different approach values will be obtained, as shown in Fig. 3.11, which plots significant approaches (25% and over) in decreasing order in relation to their respective deployment. For example, in the figure, the unit as a whole has a 30% deployment quota for approaches of under 25%; a 10% quota for 30% approaches; a 20% quota for 40% approaches; a 20% quota for 60% approaches and so on. Read in cumulative terms, 70% of the unit has approaches with a score of more than 30%, 60% of the unit has approaches of more than 40%, and so on, up to the point where 10% of the unit has approaches with a score of more than 80%. Establishing approach-deployment pairs is therefore somewhat arbitrary. If a high approach value is taken, deployment will be low; if the approach value is lower, the deployment value rises. In practice, graphs of this type are not normally plotted and the assessor estimates the deployment score. Even if the assessor is aware of the relationship between approach and deployment, the reliability of the result is often low. But if deployment is taken to mean 'portion of the unit whose approaches are higher than the significance threshold' (25% here), then greater objectivity can be exercised in estimating deployment (in Fig. 3.11 deployment would

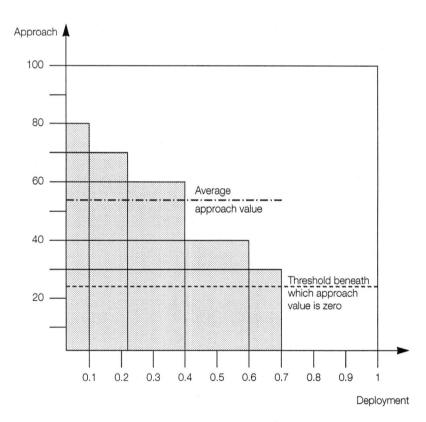

**Fig. 3.11** The significant approaches/deployment graph. For each significant approach value (ordinate), the graph shows the percentage of the unit (abscissa of the vertical part of the step) whose approach score is equal to or higher than that value. The grey area is the product of average approach multiplied by deployment (in the figure, 54 × 0.7 = 37.8), in other words, the aggregate parameter. This value will be compared with and added to effectiveness to produce an average.

be 70%). If approach is taken as the *average value* for the portion of the unit with a significant approach, i.e., the portion to which deployment refers, then a correspondence clearly exists between approach and deployment. In Fig. 3.11, the average approach value is about 54% and deployment is 70%.

Methods based on the awards usually assess deployment – like approach – as a percentage. The average value for approach and deployment is then calculated and taken as the *final score for the element*. This method is not recommended, because the average is calculated by combining two different types of value, and the number obtained is not greatly significant. It is much more useful to express deployment as a number between 0 and 1 (see figure) and take the *product* obtained by multiplying approach and deployment as the final score for the element. For example, an average approach of 54% and deployment of 0.7 would give a value of 37.8 for the element. Many would object that when approach is multiplied by a number that is always less than 1, the final result is always less than the approach value, and a great deal less if deployment is low; whereas if the average of approach and deployment is calculated, deployment often helps (unjustifiably!) to raise the final result, or at the least to ensure that it is not too low. Clearly, reasonable values must be given to average approach and to deployment, but the above criticism is not sufficient to justify a calculation criterion based on faulty logic. With the system described above (taking into account only the approaches with a value in excess of the 25% threshold; taking the average approach value as the measure of approach; calculating deployment with reference only to the above-average sectors of the unit), the final score of the element (the product of approach and deployment) is represented in Fig. 3.11 by the percentage ratio of the grey area to the total area of the rectangle (whose sides are 100 for approach and 1 for deployment).

As noted above, in smaller units which are not physically dispersed, where an overall assessment is possible, the expert assessor can omit the details of Fig. 3.11, and directly assess the average approach value for the whole unit, by mentally associating approach with deployment. Whichever method is chosen, however, deployment must always be estimated with a managerial approach, and never on the basis of a simple headcount. This applies to every area of self-assessment.

In all cases, the assessor should use Fig. 3.11 to calculate overall deployment at division or company level, beginning with the assessments of the individual units. The important point is that approach and deployment should not be combined to produce an average; a significant figure is obtained by multiplying the average approach value (percentage) with deployment (fraction). The discussion of effectiveness below supports this.

### 3.5.3.3 *Effectiveness*

This is one of the distinguishing characteristics of the self-assessment method described in this book (and elsewhere over recent years [6]). Effectiveness expresses the degree to which the 'approach' has had the desired effects in the view of those presumably involved, especially the 'users' of the approach (as opposed to higher-level management, which is the 'supplier' of the approach). Effectiveness is measured through a survey of a representative sample of the entire company population – or population of the unit concerned – (excluding top management, Chapter 6), in which everyone is asked to reply to a series of questions corresponding to the various assessment elements, strictly from the point of view of their particular role in the company. The questions (which will be formulated in simple terms, but will refer to systemic factors) will be designed to investigate people's assessment principally of the intangible 'tools' provided by the company to enable them to achieve the goals of their specific roles.

Figure 3.3 shows that assessment of systemic factors is based on the 'voice' of people who work in the company. As we have seen, the voice of those responsible for defining systemic factors is recorded through individual and group interviews and provides input for evaluating approach and deployment for each assessment element. This is the situation 'as seen from the right', or 'as it should be' according to those responsible for providing organizational tools. Many factors, however, especially those in the leadership and human resources categories, cannot be properly assessed unless the voice of those who use these organizational tools is also heard; in other words, unless a picture is built up of the situation 'as seen from the left'. The effectiveness questionnaire serves this purpose. As the example provided in Appendix A shows, the statements in the effectiveness questionnaire do not cover the full range of systemic factors; they exclude tangible, objective factors and factors for the 'experts' (strategy planning and plan development methods, for example), which involve only a limited portion of the company population.

The EQA and MBA award assessments do not include effectiveness as an additional criterion for assessing systemic factors. This is a shortcoming which should be eliminated. Assessments based solely on approach and deployment focus inevitably on the judgement of management, which tends to believe that things are as they should be. Interviewing a few people during site visits is not sufficient to rectify the balance. The findings of the effectiveness survey provide sound information for assessment of systemic factors, especially soft factors. Any differences between the viewpoints of management and the perceptions of operating personnel that emerge from the effectiveness questionnaires will be very important for diagnostic purposes.

### 3.5.3.4 Calculating the global score for the element

In effect, the assessment provided by the effectiveness survey can be regarded as an assessment of approach by deployment (assuming that the effectiveness questionnaire has been distributed to a truly representative sample of the company population). It will therefore be consistent with the result of the judgements on approach and deployment expressed during interviews. This supports the above theory that average approach and deployment can be multiplied to produce a single result. Thus assessment of each element will produce two numbers: the first (the product of the approach and deployment scores obtained from the interviews) mainly represents the opinion of management; the second, obtained from the questionnaires, mainly represents the opinion of operating personnel. If the average of these two figures is calculated, a final score is obtained in which equal weight is given to the viewpoint of management (which must guarantee that systemic factors are adequate) and the viewpoint of the users of systemic factors.

To sum up, the global score for the element (eS) is obtained from the partial scores for approach (aS, expressed as a percentage), deployment (depS, expressed as a number between 0 and 1) and effectiveness (effS, expressed as a percentage), using the following formula:

$$eS = (aS \times depS + effS): 2$$

# Assessment of results, processes and systemic factors

## 4

In line with the goals/results-based, right–left self-assessment approach, both cross-diagnosis, which is discussed in the next chapter, and analytical, category-by-category assessment, which is examined in this chapter, take the results of the right side of the model as their starting point; then they consider processes and finally systemic factors. This is the exact reverse of the procedure adopted today by the award assessments and by award-related self-assessment. The following observations illustrate how much more rational the right–left approach is. The strategic importance of self-assessment is directly proportional to the strength of its relationship with the company's strategic goals. If self-assessment is clearly and closely related to goals, then it will be integrated easily into the corporate strategic planning process. On the other hand, if links with goals are vague and uncertain, it will be difficult to assert the strategic importance of self-assessment.

A strong relationship between self-assessment and strategic goals is possible only if goals are the starting point for self-assessment; if the results measured refer to those goals; if the processes assessed are the processes that generate those results; if systemic factors are assessed in the context of those goals/results and those processes. In other words, self-assessment *must* begin from the goals area (right side of the model). The self-assessment kick-off should be a top management session at which the company – or the division – defines its key strategic goals, with reference to the model. This is important: reference to the model obliges people to focus on all the company's goals, especially its strategic goals, and on all the 'users' of these goals, including customers and stakeholders, and avoids the risk of only a limited range of issues – specifically, short-term business goals – being considered. For top management, the kick-off can be an opportunity to rethink the company and its policies, to state explicitly what was previously implicit or unstated (Appendix B discusses this). It concentrates top management's attention on the content and weights of the area of the model for which it is specifically responsible.

The kick-off should end with a list of goals/results to which the company attaches top priority and which should therefore be the focus of the self-assessment. We have been referring here to goals/results. In practice, top management is concerned with *goals*; the corresponding results will be collected by those responsible for organizing and implementing the self-assessment. Naturally, when top management has prior knowledge of critical results, it will tag them as areas for which improvement goals are to be set, but operating staff will continue to be responsible for quantifying the situation by measuring current results.

The list of goals and priorities set by top management constitutes the framework for the entire self-assessment process (this does not exclude the possibility that variations may emerge during the self-assessment itself). Consequently, in discussing assessment of results, Section 4.1 refers mainly to this list when deciding which results should be examined and in which order of priority. Similarly, Section 4.2 – assessment of processes – refers to the list of priority goals and relative results when selecting the processes to be assessed (Fig. 4.7). In Section 4.3, assessment of systemic factors will also refer to priority goals, although the processes often act as an intermediary. Without doubt, the correlations between systemic factors and results are less direct, less evident than those between processes and results. Nevertheless, they exist; thus, if assessment of the state of systemic factors begins with results and moves back through processes (right–left approach), it will acquire greater force. Assessments that begin with systemic factors (left–right approach) are always 'nebulous' and therefore less convincing.

The list of priority goals is not the only basis of reference for self-assessment, however. Once established, self-assessment is the 'Check' phase of the PDCA cycle (Section 3.3); it is preceded by a 'Plan' phase (the previous year's improvement planning) and by a 'Do' phase (the action taken to implement planning). It must therefore also refer to the improvement goals of the previous plan in order to assess the results achieved.

In short, the input for self-assessment consists of the priority goals set by top management and the goals of the previous annual improvement cycle (blocks (1) and (2) in Fig. 4.1, which is explained in full in Section 4.1).

In addition to the primary links between results, processes and systemic factors, which are examined during the right–left assessment path, countless interrelations exist within each block, among the various result categories, among processes and among the systemic factors categories. Failure to consider these links could compromise the reliability of the assessment.

Before looking at each category, the reader is referred back to Figs. 2.10

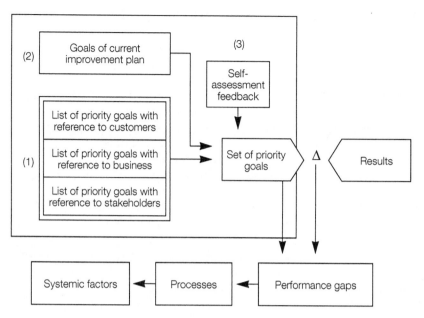

**Fig. 4.1** The input for self-assessment consists of the company's strategic priorities (1) and the goals of the current improvement plan (2); plus feedback from critical results found by the self-assessment (3) which are not covered by (1) and (2). Measurement of results will produce the performance gaps that provide the starting points for the diagnostic analyses of processes and systemic factors.

and 3.1, which illustrate the concept of the right–left approach. This is the basis for the sequential order followed in this chapter and for the logical links among the three areas and, in the next chapter, at a more systematic level, for the cross-diagnosis path.

## 4.1 ASSESSMENT OF 'RESULTS'

For each category in this area, the self-assessment first examines the results that correspond to the priority goals discussed in the previous section: the goals of the company's strategic plan, which top management has approved and arranged in order of priority for the self-assessment, and the goals of the current improvement plan (blocks (1) and (2) in Fig. 4.1). But it should also collect results outside the sphere of these goals in order to submit strategic planning and management's vision to the diagnostic process.

Since a good self-assessment may reveal unexpected weaknesses (through the voices of the market, employees and processes), the company should be prepared to accept any critical results, not only outside the area of its priority goals but even in areas where no goals exist. In addition to the two inputs mentioned above, therefore, Fig. 4.1 includes a third input called 'self-assessment feedback'. This comprises results that are unrelated to any of the goals included in blocks (1) and (2) in Fig. 4.1 but which the self-assessment has shown to be critical. These results may correspond to goals (not highlighted in blocks (1) and (2), in which case the relevant gaps or goal shortcomings will be identified; in other cases, they will refer not to goals but to other elements, such as the performance of competitors, and the gaps in relation to these references will be identified.

In short, for each category, the self-assessment will measure the 'delta' (Δ) between goals and results (or between the unit's results and the equivalent results of competitors or non-competitor best-in-class). These deltas will be the starting points for the diagnostic analyses to be conducted in the 'processes' and 'systemic factors' areas (central and left-hand blocks in Fig. 4.1). The procedure must be applied to every goal/result category.

These general remarks apply to all goal/result categories. The specific characteristics of each category and relevant assessment methods are discussed in the following sections. Application details and examples are provided in Appendix A.

### 4.1.1 Assessment of the 'customer satisfaction' category

Although the focus is on customer satisfaction, assessment of this category should aim to answer a broader type of question: how well does the company retain customers and attract new ones? To what degree do the company's image, the quality of its products and services, its approach to customers and potential customers create a propensity to buy? In a competitive environment, customer satisfaction may be a factor for consideration, but it is not necessarily a decisive factor in the final choice of supplier. The assessment should therefore be wide-ranging and composite so as to build up as accurate a picture as possible of the market's perception of the company. The following sources of information should be utilized:

1. the voices of people in direct contact with customers. The company's commercial and technical front-end, first of all, but also people who have contact with customers, on an occasional basis, with regard to specific issues (in a customer-oriented company, all corporate functions should have opportunities, planned or otherwise, for customer contact);
2. indications provided by customers, both negative (complaints) and positive (letters of thanks or praise);
3. defect-rate data collected by the technical assistance department or directly from customers, goods returned by customers, product recalls, significant problems that have created disruption in customer bases;

4. intervention rates during warranty periods;
5. discounts applied to stimulate sales;
6. ratio between successful sales and total attempted sales, and main reasons for failures;
7. variations in customer base and customer turnover: customers lost and acquired, sub-divided by size of purchase;
8. direct customer satisfaction surveys among the company's own customers and those of its competitors;
9. direct surveys of lost customers, to investigate reasons;
10. targeted diagnostic surveys to identify causes of dissatisfaction;
11. image surveys among non-customers.

Sources (1) to (7) provide indirect information about customer satisfaction/dissatisfaction, which needs to be analysed, while sources (8), (9) and (10) provide information obtained directly from current or recently lost customers in response to specific questions. For the purposes of self-assessment, the information or measurements collected during the year for points (2) to (7), and in particular for (5), (6) and (7), should be summarized and analysed in depth. Special care must be taken in analysing information from source (7), which covers the particularly important question of customer retention (especially as regards the company's largest and longest-standing customers).

Source (1), the voice of the front-end, is usually neglected, whereas it should be a key reference. The truly market-oriented company perfects its sensors so that they pick up even the weakest signals, perceives customers' moods and anticipates their moves. At the very least, it therefore obtains the same information as that provided by direct customer surveys, in greater detail, faster, and in a more systematic fashion. If this area is a weakness, suitable long-term action should be planned; for the short-term, front-end managers should be asked to fill in questionnaires correlated to the customer satisfaction questionnaires filled in by customers. The level of alignment between the answers of the front-end staff and the company's customers reflects the quality of the company's market sensors.

Source (8) is vital and provides extremely significant information if the surveys are properly conducted. The following requirements are essential [3]: the customer satisfaction tree and related questionnaire must be based on quality as perceived by users (the company's own customers and those of its competitors) and must be weighted by users; questions must be carefully phrased and directed at the right people (this is particularly important when a large company is being surveyed); global questions (i.e., those that embrace the entire customer satisfaction tree) must focus on value for money, on customer preference; a significant sample of competitors' customers must be interviewed (to assess their satisfaction with their respective suppliers). Generally speaking, answers will be ranked on a scale of five: very satisfied (5) – satisfied (4) – partly satisfied, partly dissatisfied (3) – dissatisfied (2) – totally dissatisfied (1). In the past, the total percentage of answers in categories 4 and 5 – satisfied and very satisfied – was taken as the measurement of customer satisfaction. This is not sufficient today, especially in fields where competition is particularly fierce. One of the conditions of customer retention is a very high level of satisfaction (compared with competitors). So the company should analyse the distribution of responses among categories 4 and 5.

Once the company has established a measurement method, the results, sub-divided into the various customer satisfaction components (branches of the customer satisfaction tree), should be plotted in special graphs in order to identify strengths and weaknesses as compared with competitors. The chart on the right of Fig. 4.2 shows how results can be represented in relation to a reference competitor, to enable the company to see which areas require priority action.

The importance of the various customer satisfaction components, that is, the weight of the branches of the tree, is plotted on the vertical axis of Fig. 4.3. This tree is represented on the left side of Fig. 4.2 (branches, weights and results are imaginary examples, which provide input for Fig. 4.3). The horizontal axis of Fig. 4.3 represents performance compared with a reference competitor, expressed in percentage variations. The points plotted in the grid are taken from the graph in Fig. 4.2. The left side of Fig. 4.3 shows areas of weakness. Areas requiring priority action can be identified by multiplying weight by variation, for each result in the left-hand squares. As will be seen in Section 4.2, this analysis of critical results components will be useful when identifying critical processes.

Customer satisfaction surveys measure and compare; they highlight critical areas, but not the underlying causes, and must therefore be completed with diagnostic surveys (point (10)). Specific questions and, often, direct interviews are needed to reveal the causes of problems. Evidently, the self-assessment will not investigate the merits of such surveys, but it is important to know whether the company normally adopts a diagnostic approach, in other words, whether customer satisfaction surveys are the starting point for improvement initiatives, as well as for measurement.

Surveys of lost customers (source (9)) are vital if the company adopts a customer retention policy. In this case, the company should have a specific strategy (which should emerge when the 'strategies and plans' and 'organizational architectures' categories are assessed), that provides for such surveys. Clearly, lost-customer surveys should be conducted whenever necessary, possibly in real time or at very frequent intervals. The self-assessment will simply verify whether the action taken in this area is in line with corporate strategy and whether it is performed well. Given that self-assessment will also highlight the need for improvements in plans and

(a) Customer satisfaction tree

(b) Graph of customer satisfaction results

○ company    △ competitor

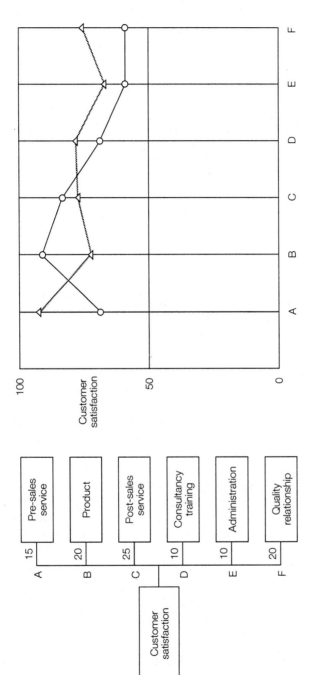

**Fig. 4.2** First-level branches of customer satisfaction tree with weights (a) and graph of corresponding results of a survey based on the tree for the company and a reference competitor (b).

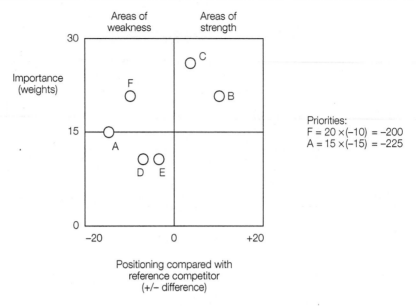

**Fig. 4.3** Identification of areas requiring priority action on the basis of importance of customer satisfaction components and positioning compared with a reference competitor (performance gaps).

strategies, any strategy shortcomings as regards lost customers can be included in the self-assessment report as weaknesses, if this is required by the company's competitive position on the market (for example, if a loss of market share can be attributed to lack of a customer retention strategy).

Image surveys among non-customers (source (11)) help the company discover how it is perceived by those who are not yet its customers. The relevant questionnaire is specific and the answers will reflect the negative or positive effects of the 'word-of-mouth' process generated by past or current customers, and the messages the company itself has conveyed to the market (advertising).

As noted in Section 3.3 and in the introduction to this chapter, all the results from the surveys described above should be compared with the company's planned goals, in particular with those of the current improvement plan, which are based on the previous self-assessment. Reference to the plan will show goals that have been reached, those that have been beaten and those that have not been reached. With regard to the last two – and in particular to goals that have not been reached – the company must decide whether the gap is due to shortcomings in the previous self-assessment, in planning or in implementation, or to unforeseeable interference. Its conclusions will provide input for the next PDCA cycle, especially for the planning stage (Fig. 4.4, upper right-hand output). This is as far as self-assessment is concerned. As regards award assessments or comparative assessments, the influence of improvement rates will have to be defined (Fig. 4.4, upper left-hand output).

The company should also always compare its customer satisfaction results with those of the best-in-class (lower part of Fig. 4.4). This comparison is another source of valuable information for improvement planning (right-hand output) and for scoring (left-hand output). Figure 4.4 applies specifically to the assessment of the 'customer satisfaction' category, but with suitable adjustments it can also be applied to the other results categories (reference to the best-in-class will often not be available). There is no need to repeat it for the other categories.

All the information from the sources listed above (1)–(11) is potentially useful for the primary purpose of self-assessment: to highlight the

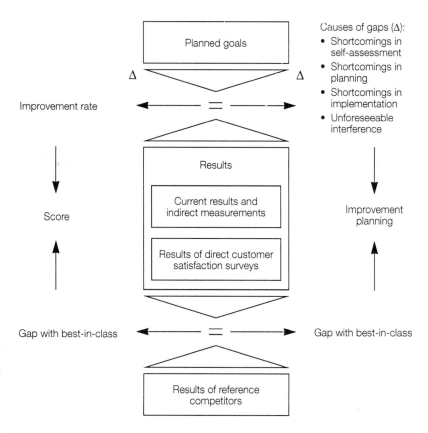

**Fig. 4.4** Assessment approach for the 'customer satisfaction' category.

company's weakness on the market (right-hand output in Fig. 4.4). These may be weaknesses in relation to the company's strategies, or weaknesses in strategies compared with competitor strategies. But it would be too complicated to use all this information for the score (left-hand output in the figure). The recommended method is to limit the score to the customer satisfaction surveys, putting the best-in-class at 100 and the average value of competitors as a whole, including the company, at 50; the score will be a percentage of this scale (Section 3.5 and Fig. 3.8). When the company operates in a variety of sectors and market segments, the weighted average of the individual scores will be calculated.

Assessment of customer satisfaction should also include assessment of the *satisfaction of internal customers*. The self-assessment of the company as a whole is based, through a series of aggregations, on the self-assessments of the various units in the organizational structure. Some of these units – and often many of them, if the company is large and adopts a function-based structure – do not have any external customers. They do, however, have internal customers, that is, other units that come after them in the value chain. Since satisfaction of internal customer requirements is one of the conditions on which achievement of the final goals set by the company depends, it too must be measured, particularly at key corporate interfaces.

Measurement of internal customer satisfaction should take assessment of satisfaction between partners as its guideline rather than assessment of satisfaction between the company and external customers. Personal interest is the sole consideration for the external customer, while the internal customer and supplier should both be working in the superior interests of the company; moreover, the external customer 'is always right' and can go elsewhere if dissatisfied; the internal customer is often tied to a particular internal supplier (if this is not the case, the customer–supplier relations model will apply). Satisfaction questionnaires should therefore consider not only the customer but also the supplier and aim to enhance the partnership. They must be designed to produce answers that show up the shortcomings of the supplier, but also those of the customer (for example, weakness in specifying expectations clearly) and above all the shortcomings of the partnership, so that direct improvement action can be taken. If a score is given, it should not be combined with the customer satisfaction score. Since scores should be used only when necessary (with the exception of awards), in this case they may be useful for key interfaces. They are always internal partnership scores rather than internal customer satisfaction scores. A map of such scores provides management with a picture of the level of cooperation among the different corporate functions.

Assessment of the satisfaction of internal suppliers/customers could also be introduced into the business partners satisfaction category, since two-way satisfaction is a characteristic common to both. It has been inserted here, so that the 'business partners' category refers to independent bodies that cooperate with the company of their own free will, normally on a contractual basis.

### 4.1.2 Assessment of the 'business results' category

The company is the beneficiary of the results of this category, and is represented for the purposes of the assessment by senior management, which is usually delegated broad powers by the owners (when the owners are not also the managers) and is responsible for drawing up a vision and missions suggested or approved by the owners. In addition, senior management has total responsibility for defining goals and strategies related to such missions and for their implementation.

In this category, the degree to which the company has reached its general business goals (operating results, competitive growth and consolidation, increase in value, adjustment of capabilities to meet future challenges) is the object of the assessment. Achievement of the current year's goals must be assessed in the wider context of the company's missions and strategies and its mid/long-term goals and strategies. The assessment will therefore consider not only results for the immediate period, but also those related to a longer term, for the part to be achieved during the current year. Self-assessment is the crucial moment in which the company examines itself at a global level, in order to identify its competitive strengths and weaknesses and check the general consistency of planning and implementation with its strategic vision.

The company's missions and goals are therefore the main reference when identifying business results and relevant indicators. For example, if one of the company's strategic goals is to move towards a TQM model or a lean organization, key indicators will be costs arising from non-quality and inefficiency (warranty costs, write-off costs, costs for returned goods, costs from discounts to move non-competitive products, costs linked to supplier non-quality), working capital and capital turnover rates, time-to-market, delivery times and so on. If development of new technological capabilities or new sales channels is a goal, then indicators that reflect competitive progress towards such goals should be assessed.

Indicators will therefore be both general, in which case comparison with other companies in the sector will be possible, and specific, in which case comparison will be more difficult and the assessment will have to be based mainly on the opinion of experts, on the level of improvement achieved (self-comparison), and on progress towards long-term goals. General indicators include financial indicators provided by the company's financial statements, productivity indicators, market share, and new product time-to-market; specific indicators include non-quality costs by product lines, the efficiency of the main processes in terms of both cost and times and the success rate in achieving goals.

During assessment, indicators should be divided into homogeneous groups. The first group includes indicators related to precise, clear goals, which the company wishes to achieve with the minimum variation. Budget indicators for which the company must fine-tune its efforts and investments in line with goals are typical examples. What is being assessed here is the ability to reach the goal exactly (and if necessary to adjust it during the year with the least possible trauma). Prudent budgeting to account for the possibility of negative variations is not the solution, due to the risk that projections may be over-cautious so as to take advantage later of large positive variations (this is particularly common when the company adopts a results-based system of incentives). Generally speaking, assessment of these indicators can be considered positive if results fall within a range between the target value and a slightly higher value (5% for example); obviously, larger positive variations are acceptable if they arise from promising opportunities exploited by the company or changes that could not have been foreseen when the budget was drawn up. As far as self-assessment is concerned, significant variations should be examined to see whether the cause lies in weak forecasting (if so, this must be taken into account when assessing the 'strategies and plans' category) or in weak implementation (if so, the 'processes' and 'organizational architectures' categories must be carefully examined). If the variation is due to external causes or causes the company could not foresee at the planning stage, then the assessment will analyse how well the company or division reacted to the negative variation or took advantage of the positive variation.

The indicators in the second group relate to areas in which improvements in relation to the previous year are planned, but where goals are regarded as minimum levels, to be beaten if possible (for example, improvements in efficiency, costs and/or times, market share). At first sight, every above-target improvement can be considered positive. But self-assessment is a corporate 'soul-searching', designed to identify and correct any distortions. And distortions often arise in reward systems. If improvement is rewarded, as it must be in companies that pursue it (in terms of greater empowerment if not in immediate financial terms), the possibility of distortion is never far away. So self-assessment must assess improvement together with the *ways* in which that improvement has been obtained. Positive improvements stem from action on result-generating processes that corrects, simplifies or establishes a more effective and efficient way to reach the result. Process improvement nearly always combines an improvement in effectiveness (quality of result) with an improvement in efficiency (costs and times). The assessment must therefore make sure that improvement is based on 'healthy' action, and not achieved at the cost of other important considerations. Just as assessment of quality improvements (customer satisfaction) must ensure that such improvements have not neglected costs, here, where better efficiency is the goal, improvement must not be achieved at the expense of quality.

A third possible group of indicators concerns factors that play an important role in relation to the company missions, for which the annual plan sets no goals but which appear during self-assessment to be in a critical situation. Critical situations that emerge during assessment of other categories in the 'results' area, indicating the need for action on business goals (the links among the various categories of the model must always be taken into account), are typical. In these cases, the company may need not only to set new goals and take action on processes, but also to create business indicators to be kept under control. One example is the loss of major customers in strategic sectors, which requires development of customer retention initiatives involving extra investments and costs; another example is difficulties in relations with strategic partners, which requires a more equitable distribution of benefits; a third is evidence that the company needs a more carefully planned incentive and bonus policy in order to retain skilled personnel. Cases of this kind may require closer examination of the criteria used to distribute income among different types of investment and to remunerate stakeholders. This third group also includes indicators related to long-term growth of capabilities and related investments. Although results are often not available here, the relevant processes and key variables should be identified in order to highlight the indicators that should be kept under control.

We said earlier that for some business indicators, achievement of goals is the main objective, while for others it is improvement. Whenever historical data is available (previous PDCA cycles in particular), the improvement trend (positive, stationary or negative) should always be assessed, since it provides a basis for the next assessment – and therefore for improvement planning – of processes, but also of systemic factors. Moreover, whenever possible, the company should compare its findings with the situation of competitors or comparable companies, since comparisons are helpful if a percentage score is given to 'business results'. If comparative data is not available, then the indicators of greatest importance for the company's missions and goals in both the first group (exact goals) and the second group (improvement goals) can be re-examined, to assess the degree to which goals have been achieved in each case. An average can then be calculated (a weighted average if required) to give the category a global score.

### 4.1.3 Assessment of the 'relations with stakeholders' category

As we have already observed, ideally this should be a win–win relationship providing mutual satisfaction. Figure 4.5 illustrates the main contributions

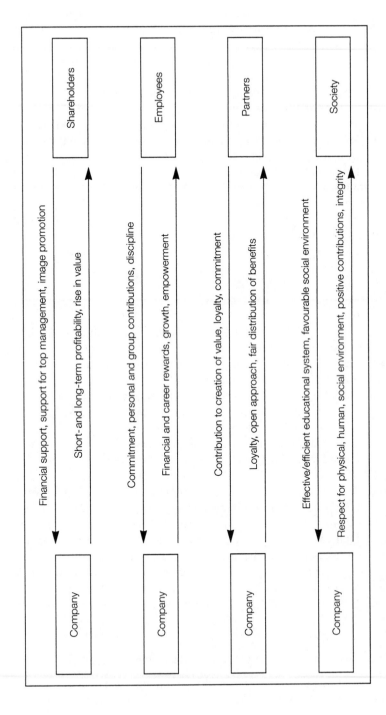

**Fig. 4.5** The expectations of the company and its stakeholders.

the company expects from its stakeholders and those stakeholders expect from the company.

The following sections illustrate assessment of each class of stakeholder in detail.

### 4.1.3.1 Relations with shareholders

As mentioned earlier, the term 'shareholders' refers to the most common form of large company ownership, but the approach also applies – in simpler terms – to other forms of ownership. For simplicity, the parties involved are, on the one hand, the company's major shareholders, those that exert control and appoint the managing director, and, on the other, the company's management, in particular top management. Assessment of shareholder relations will be based on interviews with those concerned, preferably conducted by expert consultants appointed by senior management (with autonomy and confidentiality guaranteed). Major shareholders will not be asked for their opinions about the way the company is managed: this would interfere with the broad powers delegated to management and would contradict the direct fiduciary relationship that must exist between owners and management. The interviews should address shareholders' satisfaction with results, with questions covering areas such as:

- satisfaction with the company's competitive growth;
- satisfaction with the company's image;
- assessment of short- and medium-term profitability (profits and increase in value);
- relations with top management;
- willingness to maintain current involvement with the company and, in line with growth requirements, to invest further;
- willingness to accept a possible review of the company's income distribution policy involving a reasonable sacrifice of dividends in order to achieve a more equitable remuneration of other stakeholders and/or to provide better support for company growth.

Major shareholders should also be regarded as spokesmen for the market, although, where possible, direct interviews with financial analysts and investment trust representatives are preferable.

The interview with senior management (top officers and first line) should cover areas such as:

- financial support received from major shareholders for growth requirements;
- support for management received from major shareholders;

- perceived willingness of shareholders to review income distribution policy as described above;
- relationship with major shareholders.

The assessment will highlight a series of strengths and weaknesses, which should be examined during an assessment session attended by both management and major shareholders. This session should draw up any corrective action or improvement measures (improvement in this case meaning both small–medium changes and radical changes). Since this type of assessment generally requires the presence of an expert external consultant, scoring, if required, should be left to the consultant.

### 4.1.3.2 Personnel satisfaction

This category concentrates mainly on 'personnel satisfaction', since the other side, the company's satisfaction with its employees, is already institutionalized in the form of individual employee assessments conducted by heads of department and consolidated by the personnel division. What is missing, perhaps, is the company's global satisfaction with its human resources, an element that is worth examining before looking at the main issue of personnel satisfaction. Global satisfaction should be assessed by management, in focus groups or through questionnaires (focus groups are more appropriate, but since comments may be perceived as criticisms of the personnel division, questionnaires may provide a more accurate picture in certain cases). Questions should cover the ability of the company's resources, in the various functions (marketing, R&D, sales, administration, personnel, etc.), to perform the tasks assigned; preparations for the future (consistency with vision and missions); motivation and sense of belonging; ability and willingness to work in a group; ability to meet the challenges of the future. The survey results should be taken into account later, when examining personnel management and development (left side of the model), as part of the investigation of the methods used to ensure that the company's human resources are adequate.

Moving on to the main question of personnel satisfaction, the assessment will consist of two types of survey: direct surveys, often known as 'climate' surveys, and indirect indicators. Direct surveys are usually conducted with questionnaires and investigate satisfaction levels in the following areas:

- working environment (physical and social);
- financial remuneration (since there is tendency towards dissatisfaction on this point, questions must be formulated in such a way as to be understood in relative terms, that is, in relation to comparable companies, to the social environment, to the company situation; in any case, satisfaction levels will inevitably be lower than the questionnaire average);

- recognition;
- growth and career prospects;
- job security;
- respect for people;
- empowerment, delegation, responsibility, participation;
- opportunities for cultural growth, training;
- equal opportunities;
- sense of self-realization;
- communication;
- awareness of the company's values, aims and strategies;
- cooperation and teamwork;
- management style;
- workload, stress;
- physical safety and health in relation to working conditions;
- services for employees, their families, the community;
- social gratification of being an employee of the company (company image).

Clearly, questionnaire-based surveys are not the only way in which the corporate climate can be directly perceived. To a great extent, the range of opportunities depends on the level of leadership: it includes conventions, retreats and forums, informal convivial occasions, management-led training sessions, award presentation ceremonies for the results achieved by improvement groups, etc.

Indirect personnel satisfaction indicators include:

- personnel turnover;
- absenteeism;
- late arrivals;
- willingness to stay in the office after normal working hours (this should be analysed with care: working late may simply be a habit in difficult work environments);
- applications to take part in improvement groups;
- level of suggestions from individuals and groups;
- participation in social initiatives.

If a score is required, it should be calculated with the data from the climate surveys only, setting the top of the scale in the questionnaire at 100. In this case, it is not easy to obtain external references. The information provided by the indirect indicators and other direct sources can be used to check and if necessary adjust the score.

### 4.1.3.3 Relations with business partners

Assessment of this category is important for the many companies whose business system includes a large number of partners: suppliers, distributors, co-makers and others. The business relationships considered here are those in which the company regards itself as the leader, that is, as the party with direct responsibility towards the external customer. They are therefore not symmetrical relationships, since the satellite companies undertake to direct their efforts towards the end customer when they enter the value chain. Specifically, they undertake to respect the conditions stipulated with regard to quality, costs and times. In entering this type of partnership, these companies will do their best to follow the main company in its efforts to win and maintain customers, even if this implies improvement of quality and reduction of costs and times. Naturally, they expect a fair return. If the relationship is to succeed it must be based on a win–win approach. For the satellite companies, a fair return means reasonable margins in a situation of full mutual visibility, but also long-term contracts, with termination of the relationship only if performance is clearly inferior to that of competitors. Transparency and correctness are the foundation of these business partnerships. If the leader company concentrates exclusively on its own interests, the relationship is not a partnership but mere opportunism. This can happen with companies that are outside the 'corporate system', but not with those that are part of it and therefore represent vital links in the value chain. It is this second type of company that we refer to here.

Assessment of relations with business partners is a straightforward procedure if joint annual reviews designed to improve the partnership are already performed. If not, they should be introduced. These joint reviews should be preceded by assessments conducted separately by each of the two parties, in the form of an agreed questionnaire. This will provide a basis for comparison, in order to smooth out any divergences, align perceptions and plan the action the partners feel is needed to improve their relationship. The questionnaire – and in particular the subsequent review – should begin by considering the 'products' which the partners exchange (products in the broad sense of hardware, software, services, information: everything the company expects from the partner and vice versa). For each product, the situation and any problems will be noted down. A second section will examine the financial value of services rendered, while a third part will consider interpersonal relations. The first two sections can be reviewed during meetings between the managers who coordinate the relationship, but the third part usually requires a broader assessment. Many partnerships fail because problems arise at operating level: too many people, parochial attitudes, arrogance, not-invented-here syndromes, etc. The questionnaire will focus on the relationship as a partnership and in terms of optimization of the entire value chain, and will be distributed to those with operating responsibility within the two companies.

As always, the purpose of the self-assessment is to identify weaknesses in order to suggest remedies. Since results are the object of the assessment here, weaknesses must be noted down for re-consideration when the left side and centre of the model – systemic factors and processes – are assessed. Any shortcomings in the partnership are likely to stem primarily from the 'leadership' and 'strategies and plans' categories (a lack of precise partnership strategies) and from the 'organizational architectures' category (translation of strategies into intercompany process management rules). But difficulties may also emerge at the executive level, at process monitoring level and so on.

Calculation of a score is a minor problem, but not to be neglected. One approach is to select the company's main partnerships, assess them with the criteria described above and allot a percentage score to each one (e.g., 100 = a perfect partnership, 75 = a good partnership, 50 = a partnership with problems but a commitment to improvement, 25 = a newly established partnership). The category score will be the average score for the partnerships considered.

### 4.1.3.4 Relations with society, the environment, institutions

Companies are open systems that interrelate closely with the environment. In addition to relationships that focus directly on business interests – relations with the market and with partners, which have been described above – the company has relationships with the physical and social environment in which it operates, whose importance is directly proportional to the prosperity and living standards of the community. On the one hand, companies increasingly need skilled human resources – and therefore benefit from the presence of high-quality educational establishments – and attractive physical environments to attract people whose high skills make them more demanding. On the other, social legislation is becoming increasingly severe as regards protection of the environment, personal health and safety, cultural heritage; moreover, each organized social system is expected to contribute to the common good.

Management usually monitors the company's satisfaction with its relations with the physical and social environment when a location is chosen and subsequently whenever it perceives constraints, damage or obstacles to the company's missions. Although self-assessment is therefore not necessary to focus attention on this area, it can be a useful opportunity to make a systematic, comparative analysis of disadvantages and benefits.

Less attention is certainly paid to the reverse situation, the community's positive or negative perceptions of the company. And since this lack of attention is creating growing problems for an increasing number of companies, the issue certainly needs to be considered during self-assessment. Full periodic reviews of the state of relations with the local community and public institutions are essential.

Assessment of this category concentrates principally on the negative and positive impact of the company on the social and physical environment in which it operates. Parties surveyed should include bodies for protection of the environment and society, central and local government departments, citizen associations, educational establishments and the media. In practice, it may not be easy to contact all these groups and in many cases they are not equipped to answer questions of this kind, particularly those concerning protection of the environment. Local government, for example, is often unfamiliar with regulations. Answers may therefore be highly subjective and must be interpreted with care. In this area, the limitations of these institutional bodies can be legitimately supplemented with objective internal data, in particular as regards respect for anti-pollution standards or other issues that are subject to regulatory control.

The assessment can be divided into two parts: the first covers the ways the company minimizes *negative impact* on the environment and society, the second highlights the benefits that the company and its policies provide for the social environment. In both cases, the assessment will be based on the direct perceptions of the parties concerned, supplemented with all the objective data needed to complete the picture.

Negative impact will depend to a large extent on the type of company. The assessment will cover areas such as:

- respect for national and local regulations concerning pollution of water, soil, air (where these exist, otherwise with reference to European and ISO standards or recommendations);
- minimization of acoustic pollution;
- compliance with legislation on the safety of people and property;
- compliance with general labour and social legislation;
- the degree to which, in the above areas, the company has shifted from a focus on non-violation of the law to active prevention of risks to people, property, the environment.

For each area, the survey will first collect negative data: complaints, public inspections with negative findings, fires, electrical shocks to customers from products or inside the factory, legal proceedings regarding product liability, etc. (The maximum transparency is necessary to ensure that all negative data is collected, a requirement that perhaps is not so keenly felt when the company is preparing for an award, when its attention focuses on collecting all positive data.) Then positive data will be collected: certifications, declarations of conformity, reduction of accident rates inside the company and from products, etc. As noted above, wherever possible the survey will listen first of all to the parties that represent society and the environment. Public utilities (water, electricity, gas, telecommunications) should monitor the perceptions of local government and consumer associations as regards the service provider's respect for its physical surroundings and its attention to minimizing damage and inconvenience arising from its operations on public and private property. The supplementary information provided by the company itself, in particular as regards prevention, will consider whether the company has – or intends to draw up – a 'code of ethics' for activities that affect society and the environment; the findings recorded on this point can be analysed in greater depth when assessing 'leadership' (in relation to values) and 'organizational architectures' (everything that has been done to develop a systematic approach to the issue of impact on society).

The question of a code of ethics and values emerges even more clearly when the assessment considers *positive impact*. In fact, if the company wishes to move beyond the episodic level, the definition of values, attitudes and strategies with regard to the environment and society is essential. This entire issue will therefore be examined in greater detail when the 'leadership', 'strategies and plans' and 'organizational architectures' categories are assessed, although here data on what the company has already done and is doing must be collected. The assessment could investigate:

- support for local educational establishments in the form of funds and teaching skills;
- support for and cooperation with healthcare structures;
- social initiatives for employees and the local community in general;
- cooperation with local government or other bodies as regards territorial development or other issues;
- support for and participation in sports and social events;
- donations to bodies with important social roles.

Again, the purpose of the assessment is to build up as objective a picture as possible, in order to highlight, first, the need for action to bring results into line with goals, and, second, areas where goals need to be brought into line with the needs of society and the environment identified through the company's surveys and its contacts with these external parties. Everything will be analysed in greater depth when assessing systemic factors and processes that impact society and the environment. Calculating an overall score for this category is not a simple task. It is relatively easy to give a percentage score to minimization of negative impact. As far as positive impact is concerned, one method is to assess the company in relation to another organization known for its positive environment and community policy, assuming the latter to have a value of 100 (in this way, the percentage can be interpreted immediately and measures the gap with the best-in-class; in the case of awards, the value of the best-in-class will not be 100, but a level that takes account of the presumed difference between the best-in-class and absolute excellence, for example 80).

## 4.2 ASSESSMENT OF 'PROCESSES'

In our description of the model, we said that 'processes' are kept separate from 'systemic factors' because of their central position between factors and results, and because they are the area in which objective company measurements can be taken. Whereas assessments based on the EQA consider organizational aspects in this category and measure global process effectiveness and efficiency during assessment of results, in the diagnostic self-assessment approach the 'processes' area focuses entirely on measurement, of both current indicators and audit results.

The first step therefore is to select the processes that are to be analysed and assessed. In the case of award assessments, the process selection criterion adopted by the company is itself subject to assessment. Clearly, this is not so with self-assessment: the goal is to acquire ever greater precision in identifying processes that require the most urgent attention, in order to draw up a shortlist of the most beneficial improvement initiatives; self-chastisement with a negative score if a mistake has been made is not the object of the exercise (this is one of many possible examples that reflect the difference in perspective between award-oriented assessments and improvement-oriented self-assessments).

At the beginning of this chapter – specifically, in Section 4.1, which examines assessment of results – we saw that the company's key strategic goals (block (1) in Fig. 4.1) provide the starting point for the self-assessment. These strategic goals will often be mid/long-term goals, but they must be examined in terms of current operations so that the annual operating plan can provide for the necessary action to be taken.

The goals in block (1) of Fig. 4.1 together with the goals in block (2) (current improvement plan) are the starting point for assessment of results. Where should assessment of processes begin? When top management sets its priority goals (input 1 in Fig. 4.1), it should rank them in order of importance, on a 1–5 scale, where 5 indicates goals of the utmost strategic importance, whose processes must be covered by the assessment. For the remaining processes, the order of priority can be drawn up by combining the order of importance of goals with the performance gaps found during assessment of results.

To illustrate how goal priority should be combined with performance gaps, customer satisfaction results can again be used as an example, but business results or any other results category could equally well be used. Let us assume that the list of priorities in Fig. 4.1 consists of five customer satisfaction goals related to five major market sectors and geographical areas in which the company operates (CS1, CS2, . . . CS5). Customer satisfaction surveys have identified negative and positive performance gaps compared with the reference competitor. The five results can now be plotted in a graph of the kind illustrated in Fig. 4.6, where the y-axis represents importance (or priority as indicated by management, on a 1–5 scale), and the x-axis represents the performance gap compared with the reference competitor. The left-hand cells indicate priority (in decreasing order, from top to bottom). The figure includes the results ranked at level 5. A priority index can be useful for these results, too, although it will not affect process selection.

Since the goals set by management are often high-level aggregate objectives, immediate identification of the corresponding processes is difficult. In this case, the procedure described in Section 4.1.1 and illustrated in Figs 4.2 and 4.3 is adopted: the goal is divided into its sub-components (in Fig. 4.2, for example, it is sub-divided into satisfaction with pre-sales service, product, post-sales service, support training, administration and quality of the relationship). The relative weights are established and results are measured; then the performance gaps are identified. Once the weights (importance) of the components and the performance gaps are available, graphs of the kind shown in Fig. 4.6 can be plotted. At the component level (e.g., pre-sales, product, post-sales), it is easier to identify the processes concerned. Figure 4.7 exemplifies identi-fication of the processes that generate the customer satisfaction results related to goals CS1, CS5 and CS3. Specifically, processes P1 and P2 are linked to goal CS1, process P3 to goal CS5 and processes P4, P5 and P6 to goal CS3.

Identification of the processes linked to a specific goal (e.g., CS1) is based on an analysis that begins with 'customers' (the users of the goal) and moves back along the customer–supplier chains. Once the processes have

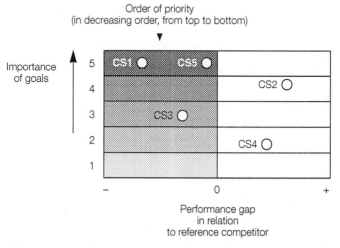

**Fig. 4.6** By combining the importance of goals with performance gaps, the areas requiring priority action can be identified.

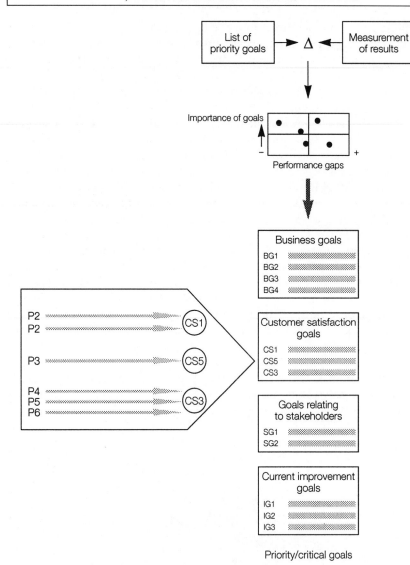

**Fig. 4.7** Identification of processes is based on priority goals and performance gaps.

been identified, it is usually best to apply Pareto's Law in order to limit the number of processes covered. A suitable weight will be allocated to each process, based on the company's experience and the data to hand, to give a final total of 100. Only the processes with the greatest weights will be selected for assessment.

The procedure used to define the order of priority of processes is explained in detail in Appendix A. It produces a list of processes in decreasing order of priority, for each category. This means Pareto's Law can be applied in every category to bring the number of processes down to a manageable level. Since shortage of resources will always be a problem, the company or division will not be able to plan more than a certain number of improvement or re-engineering initiatives. Top management will be responsible for sub-dividing that number among the various goal categories, in other words, for establishing the relative priorities of all the goals considered (even though the procedure will begin with a maximum total, it will always be possible to review this number and its sub-division at a later stage).

Assessment can now begin. For each process, data for the year and trends for key final and intermediate indicators will be collected (first assessment criterion). A team of experts should then audit the processes to verify their state of control (second assessment criterion). The audit will be based on criteria described in the literature on processes [3] and illustrated in Appendix A. For example, it could produce a score on a 1–5 assessment scale ranging from the level of a process that is totally out of control to a process under control, with excellent quality and efficiency results matching the perceptions of the user of the process output.

The findings of the assessment of 'results', conducted in the previous stage of the self-assessment, provide the third and fourth assessment criteria. The third criterion is the level of customer satisfaction, which is the final test of the ability of the process to reach its goals (here, the term 'customer' refers to the process customer, that is, the recipient of each of the results on the right side of the model). The fourth criterion is alignment between internal and external results, that is, between final process indicators and customer satisfaction results; this alignment is the gauge of the validity of the system of indicators used to control the process (or the end product of the process). The fifth criterion is the rate of improvement compared with the previous self-assessment. The sixth, when possible, is benchmarking against similar processes that have reached a state of excellence.

Figure 4.8 illustrates the types of measurement made during process self-assessment:

- current measurements
- process audits
- customer satisfaction
- alignment between end process indicators and customer satisfaction measurements
- improvement
- benchmarking.

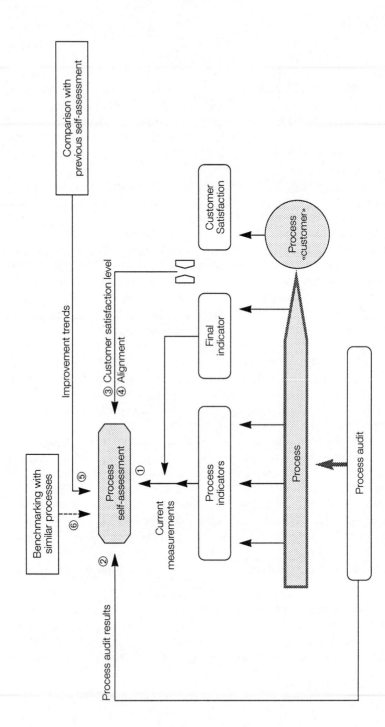

**Fig. 4.8** The main inputs of process self-assessment.

All the inputs shown in Fig. 4.8 provide information to help the company identify weaknesses and plan improvements. Process assessments may reveal symptoms that suggest that the causes of problems lie outside the process. The diagnosis should follow up these indications, or at the very least note them down for future investigation. The systemic nature of the business organization and the importance of the interrelations among its various components have been underlined repeatedly. Interrelations among processes are frequent: sales processes interact with post-sales support processes; product development processes interact with manufacturing processes; personnel recruitment and training processes interact with all company processes; planning processes also interact with most processes. The root of a problem can often be traced back to systemic factors, whose wide-ranging effects generally reach well beyond the level of individual processes. Process assessment will therefore end with a list of strengths and weaknesses for each process; where necessary, the investigation will be extended, immediately or at a later date, to other processes or systemic factors.

Identification of weaknesses is the main purpose of self-assessment, but its secondary purpose, scoring, should also be discussed. First of all: how can a final percentage score be obtained for each process from five or six different measurements? No set rules exist, so the company must establish its own method. 'Effectiveness' can be considered first, that is, the ability of the process to satisfy the needs of those who use the results of that process. One possible approach is to give the process two separate scores, one for its ability to satisfy customer needs, and one for the effectiveness of its internal indicators as advance warnings of customer satisfaction (alignment). In practice, the first characteristic depends on the second, but for diagnostic purposes it is useful to analyse both.

The first yardstick for the ability to satisfy customer needs is the level of customer satisfaction. The relevant score can be obtained directly from the 'results' area (already assessed) and if necessary adjusted to take account of the findings of the process audit. If, for example, process improvements have been introduced since the customer satisfaction surveys were performed, the current process can reasonably be assumed to be capable of producing better results. Similarly, when scoring alignment between internal indicators and customer satisfaction results, consistency with audit information should be checked. If the audit shows that process improvements have been introduced in the meantime to reduce the misalignment, the score can be raised in relation to the level of improvement expected.

As regards the scoring scale, for the first indicator (ability to satisfy the customer) the score already obtained in the 'results' area, with the adjustments described above, can be used. For the second, 100 will be the physiological minimum misalignment (e.g., a range of 5% above or below zero) and zero will be the maximum misalignment tolerated (e.g., 30%;

these values must be decided case by case, however, because alignment becomes more difficult as product/service complexity rises and market competitiveness increases, with competitors exerting greater influence on customer perceptions). An average score will then be calculated from the two scores.

This leaves improvement obtained. Scoring this factor is appropriate for an award, but less so for self-assessment, whose sole aim is future improvement. The self-assessment will consider improvement obtained mainly as a guideline for estimating current improvement capabilities and setting a goal for the next improvement phase (another example of the differences between awards and self-assessment). If, however, a score is required for the self-assessment (for internal use, not for an award), it too must take account of the degree to which the improvement stems from permanent structural roots, which can guarantee further improvements for the future.

If benchmark data is available, it will be useful for setting the 100 value on the scale. Turning to process 'efficiency', the results of the company's annual improvement plans will provide significant information if reduction of costs and/or cycle times was one of the goals for the year; current process analyses or benchmarking will also yield important data. Process analysis can be geared to incremental improvements or to a complete re-engineering of the process if the company needs to make major cuts in costs and/or cycle times. In this case, benchmarking against companies with excellent processes is particularly important.

As regards efficiency, too, the main aim of self-assessment is to identify weaknesses, or, at a more general level, to highlight every opportunity to reduce costs that produce no value added and to cut cycle times. Scoring is difficult if internal data is the only information available; less so if the company has access to benchmark data. Establishing optimal 100 values *a priori* against which to compare the company's efficiency results is difficult for both costs and times; many process re-engineering programmes have found that gains are possible in times and costs that cannot be projected beforehand. If no reliable points of reference exist, it is best simply to record the results of improvement/re-engineering initiatives, weaknesses that still exist and suggested improvement measures.

## 4.3 ASSESSMENT OF 'SYSTEMIC FACTORS'

The main characteristics of systemic factor assessment will emerge as the five categories in this area are discussed. The characteristics of the general approach are common to all the categories and are described here to avoid continual repetitions.

The assessment of the current situation, which is based chiefly on interviews, questionnaires and documentary evidence, will on one hand take account of the findings that have already emerged during assessment of results and processes (presumably critical areas that need to be investigated further). On the other, it will refer to the findings of the previous self-assessment and the goals of the current plan. In Fig. 4.9, the findings from assessment of results and processes are shown in the lower half and the comparison with current goals and the previous assessment is shown in the upper half. Gaps between results and goals provide input for improvement planning, as well as data to be used if a score is required for comparative purposes and awards.

### 4.3.1 Assessment of the 'leadership' category

'Leadership' is the most difficult category to assess, but it is also the most important. The fact that the arrival of a real leader in a company can produce a 'miraculous' turnaround, and that his departure can have the opposite effect confirms the importance of leadership [9, 10]. No model of

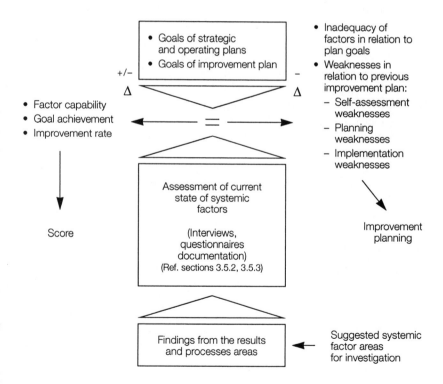

**Fig. 4.9** Assessment approach for the categories in the systemic factors area.

excellence can change a company unless it is personified by a leader. Only a true leader can create that rare situation in which the various ingredients of excellence (that can be described by a model) can blend together into reality. As we have already said, however, in illustrating a model and its application for the purposes of self-assessment, this book does not claim to offer a recipe for excellence: even if such recipes were possible, they would be accessible to an elite group of companies which already present certain prerequisites that a model alone could never create. The intention is to offer indications and guidelines to help companies improve performance by improving their critical capabilities. This is something any company can attempt; the results achieved will clearly depend on a number of variables, of which the most important is the level of leadership.

The difficulty of assessing leadership is not as evident as its importance, as the casual approach to this category often adopted by both awards and self-assessment suggests. Accepting management's point of view at face value, apart from a few routine checks; basing judgement on mechanistic criteria, on whether management does or does not do certain things; using quality experts for the assessment rather than management experts; giving examiners only a few days to study the whole range of criteria used by the model: all this raises strong doubts about the potential reliability of certain approaches to assessment of leadership. In order to ensure effectiveness (and to safeguard the good name of the awards and of self-assessment, a possibly minor but not insignificant point), a less superficial attitude is needed as regards assessment of leadership and of intangibles in general.

The first step is to use the right skills, which can and often must be different for different categories of the model. Quality management experts can assess the 'processes' area, but other skills are certainly more appropriate when assessing the 'leadership' and 'human resources' categories. Companies that are genuinely committed to self-assessment can only benefit from using the most appropriate skills for each type of assessment, employing them for the necessary length of time and requiring these experts to work in a team in order to highlight correlations and interdependencies. For reasons of cost and time, this is not feasible for award bodies. The previous chapter argued that award assessments should be based on the original assessments conducted by companies for self-assessment, and should verify the reliability of these assessments, related improvement plans and results.

The second way to make assessment of intangibles more reliable is to survey everyone who works within the company. As far as leadership is concerned, the perceptions of those who are presumably *led* are indispensable. One approach was described in the previous chapter: effectiveness questionnaires (supplemented by confidential interviews conducted by external consultants; however, these interviews are expensive and cannot cover such a broad sample of the workforce as questionnaire-based surveys). Use of both solutions – interviews conducted by specialists and perception surveys of a significant sample of the corporate population (in terms of mix and quantity) – is strongly recommended, for assessment of leadership in particular and systemic factors in general.

A common misunderstanding in self-assessments based on the award models is that leadership is often judged in relation to quality. Even though the official award documents (see MBA 95 and EQA 95) refer to total quality and quality values at a very general level, in relation to everything the company does, this restrictive interpretation is not infrequent. As the model described here makes clear, a complete corporate self-assessment/ self-diagnosis must adopt a very broad interpretation, placing leadership in the context not of quality or even total quality, but of the company's vision and missions and its related goals and strategies.

Leadership can be assessed from three perspectives:

- in general terms: how the role of the leader is interpreted, how people are oriented towards goals, how relationships within the company are viewed and established. This can be described as 'interpersonal leadership';
- in relation to the 'values' that the leadership has instilled and tends to instil in the company;
- in relation to 'entrepreneurial leadership', that is, to the way the company is managed and guided towards its missions and goals.

### 4.3.1.1 Assessment of interpersonal leadership

A precise leadership model is necessary, to provide the conceptual references required for this assessment. Every expert will have a model of preference, so here it is best to keep the discussion to the general level. Nevertheless, the following points should be considered when assessing the capabilities of the company's leaders, beginning with top management:

- the ability to create a 'vision' of the company's future, to derive clear 'missions' from that vision (the company's aims) and to achieve the widest possible support for those missions [11]. The leader learns from the past, is deeply involved in the present, but looks to the future: he or she is able to create a 'sense of direction' among staff and a 'sense of destiny' within the company [9];
- the ability to exert a significant and effective influence on the corporate system of values and thus on collective and individual behaviour;
- the ability to accord a major role to the company's human/social system;
- the ability to *integrate* this human/social system by focusing the entire organization on key values, in line with vision and missions.

At a very concrete level, especially when formulating questionnaire and interview questions, the aim is to investigate the degree to which the company's managers are – and are seen as – role models, points of reference; the degree to which they clearly express the aims and key values of the company and themselves adopt a consistent attitude; the degree to which they establish challenging visions, missions and goals and involve their staff, even at an emotional level; the degree to which they listen to their staff and provide appropriate gratification, not just in financial terms.

Clearly, the reference model is that of the team coach, which differs greatly from the hierarchical, authoritarian model. The leader is authoritative, not authoritarian; he or she manages to release the potential that individuals normally do not express, to inspire a common vision, to foster the synergies that make for a winning team. The leader's characteristics clearly stem from his or her personality. In the company that has always adopted an authoritarian, centralizing management model and a personnel strategy designed to standardize attitudes and restrict variability, senior executives will match the manager model rather than the leader model. It is very unlikely that this company will be able to change its physiognomy quickly, unless rapid, radical changes are made in top management. But even without such radical change, which is the exception, not the rule, it can start improving leadership (if top management so wishes) by taking action in a number of areas: recruitment; internal mobility; reward and promotion criteria; redefinition of values; basic education and training; definition of a challenging vision and missions; wider empowerment.

### 4.3.1.2 Assessment of leadership in relation to corporate values

This assessment examines leadership's ability to instil the values that are considered essential for success. It therefore scrutinizes the company's values, which are represented by precise paradigms that must be made explicit. A brief discussion of values is provided here, stressing once again that the suggestions offered are intended as a detailed but non-prescriptive guide to the decisions that each company will have to make for itself, in relation to its own particular situation. If, for example, a company is and wishes to remain – or wishes to become – a market leader, it is likely to place far greater emphasis on certain characteristics of personal leadership than is usual: strong focus on strategies, continuous exploration of future paths and identification/monitoring of change (in technology or markets). Accordingly, it will attach particular importance to values such as nonconformity, creativity, innovation, intellectual superiority, diversity, perseverance, continual questioning of the 'certainties' established by previous experience. All these values should always be cultivated, but in this type of company they should be far more prevalent than is normal. Since this book is intended as an aid for companies that wish to improve their performance, whatever their current situation, the values described below are not specifically geared to a leader company but to the countless companies competing on the market to survive, to consolidate their position, to stay in the leading group, to maintain or achieve the lead. The indications offered below are geared to improvement, not to excellence, and so will generally be insufficient for companies that wish to maintain or achieve the lead. These companies will have to supplement the model and adjust it to take account of their 'uniqueness' (not the only inconvenience faced by aspiring market leaders), if necessary with reference to specific literature [9].

Once core values have been identified, the assessment must ascertain the real situation in relation to such values. The awards usually examine the question of values in a foreword to their assessment guides (see, for example, in the Malcolm Baldrige Guide, the section entitled 'Core Values and Concepts'). Values are not included among the categories of the award models because, it is argued, they are a foundation for all the categories. Assessment of the leadership category considers how managers transmit values, but does not make a detailed analysis of corporate values. This is due to the lack of reference to values in the model, a shortcoming that should be rectified. In the model described here, assessment of core values is an intrinsic part of the model, a factor of the leadership category, since it provides a highly significant yardstick of the quality and intensity of the leadership provided by top management.

## The company's human and social dimension

The company is a group of people with different roles and responsibilities. If it neglects the question of interpersonal relations, inevitably those relations will be based on power and competition. It will have an entirely different 'physiognomy' if respect for people and correct interpersonal relations are valued more highly than hierarchical relations and the dialectics that are a physiological characteristic of any group of this type. A certain degree of internal conflict is deliberately encouraged in many companies; but it is difficult to control and usually too much attention is dedicated to internal conflicts, at the expense of attention to market competition. Moreover, conflict situations always generate anxiety, dissatisfaction and hostility.

Similarly, the workplace can be regarded as a place of toil and alienation that must be endured for the sake of survival; or as a place in which people express their personality by contributing to a common end and are encouraged to adopt a proactive, creative approach. One of the most important fruits of leadership is the creation of a positive human and social environment, which stimulates individuals and groups to release their potential: the benefits not only for the company's results but also in terms of personal gratification are enormous.

*The central role of the customer*

Awareness of the importance of the customer, respect for and empathy with the customer, and the desire to win and maintain customers are vital corporate values. Today, the emphasis on customer satisfaction is perhaps responsible for certain exaggerations, such as the idea that the company should be guided by the customer even in the choice of new products and services. This is going from one extreme to another: from a situation in which corporate plans failed to take due account of the expectations of the market to a situation in which the customer's word is law. Clearly, the balanced company knows that its primary goal is to not lose good customers, if anything to win them from its competitors. To do this, it must identify the conscious and subconscious expectations of the market better than its competitors; but it must also know how to combine those expectations with its own experience, creativity and technological know-how, so that it can provide the market with products and services that will enable it to achieve its primary goal. Obviously, creativity will be the dominant element for leading companies, because they need to maintain their leadership; for the crowds of followers fighting to stay on the market, knowledge drawn from customers and competitors will be the key element.

*Continuous improvement and innovation*

Continuous improvement is a fundamental concept extending to every element in the model. *Leadership must be the driving force for improvement.* Improvement should then emerge in every systemic factors category and in processes, and consequently bring improvements in results. To establish whether improvement is a corporate value, the assessment must investigate the degree to which management at every level supports and practises improvement. If improvement is preached but not practised, it is clearly regarded as a low-profile concept, and is not a core corporate value. For some companies, improvement means correcting problems in products and services: this is a first step, but it is still a low-profile view. If the concept is extended to cover problems in all the result categories on the right side of the model, the profile rises: reducing gaps between goals and business results, for example, is a matter that comes within the sphere of top management. Improvement can be further expanded to embrace strategic planning and the need for innovation. At this point, it becomes a high-profile concept, whose goal is to stimulate creativity throughout the company. At the quantitative level, this means encouraging everyone to contribute to incremental improvement in their daily work. At the qualitative level, it means creating an environment that is conducive to innovation and breakthroughs [12]. When a company views continuous improvement as promotion of widespread creativity, a stimulus for full participation in incremental improvement as well as for the necessarily more elitist phenomenon of innovation, then it has achieved a high-profile approach (and successfully overcome the sterile contraposition between incremental improvement and large-scale improvement, between improvement and re-engineering). But this requires sweeping cultural change: creativity and improvement must clearly become core corporate values. Only strong leadership can promote and support these values over time.

### Focus on facts, diagnosis and continuous learning

Acting on facts rather than opinions, on measurements rather than feelings: these cultural values may or may not be explicitly expressed and practised, and are certainly distinguishing characteristics. The ability to foster a diagnostic culture is as neglected as it is important. Companies are full of problem-makers, but they lack problem-solvers. The underlying reason is a low level of participation and sense of belonging, as a result of which people soon learn to live with problems that do not fall within the restricted confines of their personal sphere of responsibility, even if these problems cause visible disturbance. But there is a cultural difficulty here, too: very few people are familiar with diagnostic methodologies. When problems arise, the company appoints a person or a team, who will discuss and analyse the question, but usually in a non-methodical way, without getting to the root of the problem, without reference to measurements. The solutions they propose are often non-solutions or partial solutions. The self-assessment approach described in this book is a diagnostic methodology, which can be applied to any problem and any situation. It can be a tool to foster a culture of diagnosis, measurement and method.

If the company's leadership is aware of the importance of a diagnostic culture and capable of promoting it, it must be assessed positively, because the company will have acquired, or will soon acquire a substantial competitive advantage. A factual, diagnostic approach encourages continuous learning. Like people, companies learn above all from mistakes, their own and others', and the diagnostic approach, which looks for causes, is the main way to learn. Systematic self-assessment and self-diagnosis, together with benchmarking against other companies, will foster continuous learning.

### Non-conformism, curiosity, an open-minded attitude to new developments, eclecticism

This varied set of features reflects a positive attitude to the future and to the consequent need continually to change, modify and review the company's position. Awareness that the future is not an extrapolation of the past and willingness to question consolidated models are positive attitudes for a company that wants to remain dynamic and competitive.

*Other values that emerge from the model*

The values that emerge when the right side of the model, the company's missions, is examined are only touched on here, partly for the sake of brevity and partly because they will become evident as the various categories are discussed. They are reflected in the choices the company makes to achieve a balance between business goals, the primary reason for its existence, customer satisfaction and the interests of all the stakeholders. The explicit formulation of a company policy regarding the various 'users' of the company's results – and thus of the purposes to which the company and its employees dedicate their time and energies – produces a set of values and priorities, an example of which was provided above when discussing values related to human resources and customers. One value that usually emerges is that the company is *results-oriented*: every activity is designed to help it achieve its goals. Bureaucratic structures, interdivisional rivalries and power struggles do not generate value for any of the users of the company's results; on the contrary, they waste value: they are non-values and must be assessed as such. This fundamental criterion must always be applied when a company, in particular its leadership, is assessed.

### 4.3.1.3 Assessment of entrepreneurial leadership

This assessment verifies the degree of leadership provided by management, especially top management, as regards the company's missions; that is, leadership in achieving competitive success. Key characteristics therefore include the importance attached to analysing the market and competition; to building an ambitious vision of the company's market position and setting challenging missions and goals; to driving the company to achieve these goals by taking competent, decisive action to bring capabilities into line with these challenges. For a complete, methodical assessment, reference to the model (Fig. 2.4) is useful, because it provides a clear description of the company's missions and goals. The model says that leadership is the lens that focuses the attention of everyone in the company on missions, goals and strategies, and the main motor behind operations. Leadership's chief duty is to act on the left and centre of the model (systemic factors and processes) in order to develop the capabilities needed to achieve missions and goals. The first effects of entrepreneurial leadership should emerge in the definition of strategies and plans (category 2 of the model). Top management should not consider strategies as its own private domain: its role is to ensure that internally (at least) the company keeps abreast of external change and to guarantee broad-based participation in the formulation of strategies and plans, so that all the competencies and experience available within the company are involved.

To focus correctly on the market, stakeholders and competitive growth goals, the corporate organization, and the front-end organization in particular, must be equipped with sensors capable of monitoring the needs, moods and attitudes of the market, the company, stakeholders and competitors, and of relaying this information to strategy planners. Strategy and planning processes should therefore involve a broad cross-section of management, especially front-end management, but they also require strong leadership, to guarantee the correct orientation [13]. The assessment must establish whether the presence of top and intermediate management in strategy and planning processes is related to a leadership model or to a centralizing hierarchical model.

This applies to leadership in strategy and planning *processes*. As far as strategy and plan *content* is concerned, special attention must be paid to leadership's role as the driving force for improvement and innovation, a point stressed above in the discussion on values. Only top management can ensure that this force is constantly present, that it generates value, that it permeates strategies and plans and therefore human resources management, the corporate organization structure, process management and every area of company life.

Another important criterion is the degree of input self-assessment provides for the improvement planning process and, in turn, the degree to which improvement planning is an integral part of the general strategic planning process.

Next, the assessment will evaluate leadership in terms of attention to the company's human assets (category 3) and to their development, empowerment and well-being. Evidence must be found that the proclaimed value of the company's human and social dimension (see above) is matched by top management awareness of its direct, non-transferable responsibility towards its staff and, at a more general level, towards the social body of the company.

Similarly, leadership must be reflected in the management of financial, technological, information and material resources (category 4). Here again, evidence is needed that top management provides precise indications regarding the most effective and efficient use of these resources in relation to the company's missions. For example, how information technology can support the creation of new, more competitive organizational architectures or provide the infrastructure for effective internal communications.

Special attention must be paid to evidence of leadership in the development and guidance of the company's organizational architectures (category 5). This is something many companies have neglected for years; even the award models do not consider it a critical success factor. In the author's opinion, the source of this disaffection, which has gradually been transferred to the actual concept of organization, is the conventional bureaucratic-functional organization model and the adjustments that have gradually been introduced, with little success. The company's approach to organizational issues reflects its type of leadership, its understanding of the leadership concept. The external observer can only be perplexed by companies that adopt bureaucratic, microanalytical approaches to leadership assessment – based on award models – when their organizational structure is the primary obstacle to the growth of leadership: a case of searching for a mote and not seeing the beam in one's own eye. Leadership cannot grow in companies that accept hierarchical, bureaucratic structures, where corporate attitudes are dictated by organization charts; where power balances, calculation and formalities block initiative, creativity and assumption of responsibility. The speed of change in the marketplace, in society and in technology means companies must continually adapt their culture and organization in order to survive – when they are not actually anticipating change in order to lead. Thus, focus on streamlined organizational models that foster empowerment and rapid responsiveness is an indication of leadership. The leader is aware of the importance of the organization and of his or her own role as the organization's main architect.

In the 'processes' area, one important indication of the presence of leadership is the approach to the problem of cross-functional process management. Many companies are unable to decide between horizontal process-owner solutions and vertical functional solutions. And they discover that shifting responsibilities and power in one direction or the other – to whatever extent – does not solve the problem. What is missing, probably in many cases, is leadership from top management. The problem will be insoluble if top management is not involved, but simply invents an organizational formula (the process-owner approach, for example) and then leaves it to work by itself. Management of cross-functional processes is a major issue, which can only be resolved if leadership is exerted at two levels. First, through development of a corporate culture geared to partnership, to working together as a team; second, through the assumption by top management as a whole (chief officers and first line) of responsibility for supervision of cross-functional issues (such as quality, global costs, delivery schedules) that cannot be completely allocated to single functions and are normally assigned to cross-functional teams and process owners.

### 4.3.1.4 Assessment of leadership: final remarks

The previous sections provide guidelines for assessment of leadership from three perspectives: interpersonal leadership, values instilled by leadership in the corporate organization and visible indications of entrepreneurial leadership. We have also observed that all intangibles, especially leadership, require special assessments organized by experts, who will conduct the interviews and assess approach and deployment. Comparison with the opinions expressed in the questionnaires on effectiveness is vital. As always, the assessment should produce the most accurate report possible on the company's weaknesses (and strengths), as input for improvement planning. Comparison with the results of the previous self-assessment and with improvement goals is a fundamental assessment criterion, as Fig. 4.9 shows. If a score is required, it should be based on the experts' global assessment rather than on intricate mathematical formulae. Since 'leadership' is divided into three sub-categories, the assessors should certainly record the evaluation made for each one, expressed as a percentage, and base their final score on this data. But for such a delicate category, a final score that has been discussed and decided by the whole self-assessment team is more significant than calculations obtained from algorithms that may let consciences lie easy but will never be sufficiently reliable.

### 4.3.2 Assessment of the 'strategies and plans' category

The previous category, 'leadership', examines the company's vision, mission and values, since their existence and content provide significant information for assessment of the leadership of the company. The 'strategies and plans' category looks at *how* the company develops its vision of the future and defines its *raison d'être* and business missions, and from this basis how it develops competitive strategic and operating plans. It also examines deployment of strategies and plans inside the company.

The first assessment concerns *the model itself*. If the basis of reference for self-assessment is a stereotype imported model, which has not been critically reviewed and adapted to take account of the company's specific situation, this is a negative sign. Self-assessment is significant when it refers to a model that describes the company's basic missions and how the company wishes to be and to act to achieve those missions, and when it itself becomes a tool to adjust and improve the model. Of course, the company can use a non-specific model when it first tries out self-assessment, but the exercise will be purely experimental. Self-assessment becomes a strategic tool when the company personalizes the model. So the first area to assess is the extent to which the company has adapted, enhanced and analysed the details of the right side of the model, which expresses its fundamental missions and their order of priority (possibly through the use of weights); and the extent to which it has specified the systemic factors and processes that play a critical role in the achievement of those missions.

Personalization and detailed definition of the right side of the model (the company's missions) is vital if the model is itself to be an effective planning and self-assessment tool. This becomes apparent when the various right-side categories are examined as follows.

*Business goals*

For companies whose objective is market leadership, the priority will be on long-term strategic goals related to acquisition of new competencies and creation of new markets. In other words, on goals that will enable the company to keep and strengthen its competitive positioning in the future. For the follower company, the emphasis will be on short/medium-term goals related to market share, operating margins and rapid introduction of new products on existing markets. Over the long term, the key goal for this type of company could be speed of response and the ability to react quickly to the moves of the leader.

*Customer preference*

In this area, the focus will tend to be on customer satisfaction improvement goals. But the most competitive companies will also include strategies designed to ensure customer retention and attract new customers through continuous creation of new value. The goals in this category are obviously linked closely with those in the previous category.

*Relations with stakeholders*

We have already seen that a clearly defined distribution of benefits among stakeholders, possibly supplemented by the attribution of weights, is an expression of company policy. This alone demonstrates that the model cannot be non-specific, that it must be personalized to reflect the company's real policy. Weighting that does not reflect a real policy – or at the very least a clear management direction – is a useless exercise.

*The genesis of strategies and plans*

In Fig. 4.10 (which reproduces Fig. 2.8), the strategic planning process is on the one hand driven and supported by leadership, whose job is to maintain the focus on missions, as described earlier; on the other, it is supplied with information from various internal and external sources. External sources include the market, competition, technology, the social environment, etc. Key internal sources are expectations connected with the company's missions: management and stakeholder expectations as regards the future of the company, customer expectations and specific stakeholder expectations. Internal sources also include the company's expectations of stakeholders, who must make appropriate contributions to the attainment of goals. In addition, the planning process must take account of results (lower part of the figure), which reflect the company's current performance: final results – related to the right side of the model – and performance at the level of processes and systemic factors. The lower part of the figure, which illustrates results and performance measurements, is the area covered by the 'control panel' in Figs 2.10 and 3.2. The greater the accuracy of the control panel, the greater its contribution as an essential source of planning information. Self-assessment therefore provides essential input for the

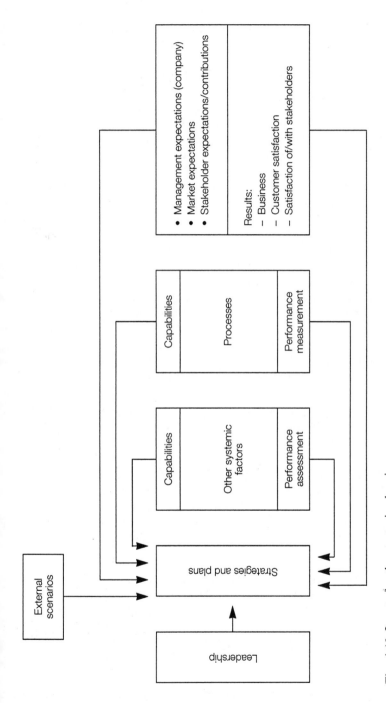

**Fig. 4.10** Inputs for the strategic planning process.

strategic planning process: quantitative information and pointers as regards the need for improvement. Usually, the self-assessment will also provide a picture of the company's strengths and weaknesses in relation to systemic factors and processes, referred to in the figure as capabilities: human resources, technological and financial resources; the company's ability to respond to market and technological challenges; process efficiency and effectiveness. In short, self-assessment provides input for dynamic planning, geared to continuous improvement of results through the improvement of capabilities. The solidity of this link between self-assessment, improvement planning and general strategic planning is a fundamental criterion for assessing 'strategies and plans'. The seed for continuous improvement, and therefore for a structural competitive capability that will be maintained over time, lies in planning.

If this category is to be given a full score, all the input classes shown in Fig. 4.10 must be active and effective, and self-assessment must be an integral part of the strategic planning process. Moreover, the process itself must be effective: a fundamental yardstick here is the extent of involvement of line managers in planning. This question has already been discussed in our examination of leadership; here, we need add only that translation of strategic plans into reliable operating plans should be based on an interactive top-bottom process (Hoshin planning) among the various levels, in order to evaluate feasibility, identify bottlenecks, plan the necessary action and involve everyone who will be responsible for contributing to the implementation of the plan.

Another area that must be assessed, which is closely related to the previous point, is communication associated with policy/goal deployment. Circulation of information about strategies and plans is essential to ensure involvement. If planning adopts the interactive process mentioned above, then information and involvement will be a natural consequence.

The final area to be assessed is how operating plans are monitored and updated during the year; that is, the effectiveness of the link between planning and operations, and the speed with which the company reacts to change. In this area, too, the results of the previous self-assessment and relative improvement plan will provide the main frame of reference (Fig. 4.9).

### 4.3.3 Assessment of the 'human resources' category

The 'human resources' category covers the methods used by the company to recruit personnel, improve their skills, satisfy their legitimate expectations (listed in the corresponding results category, Section 4.1.3.2) and make the best use of their potential to achieve the goals described on the right side of the model: success and growth for the company; winning and keeping customers; a solid, mutually satisfying relationship with stakeholders. Stakeholders include the company's employees, who are both the creators (management in particular) and the beneficiaries of the collective well-being.

The first area to assess is planning of activities of crucial importance to these goals: recruitment, development, maximum utilization, rewards and growth. The assessment will examine whether and to what extent resource planning is an integral part of general, strategic and operating planning, and its links to the organization model ('organizational architectures' category); whether recruitment planning takes account not only of the specific needs of heads of department, which often focus on the present, but above all of the company's future growth. Planning of personnel development, of the reward system and, most important, of the criteria on which career development is based will be assessed in a similar fashion.

The second area is implementation, that is, how these activities are actually managed. The assessment will examine selection and recruitment processes, as well as initial training and first-job assignment: it is important to give new employees a clear vision of the company, its missions, goals and strategies, its market and its main processes, and to foster a sense of belonging from the start. Tutoring solutions are highly effective here. The assessment will also look at the way people are developed over time and how their skills are used; that is, how training is geared to the company's present and future requirements, but above all to the development of people with a sense of responsibility, autonomy, the ability and desire to work in a team, a correct human and professional code of conduct. In addition, it will examine the way mobility is used to assist growth, resisting department heads' natural tendency to hold on to their best staff. A special assessment of management is needed here. The criteria used to select new managers and help them improve their leadership and entrepreneurial attitudes are of crucial importance for the company's future. The quality of management is the greatest competitive advantage any company can have.

Assignment of personal goals is another area that must be assessed. The first step is an analysis of the link between the personal goal assignment system and the policy/goal deployment system. If deployment is an interactive system, as it should be, the entire company will be ready when goals are subsequently assigned. Discussion of goals among department heads and their staff turns into a detailed verification of the consistency of ends and means. Management by objectives thus becomes management by objectives and means. Finally, given the importance of improvement for competitive success, the assessment will consider on one hand the development of a continuous improvement culture within the company and, on the other, the real level of involvement of people in cross-functional process monitoring groups and related improvement groups. It will also verify the significance of the results obtained by these groups and the degree of involvement of the entire corporate population in self assessment/self-diagnosis processes and improvement planning. At a more general level, it should assess the degree of involvement, empowerment and delegation in relation to all the goals on the right side of the model.

During these assessments, reference will be made, as always, to the improvement plan, but also to the conclusions reached and notes made during assessment of the 'results' block (right side of the model), especially the results in the 'employee satisfaction' category (Fig. 4.9). These earlier observations should provide indications for specific analyses and critical comparisons with the views expressed by management.

The effectiveness questionnaire will help assessors to verify the real degree to which people are geared to the company's goals (focus on the right side of the model) within a dynamic framework of continuous improvement. It should be designed to investigate cultural growth: how widespread the company's values are (assuming that leadership has explicitly identified these values). It should assess people's orientation and involvement with the company's missions and goals, that is, corporate growth and success, winning and keeping customers and mutually satisfactory relations with all stakeholders. Above all, the questionnaire and interviews should investigate the growth of a culture based on individual responsibility and personal involvement in continuous improvement: the real levels of empowerment, the ways in which a proactive approach is encouraged, the diffusion of improvement groups and cross functional process-monitoring groups, etc. The real impact of these groups on improvement results should also be assessed.

### 4.3.4 Assessment of the 'other resources' category

Here too, the assessment should examine the focus on missions. In this case, however, the link between the category and missions is usually indirect, via the 'strategies and plans' and 'organizational architectures' categories and 'processes', on which not only the effectiveness but also the efficiency of resource utilization depend (productivity of financial resources, IT resources, etc.). Reference must be made to the critical areas found during assessment of the results area, in particular 'business results' which can be correlated with this systemic factor category.

First, the company will assess management of *financial resources*. The first questions to consider are: how are financial strategies linked with general strategies and planning? How do financial strategies support planned market growth, customer retention and/or market-share expansion policies, personnel and partner policies? How are major investment decisions made? How is financial risk managed? How is the problem of fair remuneration of the various stakeholders – shareholders, employees, partners, company – resolved at financial level? Other questions concern control of financial processes, choice of process indicators and management of these indicators to improve results. Another important area is administrative and management control. In companies that adopt a process-based organization, activity-based costing is usually the most suitable cost-aggregation system; bearing this in mind, the assessment must verify whether the company's system is consistent with the goal of optimizing process efficiency. In all cases, it should verify that administrative and management control processes have appropriate indicators to enable the company to correctly assess and improve 'business results'.

*Information resources* should be assessed next. Information is the lifeblood of the organization. First, the assessment must verify whether an information strategy exists and its relation to the company's general strategies. Besides an internal information strategy, the company should have a strategy for customers and stakeholders, as well as for the market, the financial community and society in general. These information strategies should be flanked by an adequate corporate IT strategy, given the fundamental role of information technology in modern organizational architectures. To a certain extent, the self-assessment will also have to assess the IT solutions adopted by the company, but at a systemic level only: decentralized solutions rather than centralized solutions, process-based rather than function-based solutions, flexible rather than rigid, and so on.

Special attention must be paid to the company's Management Information System (MIS). The control panel concept briefly examined in Chapter 2, whose application obviously can be extended to the measurement/estimate of individual results, processes and factors, should be the guideline for the development of the MIS. The MIS should embrace and link the various elements in the company's indicator chains from systemic factors to results (business results, customer results, etc.), in order to maximize the reliability of decision processes and foster a management approach based on facts and measurements.

The third area is *material resources*. As always, the first assessment criterion is alignment with the company's missions and related planning. This area includes purchasing, an important issue for many companies. The assessment will examine the company's ability to obtain maximum value for money from its suppliers, by analysing supplier selection strategies, vendor rating strategies, supply quota distribution strategies and partnership strategies. Then it will consider the ability to minimize working capital (commercial projections, optimization of internal cycles and inventories, just-in-time, write-off control). Machinery and equipment utilization and use and maintenance of buildings will also be assessed. The final criterion is focus on continuous improvement: beginning with customer satisfaction results, which in this case will normally refer to internal customers, the company should identify processes and place them under control, identify significant indicators, measure effectiveness (quality for the customer) and efficiency (costs and times), set improvement goals and re-measure once improving action has been implemented.

*Technological resources* are the last area. Here, the assessment will explore the alignment between technological capabilities and business goals. If the company is competing for market leadership, leading-edge technology is essential, since success depends on the ability to act ahead of competitors and anticipate market expectations. If the company is a follower, the ability to monitor competitors and the market in real time and to react accordingly is more important. In both cases, the assessment will consider the company's ability to achieve its ambitions and goals. It should also analyse the technologies required by the company's processes as well as those related to the products/services offered on the market. To outclass their competitors, many service companies need processes that use highly sophisticated technologies, especially in the area of information technology and telecommunications. The assessment will consider whether the company also develops technological skills outside its specific fields of activity in order to maintain the competitive advantage it has acquired or intends to acquire. Again, reference should be made to the assessment chart in Fig. 4.9.

### 4.3.5 Assessment of the 'organizational architectures' category

Like all the systemic factor categories, 'organizational architectures' is assessed in terms of the company's missions, that is, in terms of the right side of the model. The two previous categories were dedicated respectively to management of human resources and management of other resources. The organizational architectures category is dedicated to the *way* the company organizes these resources to build flexible, mission-oriented socio-technical systems, which can be rapidly adjusted if the external scenario and the missions of the company so require.

Assessment of 'organizational architectures' is a step-by-step procedure. The first step is to check whether the company has moved or is moving beyond the bureaucratic-functional stage in which tasks are rigidly allotted to specific functions dedicated to planning, coordination and control. If the company is still at this level, it is unlikely to have a global focus on all company missions: each division will tend to concentrate on its own particular goals, which will be related only distantly, and often not entirely legitimately, to the company's goals. In this case, the assessment's verdict will necessarily be low (the remarks made for leadership also apply here).

The second step is to assess the real extent to which the company's organizational architectures (or planned organizational architectures) are geared to the missions expressed in the model (the model having already been 'personalized' in line with the company's specific types of activity). At this point, the concept of the 'customer-centric' organization, built around and based on the company's fundamental missions, is introduced, together with the concept of the lean, learning organization, which is capable of rapid adjustment in response to change. Clearly, assessments involving these concepts can only be conducted with the assistance of experts who possess comprehensive, up-to-date knowledge and know what the best companies operating in similar areas have done or are doing. Work in this field is still at the experimental stage. Many companies – and all those that operate in highly competitive markets – are hampered by the constraints imposed by traditional organizational approaches, but very few have found satisfactory alternatives.

The assessment will consider next the company's missions, one by one: attaining business goals, winning and ensuring customer loyalty, achieving a correct balance in relations with stakeholders. It will examine the specific organizational architecture adopted by the company for each category of missions and of results. For example, it will assess the ways the company intends to minimize its negative impact on society and enhance positive impact. Or the ways it intends to achieve the customer retention targets set during planning. It should be noted that the inclusion in the model of an organization category eliminates some of the problems that emerge when the EQA model is used. In that model, the correspondence between results and enablers (systemic factors) is incomplete; consequently, assessment of the organizational approaches adopted to reach the results planned by the company is linked at times with assessment of the results themselves, at others with other enablers.

The rule that the diagnostic approach is a right–left procedure, which begins with the critical points that emerge from assessments of results and processes, has been stressed repeatedly and is reiterated here. For example, reference to the problems found during examination of customer satisfaction results can highlight weaknesses in the organizational sub-system developed to identify customer preferences. In the same way, critical areas found during the examination of the 'impact on society' category can highlight organizational shortcomings in pursuing this mission. Organization of processes is a general organizational theme that requires special attention. The assessment will verify whether and how the company has set itself precise process-management rules, especially for cross-functional processes; how it has resolved the problem of the latent conflicts that always exist between vertical competencies (functions) and horizontal competencies (process owners or similar); whether it has formulated procedures to identify the processes that generate the most important, critical results and whether it maintains an up-to-date map of the state of these processes; whether it applies rules for technical process management: engineering, control, improvement, re-engineering; whether adequate training is provided for all line managers responsible for process control. These assessments will be simplified by the fact that the company will already have analysed a number of key processes (Section 4.2).

Finally, the assessment will examine process management results for the period, bearing in mind that process management should be the source of the most significant results as regards improvement of effectiveness (quality obtained) and efficiency (times and costs). Reference to the assessment of the 'processes' area – when each process is examined in detail, whereas here they are examined as a whole – will permit global assessment of the effectiveness of the organizational solutions adopted with regard to processes, one of the most important elements in the entire 'organizational architectures' category.

This global view of the company system should not lead the company to underestimate the importance of the management and quality assurance sub-system for products/services and related processes: new product/ service development and market launching; production; sales and delivery; post-sales support; purchasing and logistics. Small and medium enterprises that take the ISO 9000 standards as their basis of reference for quality should evolve towards TQM in gradual stages. But the company must make sure that the sub-system evolves towards competition at the level of customer satisfaction and costs, which is one of the missions described by the model. As we saw earlier, this requires a lean, highly integrated customer-oriented organization as well as increasingly efficient, effective processes. Assessment of the products sub-system is therefore one of the most important parts of the entire self-assessment process.

Experimentation with new socio-technical systems designed to improve effectiveness in achieving goals, raise efficiency and strengthen the company's ability to involve and gratify employees (High Performance Work Systems, HPWS), will rate particularly highly in the assessment.

In dealing with lean organizations and HPWS, organization of commun- ications should also be considered: whether and how the company gives priority to direct, non-bureaucratic communication and adopts the fastest communication paths: vertical, horizontal and diagonal; the degree to which it exploits information technology capabilities to build organizational architectures that optimize information flows: information is the lifeblood of the organization.

Once again, reference should be made to Fig. 4.9.

# Cross-diagnosis

## 5

Cross-diagnosis, to which the previous chapters make frequent references, is the fullest expression of the fundamental concept of this book, the concept that distinguishes diagnostic assessments from conformity assessments: right–left assessment. To a certain extent, this concept has already been applied in the self-assessment process illustrated in Chapter 4, in establishing the order in which the three areas of the model are analysed. The assessment begins with results, then examines the processes that generate those results and then considers systemic factors, the area in which the underlying causes of the company's main problems and its inability to become a 'high flyer' are usually to be found. This is the exact opposite to the approach that is normally adopted, which derives from the Malcolm Baldrige Award and the European Quality Award and whose roots originate in second- and third-party conformity assessments.

During self-assessment, the application of the right–left approach is necessarily limited: self-assessment is such a wide-ranging process that it would not be materially possible, nor constructive, to trace the causes of all the problems that emerge back to their roots. What the company can do during self-assessment is note down the problems that need the most urgent attention, the most complex as well as the most critical, whose real causes are not immediately apparent. The managers responsible for the processes and areas involved will then apply the approach described below.

This approach is called 'cross-diagnosis' because it follows the corporate process flow, which cuts across the organizational pyramid. Basically, it is a diagnostic approach – and as such begins with symptoms and then investigates the causes – applied to processes. Cross-diagnosis can and should always be applied every time the company wants to improve results. It should become a routine operating procedure; as we observed when discussing leadership values, it should foster a diagnostic culture within the company.

## 5.1 THE DIAGNOSTIC PATH IN A PROCESS-BASED ORGANIZATION

Figure 3.1 can be taken as the starting point. It offers a general description of the cross-diagnostic path from results through processes to systemic factors. In the systemic, process-based view of the company, systemic factors are the foundation on which the company's organizational approach is based and are therefore the area to which the origins of many problems can be traced back. Processes are all the company activities that produce results (external and internal). They may be the source of problems relating to *execution*; but in an organization where maximum responsibility is delegated to line functions, processes may also be the source of problems in the micro-organizational factors delegated to them, irrespective of whether these factors are related to personnel, customers or improvement. Since the purpose of cross-diagnosis is to identify the root causes of problems at the level at which responsibility has been delegated (those delegated to act are also responsible for correcting and improving what they do), the diagnostic path will end with the process being examined every time it identifies a root cause at the level of the powers (and therefore of the responsibilities) of that process. Otherwise, when the cause transcends this level, the diagnosis will move further back until the underlying cause is found (to the level with the power to remove that cause). The diagnostic path reaches systemic factors when the problem is not specific to the process under consideration but generalized, or when a higher-level process is reached that relates directly to systemic factors and to the level of control. The second case can be illustrated with an example: if one of the causes identified during the analysis of a process is a lack of training programmes and aids, which should be supplied by the company's human resources function, then it is best to move directly to the relevant systemic factor and establish this as the source of the problem. A process responsible for developing training programmes and aids is likely to exist, but if the owner of each primary process (those that generate the results on the right side of the model) also had to trace back the processes that generate the company's 'internal products', they would lose their way. Systemic factors materialize through 'internal products' (standards and procedures, formal and informal communications, training, documentation). In these cases, the process owner (or the process flow control team) who is conducting the diagnosis should interrupt the path and mark this truncated path as an input. The inputs from the systemic factors area will subsequently be analysed with the relevant managers. Responsibility for systemic factors generally lies with top management (of the company and its business units) and staff functions.

Before continuing our discussion of cross-diagnosis, we should examine the underlying organizational concept, in particular, the role played by

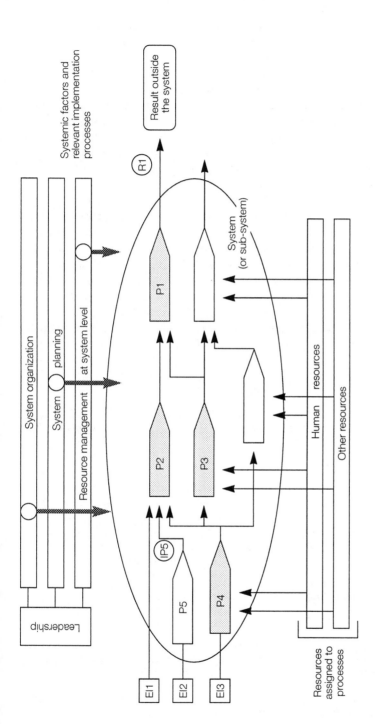

**Fig. 5.1** The system consists of systemic factors which govern the system, processes, links among processes, external inputs and outputs. Resources are assigned to and managed by processes. Shading is used to indicate the main processes in the flow that produces external result R1. External inputs are shown as EI, input from other internal processes as IP.

systemic factors and by processes. Reference should be made to Figs 5.1 and 5.2. Figure 5.1 represents an organizational system from the perspective of the model used here, with processes and the links between them shown inside the ellipse. The upper area shows the factors that govern the system. The lower area shows process resources.

Each process has a number of goals, which arise from system planning but also from joint planning among processes on the same flow. In the case of cross-functional processes, joint planning is monitored by the control team. In Fig. 5.1, for example, the goals of process P2, which contributes to result R1, will be drawn up by a control team whose members include the managers of the processes that contribute to result R1. P2's goals will have to satisfy the needs of customer process P1, which is responsible for guaranteeing result R1. In order to achieve its goals, the process will have to coordinate people, equipment and materials through the appropriate internal planning and organization, as illustrated in Fig. 5.2.

The upper half of Fig. 5.2 shows that the process is influenced by the company's systemic factors (or by specific sub-systems within the company system): respect for the rules of the game as regards planning, organization, management of human, material, financial resources, etc. Within these rules, precise process responsibilities exist at micro-organizational level (the items inside the process). As both figures show, process input comes from internal processes (e.g., IP5 in Fig. 5.1) or from processes outside the

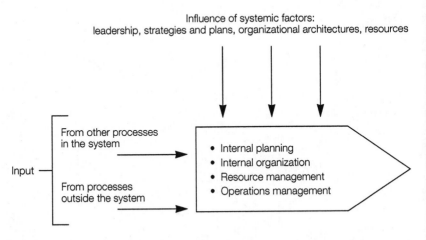

**Fig. 5.2** The process is influenced by the systemic factors (leadership, strategies and plans, organizational architectures, resources) in the company system, and may receive input from other processes in the system or from processes outside the system. Within its area of competence and compatibly with the other processes in the value chain, the process is responsible for internal planning and organization and for management of the resources assigned to it.

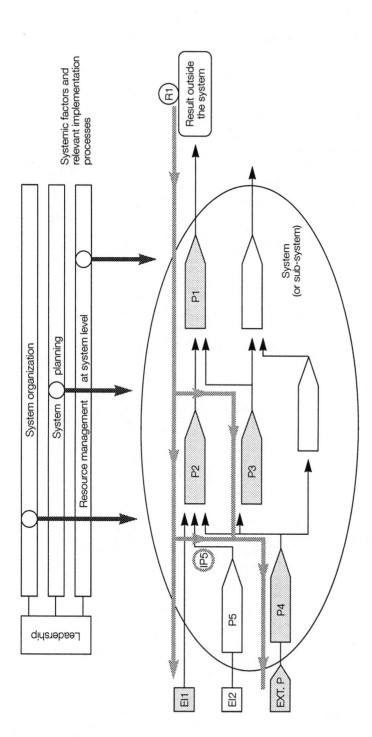

**Fig. 5.3** Cross-diagnosis begins with results and works back along the process flow to search for the causes of problems. It ends at the input level if this is sufficient to identify causes and the unit responsible for improvement; otherwise it continues back through external processes.

system (e.g., EI1/2/3). Consequently, if a problem arises at the output of the process, the diagnosis will analyse first of all the factors listed inside the block in Fig. 5.2, to identify any internal causes; then it will look at the input from other processes and at systemic influences, in order to identify and trace causes that lie outside the process.

Going back to cross-diagnosis and Fig. 5.1, let us assume that we are analysing a problem in external result R1. First, the managers of the main processes that contribute to this result – the flow control team – must be mobilized. The team will establish which processes could be contributory factors in the problem with result R1 (this preliminary assessment does not play a critical role, because it will be confirmed or modified as the diagnosis moves back along the process flow). The main contributory processes are the four processes shown with grey shading in Fig. 5.1. The team will then plot a possible diagnostic path, shown by the grey line in Fig. 5.3.

In all cases, the diagnostic path begins from the process that directly interfaces the user of the final result (the 'customer'): process P1 in the case of Fig. 5.3. An appropriate diagnostic methodology is adopted, such as that described later in this chapter. If process P1 is a complex process, it can be divided into sub-processes. Causes of the problem may or may not be found in process P1, but generally speaking some causes will require the diagnostic path to move back to the preceding process levels (P2 and P3 in the figure). The analysis will continue in this way, moving back along the process flow. Depending on the findings of the diagnosis, situations may develop that require modifications to be made in the process map and the original diagnostic path. A preceding process might be excluded from the analysis, because its contribution to the problem is considered negligible; on the other hand, a process that was initially excluded might later be included, because it appears to have a significant role. In other cases, the contribution of a particular process may be significant, but stem from systemic factors (as in the example relating to training that we looked at earlier); if so, diagnosis is postponed until systemic factors are analysed and the process is marked as an input (IP5 in Fig. 5.3). When an external input is encountered, its significance in relation to the problem being diagnosed must be assessed: if the input is very important, the team could decide to extend their diagnosis to the supplier process (EXT.P in the figure); if not, it will interrupt the path and ask the supplier to continue the analysis in its area of jurisdiction (EI1 in the figure).

As the diagnosis continues, the causes stemming from the company's processes will gradually be identified. This leaves systemic causes. Some systemic causes – those related to processes that supply 'internal products' of systemic origin, such as training, procedures, plans (input IP5 in Fig. 5.3) – will have been identified during the process analysis. Indications and hypotheses regarding other systemic causes will have emerged during the

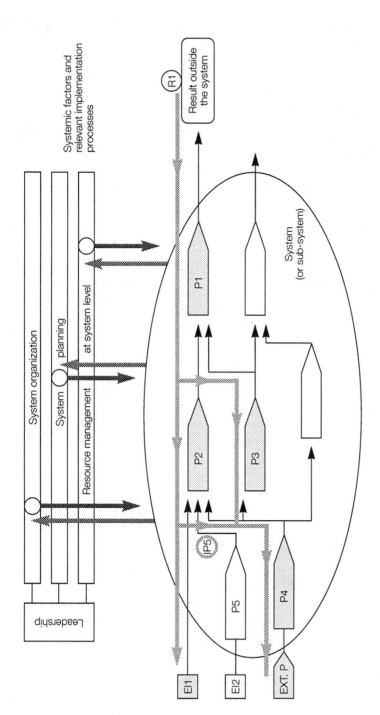

**Fig. 5.4** Investigation of causes may extend to systemic factors.

process analysis, and will need to be confirmed. Causes that recur systematically as processes are examined (e.g., organizational weaknesses) offer particularly important indications. The process analysis will therefore frequently end with a list of problems whose root cause has not yet been found. The extension of the diagnosis to systemic factors, illustrated in Fig. 5.4, requires the involvement of the relevant managers.

If the diagnosis ends by identifying systemic causes, the findings must be used to supplement or modify the self-assessment report (see previous chapter) on the relevant systemic factor (assuming that the cross-diagnosis has been performed after a self-assessment; as noted earlier, cross-diagnosis is not necessarily linked to self-assessment).

## 5.2 IDENTIFICATION OF CAUSES

Well-known tools like the Ishikawa diagram or more sophisticated instruments such as matrix-based analysis can be used to identify causes inside a process or systemic factor. To avoid complicating the conceptual framework of the approach suggested here, the discussion begins with the simplest tool, the Ishikawa diagram – or fish-bone diagram – as formulated for processes [14] (Fig. 5.5).

For cross-diagnosis, both process-related causes and system-related causes must be shown on the diagram. Another version of the diagram is therefore suggested (Fig. 5.6), using the upper half for processes (and related inputs) and the lower half for systemic factors.

The linear sequence of processes should not be taken literally. Normally,

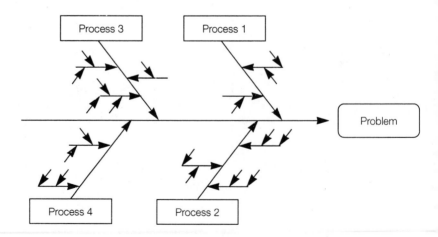

**Fig. 5.5** The Ishikawa diagram for processes.

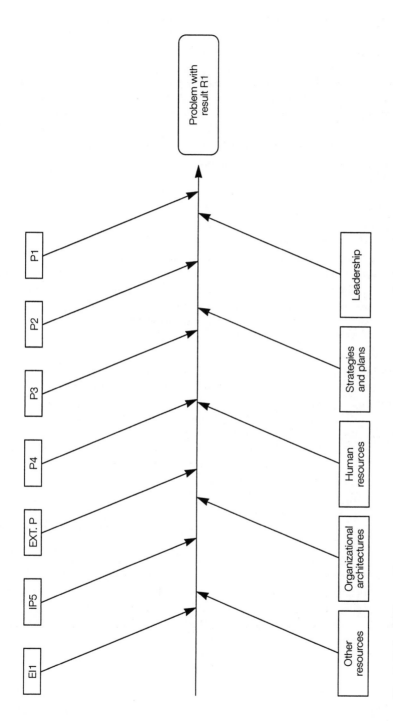

**Fig. 5.6** The Ishikawa diagram adapted to the needs of cross-diagnosis, for the process flow in Fig. 5.3.

processes will form a network, not a linear sequence (the flow in Fig. 5.1 is a very simple example). The processes in the flow being examined should be numbered, beginning with the last process (the one which ends with the user of the result); then they can be set out in order on the Ishikawa diagram, beginning from the right, remembering that, for example, process P3 does not necessarily precede process P2 (Fig. 5.1).

The first step is to assess the percentage degree to which each process contributes to the problem (Fig. 5.7). In this way, Pareto's Law, a fundamental principle for the management of complexity in the solution of any problem, can be applied right from the start. The percentages will be approximate estimates, and do not require absolute precision. Data will normally be available, but if it is not, brainstorming sessions with the managers of the processes concerned should be sufficient to obtain these estimates. In this way it will be possible to exclude immediately processes whose effect on the problem appears, on a preliminary examination at least, to be negligible, thus simplifying the analysis. If subsequent analyses – and above all subsequent checks – show that one of the causes initially regarded as negligible is actually significant, the appropriate adjustments will be made. Since causes of problems can stem from inputs as well as from processes, percentages should be assigned to inputs, too (total weights = 100). Weights are not allocated to the branches in the lower half of the diagram, which represent systemic factors, since these branches are component parts of causes located in the upper half of the diagram. In short, all causes stem from processes or inputs (to give a total sum of 100), even though some of them may have roots at the systemic factor level. In Fig. 5.7, process P2 and inputs IP5 and EI1 can reasonably be excluded from the analysis, at least to begin with.

The second step is to begin internal diagnosis, process by process, starting with P1, and using typical problem-solving methods (brainstorming, data collection and analysis, experimental checks). The reader is assumed to be familiar with these methodologies, which are not discussed here. Four areas are usually covered when the Ishikawa diagram is used: men, materials, means or machines, methods, the four Ms. This approach can be applied here, but it is advisable to refer to the four areas listed in Fig. 5.2, which are more consistent with a process-based view. The first area, 'internal planning', means that the diagnosis should examine the methods used to set process goals [3], bearing in mind that the ideal approach begins with the customer, uses quality function deployment methodologies and adopts a team approach involving the managers of the preceding and subsequent processes. The second area, 'internal organization', relates the analysis of causes to the process-based organization, once again with reference to the 'ideal' situation, where processes are described and controlled, and appropriate indicators, measurement systems and feedback loops operate. The third area, 'resources management', is really a multiple

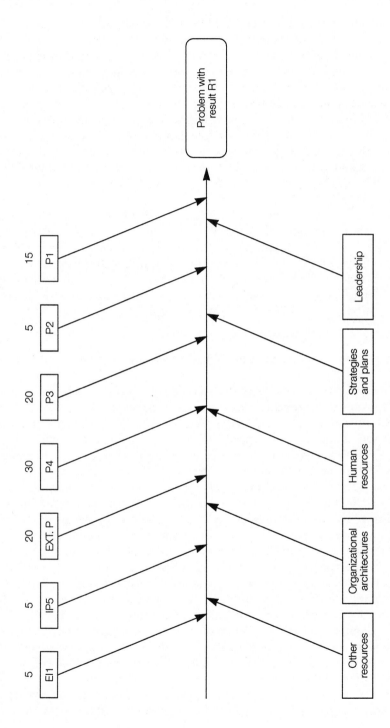

**Fig. 5.7** Assignment of percentage weights to processes and inputs.

item, which includes both human and material resources. With regard to human resources, the analysis will check consistency between skills and roles, training, the workplace environment, etc. With regard to material resources, it will verify the adequacy and state of equipment (instruments, machinery, information systems) and materials. In the fourth area, the analysis will consider activities in relation to the problem being diagnosed, examining the real state of process control, the collection and utilization of process data, particularly data on anomalies and defectiveness, etc.

As each process is analysed, the corresponding branch in the diagram will be expanded with second- and third-level branches, according to the causes found. The upper half of Fig. 5.8 exemplifies process-associated causes.

Some of these causes are marked with an asterisk: the process analysis has found that the root causes are likely to be systemic. These causes have therefore been transposed to the lower part of the diagram, which represents systemic factors. At this point, a new diagnostic phase begins. It uses the same problem-solving tools as the previous phase, but it analyses the systemic factors described in Chapter 4, and is conducted with the participation of those responsible for systemic factors.

## 5.3 HOW TO USE CAUSE–EFFECT MATRICES

Fish-bone diagrams are satisfactory when dealing with a single, relatively simple problem. In practice, however, circumstances often pose a large number of complex, interrelated problems. The problems that emerge during self-assessment are typical. When a negative result is found or a marked improvement in performance needs to be planned, the company usually has to deal with numerous complex problems. Take the area of customer satisfaction, and the specific component of post-sales service. Imagine that the company has to identify the causes that have led to significant customer dissatisfaction with post-sales service, a state of affairs confirmed by a comparative survey with a reference competitor. A variety of causes may have contributed to this negative result: slow response times; inadequate technical skills; poor resource distribution; service calls that fail to resolve difficulties; poor spare parts logistics; low product reliability; poor communications with customers, etc. With such a broad range of possible causes, a whole series of Ishikawa diagrams would be needed, one for each component of customer dissatisfaction. And since many of these components are the result of several process flows, more than one diagram could be required for a single result. The diagram would become increasingly complex graphically as the number of branches rises, and it would be difficult to allocate weights, quantitative data, etc. It would also be practically impossible to keep track of the relationships between the

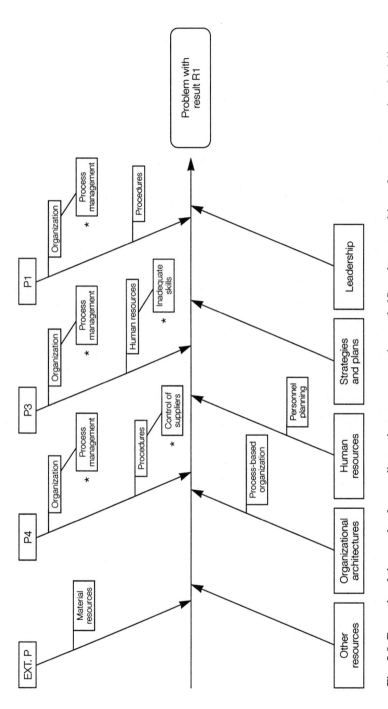

**Fig. 5.8** Example of the result of cross-diagnosis on processes (upper half) and transposition of some causes (marked \*) to systemic factors (lower half).

branches in the diagram and between different diagrams that converge on the same result.

For all these reasons, a matrix-based approach to cross-diagnosis is preferable, using matrices similar to those adopted for Quality Function Deployment (QFD) [15]. For full details, readers are referred to the software program developed by the author [16], which offers a complete, easy-to-use tool for systematic cross-diagnosis. Here, a brief outline of the basic concepts of the matrix-based approach is provided.

A chart of the process flow or flows that contribute to the result is helpful for matrix-based diagnosis, but not essential. If the flow has not been charted, the diagnosis follows the effects–causes chain until it identifies the root causes of problems and the units concerned; this diagnostic journey will help the company formulate *a posteriori* a process flow chart. In Fig. 5.9, the entire flow is represented by a single box, PF, which can then be exploded into the various sub-processes if required.

The lower part of the diagram shows that more than one flow may converge on the same 'customer'. For this reason, it is useful to insert a box between the process flow (or flows) and the customer, to be called 'front-end'. This box represents the entire company, which presents a unified face to the customer, irrespective of the number of process flows and responsibilities that converge on that customer.

The first matrix to be created is the customer/company matrix. In line with Fig. 5.9 and the observations above, this matrix covers the interface between the customer and the front-end (Fig. 5.10).

It transforms problems as perceived by customers into the company's quality shortcomings that are the immediate cause of those problems. This is a typical QFD transformation; above all, it is a 'linguistic' transformation, from customer language into the company language. It is also a transformation from characteristics perceived by customers – which can

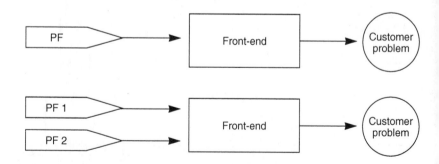

**Fig. 5.9** One or more process flows may converge on the problem being diagnosed. The 'front-end' block represents the unified face presented by the company to the customer.

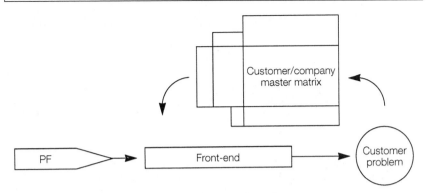

**Fig. 5.10** The customer/company master matrix transforms 'customer problems' into the primary quality shortcomings that cause these problems.

therefore be measured only through customer surveys – into characteristics that can be measured by the company.

For example, the problem perceived by the customer as 'too much time taken to restore service' can be transformed into the global characteristic 'difference between maximum guaranteed time and actual service time' (and the corresponding performance measurement could be the percentage of cases in which this difference is positive, that is, cases in which service is provided within the guaranteed time). For obvious reasons of control and diagnosis, the company will usually prefer to sub-divide total time into significant phases, for example, service access time, diagnosis time, restore time. In this way, it will be able to set goals for each phase and measure the relative differences.

The entry table of the customer/company master matrix (Fig. 5.11) can describe all the customer problems that emerged during the customer satisfaction survey, or just those selected during self-assessment for cross-diagnosis. The ability to analyse a number of often interconnected problems is the great advantage of the matrix-based approach compared with fish-bone diagrams.

As the figure shows, the entry table is associated with an entry matrix showing customer assessments. The first assessment is the weight customers give each problem. The reader should refer to Fig. 5.12, which illustrates the example discussed here – problems in post-sales service.

Weights are given on a 1–5 scale, as provided by customer perception surveys. Customer satisfaction surveys are the source for customers' assessments of the company's performance and that of competitors, shown in the second and third columns (Fig. 5.12 considers just one competitor). An analysis of these weights and performance assessments will indicate which problems are considered most critical by the market. If required,

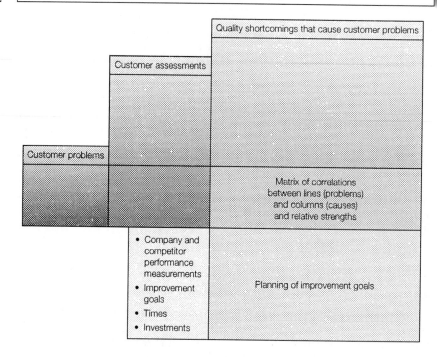

**Fig. 5.11** The master matrix, which transforms problems perceived by the customer into quality shortcomings expressed in the company's language. The lower part of the matrix is used for improvement planning.

improvement targets can already be set at this stage (expressed in terms of the customer assessment scale).

The upper right area of the matrix in Fig. 5.11 identifies the quality shortcomings that cause the problems perceived by customers. As we saw earlier, these shortcomings must be expressed in the company language and must be measurable. The cause of a problem may be an activity that is poorly performed, but it could also be the absence of an activity. For this reason, and to allow greater flexibility, the column headings can be expressed in terms both of causes and of remedies. (Fig. 5.12).

The central area beneath this upper block describes the correlations between the lines and columns of the matrix. Three symbols are used to express the strength of these correlations: a circled dot for a very strong correlation (the quality shortcoming described in the column is a major cause of the problem in the line with which it intersects); an empty circle for a medium correlation; a triangle for a weak correlation. A value is assigned to each symbol; in the example, these values are 9, 4 and 1 respectively.

| Customer problems | WEIGHTS | COMPANY | Competitor XX | | | CRITICAL ELEMENTS | TARGET | Defect rate | Start-up, diagnosis, activation of assistance | Repairs | Customer call forwarding | Customer management procedures | Problem causes/remedies |
|---|---|---|---|---|---|---|---|---|---|---|---|---|---|
| Communication difficulties | 4 | 3 | 4 | | | | | | O | | ● | ● | |
| Frequent faults | 3 | 3 | 3 | | | | | ● | △ | O | | | |
| Delay in service recovery | 5 | 2 | 4 | | | × | 4 | | ● | ● | O | | |
| Insufficient info on new products/services | 3 | 1 | 3 | | | | | | | | | | ● |
| Absolute importance | | | | | | | | 27 | 64 | 57 | 56 | 63 | |
| Relative importance | | | | | | | | 10.11 | 23.97 | 21.35 | 20.97 | 23.6 | |
| Measurement unit | | | | | | | | f/y /100 customers | Average minutes | Average hours | 1–5 scale | 1–5 scale | |
| Current performance | | | | | | | | 20 | 35 | 8.2 | 3 | 3 | |
| Critical elements | | | | | | | | 2 | 5 | 5 | 3 | 4 | |
| Organizational difficulties | | | | | | | | 5 | 5 | 4 | 4 | 4 | |
| Improvement targets | | | | | | | | | <10 | <4 | 5 | 5 | |
| Improvement goals | | | | | | | | | <15 | <6 | 4 | 4 | |
| Period | | | | | | | | | | | | | |
| Investments | | | | | | | | | | | | | |
| Payback (months) | | | | | | | | | | | | | |
| | | | | | | | | | | | | | |
| | | | | | | | | | | | | | |
| Column carry-forwards | | | | | | | | | 1 | 1 | 1 | 1 | |

**Fig. 5.12** The customer/company master matrix.

The lower part of the matrix is used for measurements and improvement planning. This area cannot be filled in until the cross-diagnosis is complete, but goals should be set right from the start if the company wishes improvement to be a continuous challenge for its capabilities and knowledge rather than a static response (planning to do only what a feasibility analysis shows can be done). Long-term improvement goals ('targets' in the matrix) and goals for the current year ('goals') must be set in line with the requirements of the competitive scenario (the future rather than the current scenario), not on the basis of what the company knows how to do. Improvement should be the spur for continuous breakthroughs; despite the possible difficulties, it should adapt the company's competencies in line with the need for survival, growth and success.

In the lower part of the matrix, therefore, when the measurement boxes have been filled in, managers should set preliminary improvement goals, to be analysed at a later stage once root causes have been identified and possible improvement action defined. In other words, goal feasibility will be assessed together with investments and times.

The customer/company master matrix provides the basis for the construction of a second matrix where the causes/remedies in the columns of the master matrix are distributed among the company's processes (if a process flow chart is available). Imagine that the company wishes to investigate the causes of delays in service recovery and the reasons for the inadequacy of information on new products/services (third and fourth lines of the matrix in Fig. 5.12). The analysis will therefore focus on columns 2, 3, 4 and 5 of the main matrix in Fig. 5.12. Imagine that the relevant process flows are those shown in Fig. 5.13. Figure 5.14 illustrates the matrix that can be created from Fig. 5.12 using columns 2, 3, 4 and 5 as input (the columns become the entry lines of the secondary matrix).

If the processes and inputs of Fig. 5.13 are entered in the columns of the sub-matrix (upper area), the result resembles the upper part of the fish-bone diagram of Fig. 5.6, with the difference that the matrix can accommodate an Ishikawa diagram for every line and that the process weights (relative importance line) are the sums of the corresponding weights in the various Ishikawa diagrams. It should be noted that in the matrix in Fig. 5.14 – and in all sub-matrices in general – the strength of the correlation at the intersections between lines and columns is expressed in fractions. In this way, the numbers that indicate relative importance, in any column of any sub-matrix, always represent the percentage weight of the cause in the column in relation to the sum of the causes of the problems being investigated (that is, of the total of the causes of dissatisfaction examined in the master matrix).

If the process flow is not available, the creation of sub-matrices from the master matrix (Fig. 5.12) would be based on other criteria. A first matrix could be created by grouping together the three columns concerned with service and a second with the column covering normal customer management operations. If the diagnostic path is followed carefully, the analysis will move back along the process flow, even though this flow has not previously been charted. This is because the 'why' questions that must be answered during the analysis at each step back from effect to cause are usually linked with a 'who' question, to identify the party that performs the

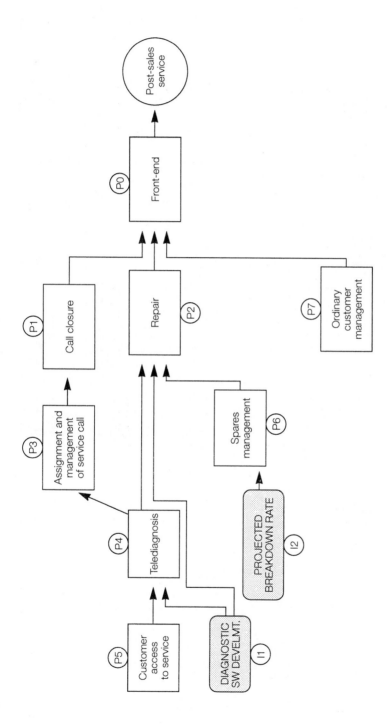

**Fig. 5.13** Process flows for post-sales customer needs. The two processes analysed are ordinary customer management and extraordinary management when problems arise.

| Level 1 causes/remedies | Relative importance | Measurement unit | Current performance | Critical elements | Organizational difficulties | Improvement targets | Improvement goals | P1 Closure of call and customer communication | P2 Repair | P3 Assignment and management of service call | P4 Telediagnosis | P5 Customer access to service | P6 Spares management | I1 Diagnostic sw development and management | P7 Ordinary customer management |
|---|---|---|---|---|---|---|---|---|---|---|---|---|---|---|---|
| Start-up, diagnosis, activation of assistance | 23.97 | Average minutes | 35 | 5 | 5 | <10 | <15 | 0.10 | | 0.20 | 0.45 | 0.20 | | 0.15 | |
| Repair | 21.35 | Average hours | 8.2 | 5 | 4 | <4 | <6 | | 0.25 | 0.40 | | | 0.20 | 0.05 | 0.70 |
| Customer call forwarding | 20.97 | 1–5 scale | 3 | 3 | 4 | 5 | 4 | | | | | 0.30 | | | 1.00 |
| Customer management procedures | 23.6 | 1–5 scale | 3 | 4 | 4 | 5 | 4 | | | | | | | | |

**Unit concerned / Level 2 causes/remedies**

| | P1 | P2 | P3 | P4 | P5 | P6 | I1 | P7 |
|---|---|---|---|---|---|---|---|---|
| Relative importance | 2.13 | 5.34 | 13.33 | 10.79 | 11.09 | 4.27 | 4.66 | 38.28 |
| Measurement unit | | | | | | | | |
| Current performance | | | | | | | | |
| Critical elements | | | | | | | | |
| Organizational difficulties | | | | | | | | |
| Improvement targets | | | | | | | | |
| Improvement goals | | | | | | | | |
| Period | | | | | | | | |
| Investments | | | | | | | | |
| Payback (months) | | | | | | | | |
| Column carry-forwards | 1 | 1 | 1 | 1 | 1 | | | 2 |

**Fig. 5.14** Sub-matrix for processes.

activity in question. As a result, the internal supplier–customer chain, that is, the process flow, is automatically followed.

Pareto's Law can be applied to the data in the 'relative importance' line of the sub-matrix (Fig. 5.14) to decide which branches of the tree of causes should be followed up and which should be abandoned. In our example, the company decides to analyse the causes related to fault repairs and to normal customer management operations. To avoid a proliferation of matrices, the five processes related to repairs (processes 1 to 5, the first five columns) are grouped into a single matrix, while the last column will be considered in a separate matrix. Further matrices can be created from these two sub-matrices, until root causes have been identified. For further details, see the software package developed by the author [16].

| | Relative importance | Customer database | Customer visit planning | Proactive complaints mngmnt | New product information | Retention policy | Personnel training | Lost customer surveys | Customer communication logistics | Level 3 causes/remedies |
|---|---|---|---|---|---|---|---|---|---|---|
| **Ordinary customer management** | 38.28 | 0.10 | 0.10 | 0.05 | 0.05 | 0.25 | 0.20 | 0.05 | 0.20 | |
| Relative importance | | | | | | | | | | |
| Measurement unit | | 1–5 scale | 1–5 scale | 1–5 scale | 1–5 scale | 1–5 scale | 1–5 scale | yes/no | 1–5 scale | |
| Current performance | | 2 | 1 | 1 | 3 | 1 | 2 | no | 1 | |
| Critical elements | | 5 | 5 | 2 | 2 | 5 | 4 | 3 | 5 | |
| Organizational difficulties | | M | L | M | L | H | M | L | M | |
| Improvement targets | | 5 | 5 | 5 | 5 | 4 | 4 | yes | 5 | |
| Improvement goals | | 5 | 4 | 4 | 4 | 3 | 4 | yes | 5 | |
| Period | | | | | | | | | | |
| Investments | | | | | | | | | | |
| Payback (months) | | | | | | | | | | |
| Carry-forwards to systemic factors | | | | | | 1.a | 1.c | | | |
| Column carry-forwards | | | | | | | | | | |

(rightmost column: Unit concerned)

**Fig. 5.15** 2nd level sub-matrix (H = High, M = Medium, L = Low).

So far we have discussed diagnosis in relation to causes whose roots lie in the processes considered or in processes that provide input for these processes. How should the diagnosis deal with causes whose roots are thought to lie in systemic factors? How does the matrix-based approach handle the area covered by the lower part of the Ishikawa diagram in Fig. 5.6?

The answer is provided in Fig. 5.15, which illustrates the second sub-matrix derived from the matrix in Fig. 5.14 (since the aim of this discussion

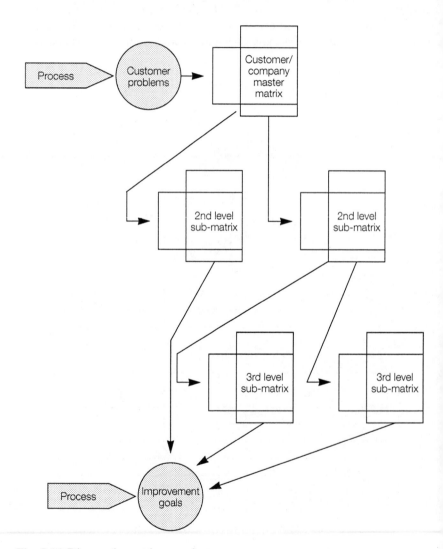

**Fig. 5.16** Diagnostic matrix cascade.

is to offer a brief outline of cross-diagnosis, the first sub-matrix is not illustrated). In the sub-matrix in Fig. 5.15, a line named 'carry-forwards to systemic factors' has been added. The various carry-forwards are shown with a 1–5 numbering, where 1 is leadership, 2 is strategies and plans, etc., following the right–left order in Fig. 5.6. The letter that follows the category number identifies the specific factor within the category (see Appendix A for a detailed description of factors). As we saw when discussing the Ishikawa diagram (Fig. 5.8), the conceptual basis for diagnosis of systemic factors is similar to that of process diagnosis. Diagnosis of systemic factors should not begin until the cross-diagnosis has been completed and all possible systemic causes have been identified. The managers who conduct systemic factor analysis will usually be senior to those who conduct process diagnosis.

Figure 5.16 represents the typical cross-diagnosis matrix cascade.

Once this cascade is complete, the company can expect to have not only a clear picture of the causes of problems, but also reliable indications regarding the general lines of action to be taken to improve performance. The reason, noted earlier, is that use of cause–effect matrices stimulates the company to plan improvement planning concurrently with diagnosis (when the lower part of the matrices is filled in), even if this planning process is interactive; in other words, it begins by setting 'external' goals (what the market or the internal customer demands) and gradually, through feasibility checks, builds up 'internalized' goals that are consistent with the company's capabilities.

## 5.4 CONCLUSIONS

Cross-diagnosis is by nature a highly interactive process. Matrix cascades are built one after another, but the company will frequently have to go back and make adjustments, since the approach proceeds on the basis of hypotheses that must be subsequently verified. In each matrix, the lines represent effects, the columns represent relative causes or remedies. The diagnosis can begin with brainstorming sessions, but the various hypotheses must be substantiated by quantitative data, which means going back to the matrices to add or modify data. This applies to the estimated percentage weight of each cause on an effect (the 'strength of the correlations' in the boxes where lines and columns intersect); it applies to measurement of current performance, where preliminary measurements are often approximate and need to be gradually adjusted as the diagnosis proceeds; it also applies to long-term improvement targets and current improvement goals.

Matrices are invaluable tools, because they enable all the necessary data to be allocated easily; moreover, if a standard procedure is introduced, they actually *oblige* the company to insert data and take measurements.

For this reason, a specific software tool can provide extremely useful support [16]. It also performs automatic updates of sub-matrices when adjustments are made in higher-level matrices [16]. For a highly interactive process of this type, this updating capability is clearly a great advantage.

The master matrix becomes the improvement planning 'chart', the master document, while the sub-matrices provide the back-up details. The managers of all the processes that converge on the result the company wishes to improve should refer to these documents and go back to them every time changes are made or proposed.

This discussion of cross-diagnosis ends by emphasizing once again that approaches of this type may have a significant impact on the company culture. A diagnostic culture can be of benefit to every company and can only be developed through a *method*. Approaching problems in a rational, orderly, diagnostic manner, if possible with tools that encourage a methodical attitude, will foster the spread of a diagnostic culture, which is the preliminary requirement for any company that wishes to become a *learning organization*.

# Introducing self-assessment into the company: preparing for and implementing the self-assessment process

**6**

The introduction of self-assessment into a company is too important an event to be delegated in full, even if the delegated company officer is a first-line manager (and therefore reports directly to top management). Ownership and control must be retained by top management. If the company has a quality function (or, better still, a quality and organization function: an increasingly frequent combination in companies that seriously intend to implement a process-based organization), which reports directly to top management, this is the unit best suited to act as top management's operating arm. Its role is to guarantee that the strategic goals set by top management are properly communicated and ensure that a consistent approach to self-assessment is adopted throughout the company (a self-assessment guide setting out the basic requisites is a useful tool). Methodological consistency does not rule out the necessary adjustments to cater for specific differences; indeed, such adjustments are essential. It means limiting them to the indispensable minimum, in order to avoid differences for differences' sake and to permit comparisons and foster the growth of a homogeneous corporate culture (adopting continuous improvement as a company value should always favour exploration of new avenues: but to avoid chaos, these investigations must always be conducted on an experimental basis, leaving current practice unchanged until the experimental initiative is shown to be better and can therefore formally replace the former method in the corpus of rules). The function delegated to self-assessment must also coordinate the sectorial self-assessments, collect suggestions and encourage cross-referencing (in particular, internal benchmarking). It will then consolidate the sectorial self-assessments and organize top-management self-assessment (interviews with the chief executive officer and his first line, which will normally be carried out by a suitably senior external consultant). Finally, it will organize the review sessions at which the chief executive and the first line analyse results and draw their final conclusions, and then set strategic improvement goals in line with the findings of the self-assessment and with the company's business strategies.

Although the delegated function will have broad operating powers, top management must be a clear, continuous and tangible presence. The reason is that if self-assessment is seen as an initiative of the quality function, it will be perceived as an activity that refers to quality rather than to the company's general business; if it *is* perceived as business-related, it will be regarded as an overstepping of duties, an irritating interference or, at best, an additional burden of uncertain value added. But if top management clearly assumes ownership and states that it wishes the entire company to regard self-assessment as a fundamental stage in corporate self-diagnosis and reflection, then it will be clear to everyone that self-assessment refers to business and not to quality (it simply uses quality tools) and that the subsequent improvement planning must be fully integrated with business planning.

If self-assessment is introduced correctly, if top management understands its strategic dimension and assumes ownership and if the first line fully shares top management's vision, then it can become a milestone in the company's history, a value that endures over time irrespective of the changes in external scenarios. Self-assessment does not in fact come under the necessarily variable heading of 'what' the company does, it comes under the heading of 'how' the company does things. Specifically, it does not examine the content of strategic plans, it assesses their feasibility and aims to boost their success rate. It also introduces a corporate management style based on periodic introspection, on self-diagnosis. Taking the gaps between goals and actual achievements (or between future objectives and the present) as its starting point, the company learns to identify its weaknesses (or the new strengths needed for the future). Introspection and self-diagnosis skills will continue to be important factors for success, today and in the future, when the 'things to be done' will be totally different. They are typical skills of the learning organization.

If self-assessment is introduced via the back door, or attracts management attention simply as a means for the ambitious (often presumptuous) company to win an important award, then it will end up in the scrapyard of abandoned good intentions.

## 6.1 INTERNAL RESISTANCE

Correctly understood, self-assessment is a major change. Strong internal resistance is therefore inevitable. The first source of opposition may be top management, once it realizes the full significance of self-assessment. It is not uncommon for top management to accept a self-assessment approach of the kind adopted by the quality awards, either because it is confident that the results will justify the company's application for the award, or because it is attracted by the opportunity to have greater visibility over the state of the various corporate sectors and, specifically, to identify any 'black sheep'. In these cases, the process is usually more of an audit than a self-assessment: active involvement of the company population is limited and little significant disruption is caused. Quantitative analysis is what interests top management most, the relative scores of the different sectors and, at global level, comparison with the scores of the companies that win the awards. Improvement is of interest too, of course, but it is not always understood that improvement should relate to the company's business in general. Many large organizations set up an internal award (or series of awards) related to the assessment; this aspect also attracts the interest of top management because it creates a climate of competition among the various sectors, which fuels short-term improvement.

When top management is confronted with a strategic vision of self-assessment of the kind described in this book, where the entire company system and all the company processes, including strategic processes, are involved, where everything and everybody in the company could be brought under scrutiny, including top management and the most solidly established traditions, resistance and perplexity are natural reactions. The chief executive will necessarily respond with the greatest caution to such radical developments. All the folklore surrounding scores and awards must be set aside and the true significance of self-assessment clearly explained; the advantages, costs and risks must be illustrated in full. It is essential that the chief executive be absolutely convinced that self-assessment is a strategic tool for the company's competitive growth. He and his first line must therefore have complete, well-organized and convincing information. This is best achieved through meetings with distinguished *external* experts, who will be credible bearers of the self-assessment message. If top management still fails to understand the importance of extending self-diagnosis to the entire company, or decides that the risks outweigh the benefits, or does not assume ownership, then it is better to let the idea drop altogether rather than adopt a self-defeating low-profile solution. Opposition may also come from the company's functions (or divisions, or business units): if they fear encroachment on their personal territory or suffer from the not-invented-here syndrome, they may attempt to contain an initiative they regard as an expansionist tactic by the function delegated to handle self-assessment, particularly if that function is quality. In every company, one function prevails over the others – usually the most reactive function. Examples abound of companies in which the personnel function, especially if it has responsibility for organization, has viewed with alarm the entry of the quality function into areas that appear to interfere with its own sphere of competence. Functions that consider themselves damaged in some way may openly oppose self-assessment or, more frequently, question the value added for the company or the reliability of the data collected; or they may underline the costs of the operation (which can be high, considering the amount of time people dedicate to self-assessment interviews and questionnaires). The only way to overcome this resistance is to ensure the direct involvement of those functions that react most negatively to the attribution to another function of operating responsibility for self-assessment. The best results are obtained when the quality, personnel and organization and strategic planning functions work closely together on planning and implementing self-assessment. In addition, a steering committee chaired by the chief executive should be formed, which involves the entire first line in the supervision of the self-assessment and subsequent improvement planning. Specifically, the steering committee will analyse the underlying strategic issues to ensure that the model truly reflects the company's particular situation and is acceptable to everyone; decide how the new values incorporated in the model are to be established; define the corporate PDCA self-assessment and strategic improvement planning cycle and integrate it with business planning; establish and implement the checkpoints for the planning cycle.

The problem of resistance should not be underestimated. Plans should be made from the start to maximize the involvement of all company functions, beginning with those that carry the greatest weight with top management and, generally speaking, within the company as a whole.

## 6.2 ASSOCIATING SELF-ASSESSMENT WITH AN INTERNAL AWARD

We noted earlier that self-assessment is often associated with an internal award, especially in larger companies. Experience has shown the advantages and disadvantages of this approach. By far the greatest advantage of the internal award is that it stimulates extensive involvement in self-assessment. In some cases, the level of awareness and contributions to the improvement of individual sectors would never have been achieved without this type of incentive. Awards are excellent springboards for self-assessment and improvement plans. They can also bring significant results quickly; but much more is needed to maintain these results: assimilation, competence, method, patience, constancy. Awards are one way – a springboard, as we said – for the company to reach its goal, which is to establish an annual process of diagnostic self-assessment and improvement planning.

The danger with awards is that the means may prevail over the end: that the desire to win – and therefore to emphasize the sector's strengths – may blind people to the ultimate purpose, which is to identify weaknesses in relation to goals in order to correct them. Experience shows that this is inevitable. Despite all prior warnings to alert everyone to this risk, the award will become the main concern and chief goal. Companies therefore require a strategy that adopts the award as a tool during the first stage, but other means for later stages. The best strategy is probably what could be described as a 'fade-out/fade-in' approach: the emphasis on awards diminishes while the emphasis on self-assessment grows. During the first year, the main focus is on the award and therefore on the assessments conducted by assessors from outside the sector. In the second year, each sector begins to assess itself with internal assessors (supported by external assessors), following the procedures established at company level. In this way, the emphasis on self-assessment and the improvement plan grows. A competitive company award can be retained, but greater importance should be attached to awards for 'scores' (attainment of specific scores levels on the conventional 0–1000 scale) and to improvement awards. Partnership awards – for cross-functional/cross-divisional processes – could also be introduced. The main task of the external assessor is to check methodology and ensure alignment among the various self-assessments. By the third year, self-assessment should clearly prevail, and become part of the corporate planning cycle. Company awards are still useful, especially if they focus on resolution of weaknesses, in particular cross-functional/cross-divisional weaknesses or weaknesses in relations with external partners. Prizes may also be given for the most significant improvements and for attainment of levels of excellence as compared with competitors and the best-in-class.

The importance of partnership has been stressed. This is an area in which awards have a negative influence. They lower willingness to accept comparisons and internal benchmarking and to share positive results. All awards, beginning with MBO incentives, have the drawback of stimulating individualism and sectorialism, frequently to the detriment of the corporate interest. Individual and group initiative can be stimulated, but cooperation, the feeling of being in the same boat, placing the company's interests above those of the sector, the ability honestly to balance personal interests with the company's interests are values that must not be lost and must be fostered where they do not exist.

## 6.3 PREPARING FOR SELF-ASSESSMENT: THE COMMUNICATIONS PLAN

Careful preparations must be made when a major initiative is launched; nothing should be taken for granted. The first step is to establish clearly and fully the goals that are to be reached and then tell people what those goals are. Self-assessment is a strategic tool, but it is subject to incomplete or distorted interpretation; so it is particularly important that everyone, not just those who will be directly involved, knows what the company's intentions are. Too often, companies assume that the usual communication channels are sufficient or that a few extra mass communication channels (conventions, house organs) will ensure full communication. This is not so. When special emphasis has to be given to a particular message in the everyday sea of information, special transmitters, channels and repeaters are needed to attract attention. Every new message has to overcome people's preconceptions and prejudices.

The solution chosen will depend on the specific situation and above all on the size of the company, but great attention must be given to the content of the message and the choice of communication channel, to ensure that the message is clear and people's interest is caught. With regard to *content*, the following main concepts must be conveyed: to stay on the market and improve competitiveness, the company must improve continuously; to improve performance, the company has to conduct an annual self-diagnosis or check-up, so that it can identify weaknesses and apply the appropriate remedies; everyone is asked to contribute on the basis of their particular experience, in their particular role. Everyone will be involved in the collection of data, some people will be interviewed, many more will be asked to fill in a questionnaire; those who do not receive the questionnaire – if the company is large, the questionnaire cannot be sent to everyone for reasons of cost – will still be able to make a useful contribution by discussing the issues covered with the people who do receive the questionnaire or with their direct superior; everyone has a valuable contribution to make; the findings of the self-assessment will be published and discussed at follow-up meetings; after that, everyone – or a large majority of the company population – will be involved in the improvement measures planned on the basis of the findings of the self-assessment.

In addition to the usual *communication channels* – kick-off ceremonies, articles in the company house organ, posters – top-down cascade communication, from manager to staff, has an important role to play. It must be supported by documentation that briefly covers all the main issues, in order to avoid the risk of distortion as the process proceeds. At each level, the manager, with the support of the documentation, will illustrate the goals of self-assessment, the reference model, the significance of that model for the company and the sector, the self-assessment methods, and the subsequent improvement plans. In particular, he will emphasize the importance of self-assessment as an event that depends on full participation, that requires everyone, whatever their role, to contribute from the basis of their experience to the improvement of the company. He will point out that everyone who is interviewed or asked to fill in an effectiveness questionnaire should do their best to respond not as an individual (the contribution of the individual is covered by the climate questionnaires) but in terms of their role; they should therefore exercise the greatest objectivity when assessing the actual situation (i.e., the hard and soft tools available) in relation to the goals the company has set itself. Metaphorically speaking, people should ask themselves whether the 'toolboxes' the company provides them with are sufficiently well equipped to reach the goals the company has set, the 'tools' being the hard and soft factors shown on the left side and centre of the model (systemic factors and processes).

The company should draw up a *communications plan*. Like all quality-related initiatives, this plan should be flexible and non-bureaucratic, but it should ensure that the fundamental requirement for the success of the self-assessment is fulfilled: that everyone, and especially those who will be directly involved, is fully aware of what they are doing. The plan should also provide for top-down follow-up meetings, at which the findings of the self-assessment will be illustrated and discussed.

## 6.4 PREPARING FOR SELF-ASSESSMENT: THE ACTIVITIES PLAN

Since self-assessment considers the perceptions and views of a multiplicity of customers and stakeholders (see model, Fig. 2.4(b)), the company must organize the necessary surveys and interviews and hold preliminary meetings with stakeholders to inform them about the self-assessment. The quality of the information obtained will depend on the degree of interest aroused. The full involvement of top management should be ensured at this preliminary stage to prevent opposition from developing, by bringing on board all those who should play an active part and those whom it would be unwise to exclude. Top management should formalize the various roles and possibly also immediately form the steering committee.

The next step is the sub-division of the company for the purposes of the self-assessment. After the first, natural segmentation into functions/divisions and central staff, the criteria for segmentation within these units are size (not less than 200–300 people per segment, more if the company is large, but this also depends on the next two criteria); non-excessive segmentation of processes (ideally, processes should be assessed in their entirety); geographical location. Self-assessment should be a bottom-up process that gradually covers the entire company, but not necessarily from year one. Its introduction will depend on the company's size and structural organization. In a large company, for example, a full-scale start-up could have serious negative repercussions: the inevitable imperfections would be amplified and could become lethal weapons for sectors that have submitted unwillingly to self-assessment, or, more generally, for people who tend to mistrust change or to criticize. A soft start-up is preferable, if possible among the sectors where awareness of self-assessment issues is greatest or those that wish to take part in the trial run (which is what the first self-assessment cycle is). Usually, the sectors that are most sensitive to self-assessment are the front-end sectors in service companies and the production sectors in manufacturing companies. Where to start is a delicate question, which should be examined with great care by top management. If the self-assessment begins with a restricted number of sectors (but including all those that belong to the chosen area, be it a division, production operation, territorial unit) then the start-up phase will be easier to manage. On the other hand, excluded areas might feel resentful. The best solution is for the steering committee to establish the sequence of participation, if possible including the sectors (divisions or functions) that wish to participate. At this experimental stage, it is important that the self-assessment be performed by willing sectors that are likely to become convinced supporters.

During the preparatory stage, the company must also decide where and to what degree it will use the services of external consultants. It would be a serious mistake fully to outsource management of the self-assessment, with the company's personnel – those who procure data for the assessment and who are the subject of interviews and questionnaires – playing a passive part. Total outsourcing would deprive the company of the most important fall-out from self-assessment: the chance to learn and to improve the company's diagnostic culture. On the other hand, consultant services are essential, especially for assessment of systemic factors. The best solution is to set up a joint team of company representatives and consultants: the latter will be responsible in particular for methodology, for establishing the criteria used to assess the various categories of the model, especially the 'soft' categories, and for the most delicate interviews; the company function delegated to handle the self-assessment will retain leadership of the entire process. The company should choose consultants who offer, first of all, experience in diagnostic self-assessment and, second, management and organization experience. The consultancy team should also possess expertise in the areas of leadership, human resources and organizational architectures.

These remarks – and this chapter in general – refer chiefly to the large company, in other words, to the most complex situation. The simplifications that can be made for small and medium-sized companies are explained in some cases, in other cases they are self-evident. As far as consultancy is concerned, small/medium companies, like larger businesses, require the support of external experts. In particular, they should look for a consultant with wide-ranging experience of the small business sector and organizational issues in particular. This may prove difficult since few consultants offer such knowhow today.

Since the introduction of self-assessment is a delicate and risky undertaking, which can fail if adequate arrangements have not been made, the function delegated by top management to handle self-assessment should draw up a complete activities plan to be submitted for the approval of top management and illustrated to the steering committee.

## 6.5 DRAWING UP THE SELF-ASSESSMENT GUIDE

Assessment of systemic factors (left side of the model) is a difficult process, which requires experience. Assessment of categories such as leadership risks being highly subjective if the factors and their constituent elements have not been defined in sufficient detail (and even if the key elements have been clearly defined, with examples provided in the areas being assessed, the difficulty of understanding the real situation in relation to the stereotype remains). Moreover, conversion of the assessment (a set of strengths and weaknesses) into scores will inevitably be a somewhat subjective and arbitrary process; however many rules and criteria have been provided. Experience is therefore essential, each assessment should be conducted by at least two or three assessors (possibly more, see below) and alignment sessions attended by all the assessors should be held. Continuous contact and cooperation among the assessors working in the various company sectors is equally important.

For companies embarking on self-assessment for the first time, the support of an experienced external consultant (see above) is indispensable. But they also need a self-assessment guide or manual, which describes the entire process and illustrates in the greatest possible detail the various criteria used to assess the 'systemic factors' area. This text will be the reference for interviews, surveys and every other type of analysis. Chapter 4 and Appendix A provide all the information the company needs to prepare the section of its guide that deals with 'systemic factors'.

Measurement in the 'results' area is less complex than measurement in the 'systemic factors' area. On the other hand, significant problems arise when it comes to deciding which goals, and therefore which results, are to be assessed. Once again, Chapter 4 and Appendix A provide detailed information on this point. It is worth noting here, however, that besides the usual customer satisfaction surveys, the Personnel Function will be required to organize an employee satisfaction survey, while the other relevant functions will investigate satisfaction of business partners and impact on society. Appendix A also provides detailed information about preparation of the section of the guide that deals with assessment of 'processes', to supplement that provided in Chapter 4.

The guide should be drawn up during the preparatory phase that precedes the first self-assessment, because it can be an effective communications tool to describe the process to all those who will be taking part. Indeed, since the guide illustrates all the criteria against which the company wishes to assess itself, derived from a model that has been personalized by the company for its own use, it should be distributed to all employees. It should also be part of the material used in training courses on corporate values and the organizational behaviour the company expects from its staff.

When the process turns from an assessment conducted by external experts into widespread self-assessment, the guide must be extremely detailed to assist learning of the techniques involved. The danger here is that it will be interpreted in a mechanistic, bureaucratic fashion, which can be counter-productive as regards assessment of immaterial factors. Assessors should be aware of this risk and take steps to simplify the criteria, once the methodology has been learned (second year of self-assessment).

The guide itself is open to improvement: it should be reviewed every year on the basis of the feedback provided by assessors and assessed parties. Nevertheless, it must begin life in complete form, describing the entire assessment process, assessment criteria, scoring and preparation of the self-assessment report in the greatest detail: any difficulties the self-assessment teams encounter due to lack of clear indications in the guide can fuel opposition.

## 6.6 ORGANIZING INTERVIEWS, FOCUS GROUPS AND QUESTIONNAIRES

The ways in which the various corporate levels take part in the self-assessment/self-diagnosis will depend on the size of the company, bearing in mind that the two fundamental aims are to give voice to the people who work with the company system and processes on a daily basis and know their good and bad points better than anyone else; and to create a climate of widespread participation and a corporate sense of belonging.

This section discusses the way participation can be organized in large companies (in small companies, the whole process is simplified; in particular, questionnaires may not be necessary). The company population is divided into two categories: the people in the first group are those whose role is mainly managerial (not just people who direct others but also those who play a prominent part – at the engineering or implementation level – in the formulation and monitoring of the company system and processes); the people in the second group are those whose role is mainly operational. The sub-division refers to people's *main* role because, apart from top management and employees at the lowest level, all intermediate levels play both roles, to differing degrees: moving downwards from the top, the managerial role gradually diminishes and the operational role grows. This sub-division is not dictated by a 'class-based' system, it is useful for the self-assessment survey, which focuses on *systemic factors* and on people's different roles in relation to these factors. The managerial category should include people whose main responsibility is to define and implement systemic factors, that is, the 'tools' with which the company organizes its processes and achieves its *results*. The operational category includes people whose main role is to use these tools. If questions on the same issues concerning systemic factors are put to the two groups, their replies will tend to complement each other. This will give a picture of the situation 'as seen from the right' (by the group that can be considered the 'supplier' of the company tools) and 'as seen from the left' (by the group that could be described as the 'customer', or user of these tools). However much care is taken to ensure objectivity, the members of the first group will tend to describe the situation 'as it should be' (they will inevitably be influenced by their efforts to make it thus), while the second group will tend to describe the situation 'as perceived'. Application of leadership, empowerment and vertical integration should assist a convergence between these two views. The degree of alignment is therefore an important indication of the state of unity with regard to the assimilation of systemic factors.

Given their restricted number and the importance of having a complete, clear picture of the situation 'as it should be' for verification against the situation 'as perceived', the members of the managerial category will be questioned directly, through interviews. If the unit being assessed is large, the managerial category can be further sub-divided into unit director, first line and others. The unit director will provide the assessment team with all the elements in his possession, at the beginning, during and at the end of the assessment. His relations with the team must be as direct as possible, and the team must have access to him whenever necessary, but without allowing its judgements to be overly influenced by him. The first line, of which the team members will normally be part, can be interviewed together on a day set aside for this purpose, but the various individuals should be available whenever necessary. The remaining managers and the higher level office staff in the managerial category will be sub-divided into focus groups and interviewed as such, taking the self-assessment guide as the basis of reference.

The second category – operating office staff and workers – will be surveyed with a questionnaire covering the various aspects of the systemic factors of concern to this group (Fig. 6.1 illustrates the criteria described).

The questionnaire will be drawn up with reference to the self-assessment guide; for every element of the guide that is considered pertinent, one or more statements will be formulated that express the underlying concepts in an appropriate language. The statements will be positive or negative and will refer to the situation of the unit in which the respondent works. The respondent will be asked to say whether he agrees or disagrees with the statement. Consider, for example, the element in the guide that investigates the degree to which people are aware of the company's goals and plans. The questionnaire might include questions such as: 'In my sector we all know how our work fits in with the company's goals', or 'Our bosses do not inform us about what is happening around and above us'. (See Appendix A for an example of the questionnaire.) The possibility of mechanistic or 'guided' responses can be limited by alternating positive and negative questions, re-arranging the order of questions compared with the sequence in the guide and introducing redundancies. The questionnaire should not contain more than 50–60 questions, which should be clear and unambiguous. Answers can be given on a 1–5 scale (totally disagree – disagree – half agree, half disagree – agree – fully agree). They will then be processed in relation to the assessment elements in the guide, so that they can be compared with the opinions expressed in the interviews.

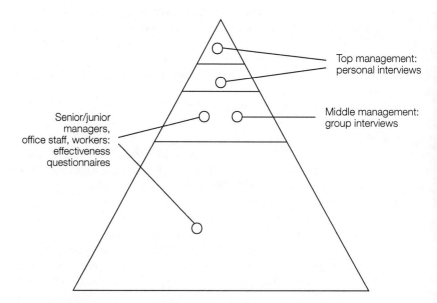

**Fig. 6.1** Criteria for assessment of systemic factors: interviews and a survey based on questionnaires.

The sample of people who receive the questionnaire will be selected from the corporate population in the second category, ensuring that all sectors and levels are properly represented. Anonymity must be guaranteed. The sample should be sub-divided into segments for the purposes of organizational diagnosis, but these segments must be broad enough to avoid the risk of the individual respondent being identified. This can be achieved by asking respondents to indicate on the questionnaire the area in which they work. Vertical segmentation into the various corporate levels is the required minimum.

Experience has proved the usefulness of distributing the questionnaire to a significant sample of people in the first category who have already taken part in the group interviews, that is, to the intermediate section of the corporate population, which plays a critically important role in establishing new management style. The information that emerges from the anonymous questionnaires often differs from the views expressed publicly during the interviews. Extending the questionnaire is advisable if there is the suspicion that the intermediate section might resist change, obviously keeping this second group of respondents separate from the rest. In these cases, the questionnaires can provide very useful pointers as to the real situation.

To minimize the risk of uninformed responses, the questionnaires should be filled in only after suitable preparation (see the section on communication above). The significance and reliability of results will depend on the degree to which employees know that the company is conducting a diagnosis in which everyone is asked to identify areas that can be improved, and that their contribution will be considered seriously. Transparent management of results is important too, to ensure that the process comes full circle for those who take part, with follow-up information and, where necessary, discussion sessions.

Process owners or their equivalent form a third category of people who should be interviewed. The key interviews will concern the cross-functional and cross-divisional processes that play a critical role in achieving the goals on the right side of the model. They will investigate state of control, alignment with customer results and results of any cross-diagnoses conducted to trace the source of critical results, as well as cooperation between the various functions involved in the process.

## 6.7 FORMATION OF ASSESSMENT TEAMS

For every self-assessment, a team of assessors must be formed who will be responsible for building up the most objective picture possible of the sector's strengths and weaknesses in relation to its missions and goals, and for allocating scores. Large companies may have a number of teams operating at various levels. For example, if the company consists of a series of divisions made up in turn of functions and large territorial units, it may be best to conduct the self-assessment at the three levels, with a team for each unit at the lowest level, a team for each division (responsible for consolidating and integrating the lower-level assessments into the division assessment) and a company team, which consolidates the division assessments and integrates them with the central staff self-assessment. This hierarchical structure may seem somewhat complex and bureaucratic, and may indeed become so if rigidly organized from central level. If, however, this approach is viewed in terms of decentralization of responsibility (with the necessary checks, see below), then the aggregation/consolidation method of self-assessment can be much more simple – and above all more reliable – than a single giant assessment covering the entire company.

In discussing division and company assessments, we said that the lower-level assessments were not only aggregated but *integrated*. In other words, the higher-level assessment is not just a consolidation of the assessments of the component units, it is also an assessment of relations among these units. Specifically, it will analyse control of the key processes that cross these units: whether each unit simply controls its own segment of the process and considers the others simply as internal customers or suppliers, with the formalities and rigidities that so often hamper relations among different organizational units; or whether the fundamental integrity of the company's processes (the primary interest of the company over and beyond sectorial interests) is guaranteed by unified control of the entire cross-functional/cross-divisional process, which adds rather than subtracts value from the individual responsibilities on each segment. Figure 6.2 illustrates this concept.

To give the company time to become familiar with self-assessment and enable knowledge to be transferred from the initial group of experts to the local self-assessment teams, a transition period (typically two years) should be provided.

During the first year, the central function should take the lead. It will form a central team (or teams, if a large number of units are to be assessed; although to begin with, it is best to keep the number down) composed of external experts and the first group of trainee internal assessors. The units to be assessed will be asked to prepare an application report (to use the terminology of the awards), that is, a description of the situation of the unit in relation to the model, drawn up in accordance with the instructions in the guide. The application report will be used by the central team to make a preliminary assessment. It should highlight strengths and their relative diffusion as well as the areas it considers weaknesses. For this purpose, the unit should form a team, which, in view of its role in the following years, could already be regarded as a self-assessment team; at this stage, however, it will not make any judgements or allot scores. The local team's

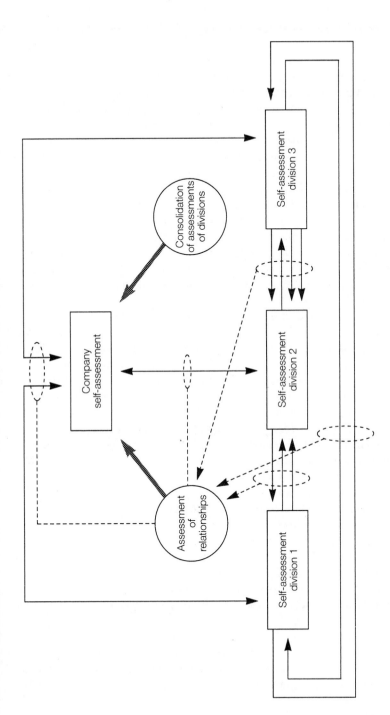

**Fig. 6.2** Self-assessment at the company level consists of: (1) consolidation of assessments of units at lower level; (2) assessment of relationships among units and among corporate staff and units; (3) self-assessment of corporate staff.

first duty is to organize training and guide-illustration sessions for all managers and everyone in the unit who will be involved in drafting the application report. It will then make preparations for the 'site visit' of the central assessment team – organizing support material, arranging any interviews that have been requested, distributing effectiveness question-naires, etc. – so that the central team can make its assessments quickly. The central team will analyse and assess the reports (each report will be examined by at least three people), and record its preliminary judgements and everything it wishes to investigate further during the assessment visit. At least two or three members of the central team will take part in the visits to the units involved in the assessment. The local team will use the visit as an opportunity to study interview techniques, criteria for assessment of weaknesses and strengths and allotment of scores. Naturally, the central team will operate on the principle of full transparency if the company's chief aim is to rapidly build up a widespread self-assessment capability. Transparency should also be the rule when the self-assessment is being conducted for an award, although understandable difficulties can arise.

Returning to the definitions in Chapter 1, the first year appears to resemble a management audit rather than a self-assessment. But although the process takes the form of a management audit, its objective is different: to enable the company to improve its self-assessment capability in preparation for the subsequent decentralization. If the company follows the approach suggested here and feels that the time is right, as early as the second year it will be able to transfer the process to the units concerned, allowing them to perform a fully fledged self-assessment. Nevertheless, the central team (or central teams) will make a visit to each unit to check on the self-assessments and review judgements and scores together with the local team. This ensures correct methodological growth and a gradual alignment among the various assessors, particularly as regards scores. Uniformity of judgement is essential where awards are concerned.

The central team plays a supporting role in relation to self-assessment and an auditing role in relation to scoring for the award. Clearly, its supporting role will tend to diminish as the years pass and the local units master the self-assessment method (which is designed to improve the diagnostic ability to identify weaknesses in order to remedy them); but the importance of the auditing function when an award is at stake will remain the same.

The company will therefore have to decide if and how to reduce the role of the central team in relation to these two requirements. Depending on the results of the second year – after comparison of central and local assessments – the company will decide whether to move to a sample audit in the third year. If the award is continued (or if management requires comparative scores for the various divisions/units), audits will be necessary and the central team will provide support and verify methodology within its role as auditor.

To ensure transparency and a correct methodological approach, the local self-assessment team should include at least one assessor from outside the unit. This also improves diagnostic capabilities, since problems will be viewed by a fresh pair of eyes. Moreover, a wider range of experience will accelerate the growth of the skills of the company's assessors. The external members will not usually take part in the entire process, nor is this necessary. Their participation is particularly important in the final stages – the site visits – when the unit's application report is analysed and discussed, methodology is checked and scores are given. The internal members of the self-assessment team should rotate, too, although the continuity of the PDCA cycle must be safeguarded (this is usually ensured by the presence of a methodological guarantor, a representative of the function delegated by top management to handle the self-assessment).

To ensure effectiveness, all the members of the teams must receive adequate training and at least one, preferably more, must have some previous experience. This may appear to contradict the requirement that, whenever possible, the team members should be high-level managers. In practice, this difficulty emerges only when the fact that self-assessment should be a high-profile process has not been assimilated, so the idea of senior managers taking an assessor course seems illogical. In companies that view self-assessment as a fundamental process in which the unit analyses itself in order to respond better to the challenges of its business goals, top management will not want to delegate assessment to others.

Naturally, the unit's senior managers in the self-assessment team are not required to collect documentation or write the report personally: these tasks will usually be delegated to staff. The group interviews, too, can be conducted by skilled staff of sufficient seniority. But the senior managers will want to coordinate the process and monitor the work of their staff. They will also attend the team meetings, when the material collected will be presented and the self-assessment report will gradually be drawn up. They will conduct interviews with top management and first-level managers, and will handle external reports and reports of a critical nature.

The corporate culture should encourage managers to take part in this type of training and create a climate in which the 'organizational assessor' is a highly regarded figure.

The company's approach to the question of assessor training will depend on its size. A small company will use external courses, a large company can organise internal courses. Attendance at these courses should be a condition for entry on to a self-assessment team. The company should also ensure that each team includes at least one lead assessor, having previously decided what exactly this role entails. It would be reasonable for a lead assessor to have taken part in three or more self-assessments, of which at least one should have been outside his or her sector of activity; moreover, at least one of these self-assessments will have successfully undergone a positive audit by the central team. The need for at least one lead assessor is why it was suggested that central-team assessors should provide support beyond the first year, until the local assessors – and similar assessors in other sectors – have acquired the necessary experience.

## 6.8 TRAINING ON THE MODEL

It is worth repeating the key concept that self-assessment differs from management audits because it requires the active participation of the entire population of the unit concerned. Since everyone must be involved in improvement, everyone should contribute to analysis and diagnosis (and the unit itself will be the first to benefit). Informed participation depends not only on correct information, but also on effective training (in addition to the specific training for assessors, discussed in the previous section): specifically, training that focuses on the model, given that the unit assesses itself with reference to the model and its specifications as illustrated in the self-assessment guide. Since the main purpose of training is to change people's attitudes, it will insist on the new values on which the model is based. Self-assessment cannot reach its full potential until the model's fundamental values have been assimilated and the cultural transformation that is its main premise has begun. Until this happens, a full understanding of the model's categories and factors is not possible; this is why the first assessment usually resembles a management audit (with the specific characteristics described in the previous section).

In large companies, unfortunately, top management is usually excluded from training. This is unacceptable. As G. Hamel and C. K. Prahalad say: 'Senior executives are prone to believe that their organizational status confirms that they know more about the industry, customer needs, competitors and how to compete than the people they manage. But what they know more about is, all too often, the past. The rules of competitive success in yesterday's world were etched into their minds as they climbed the corporate ladder' [9].

The company's top officers may appear to accept a business model of the type described here, but the depth of their understanding would be questionable if they were not the first to agree to a period of training, first-hand experimentation, checking and correction. At a time of rapid change, top management cannot simply be 'informed'. Information (usually by means of short briefing sessions) is always filtered by interpretative keys acquired previously when the manager had the time to study and test concepts. Interpretative keys, however, are subject to rapid obsolescence.

Without the necessary training and direct experience, it is not possible for anyone to replace the old management theories with the new concepts of leadership, the old approach to personnel management with the new concept of empowerment, and so on for strategies and organizational architectures. Of course, the chief executive may reject the new concepts as unconvincing or even dangerous, or dismiss them as fashionable fads. But if he accepts them, he must be the first to undergo the training that he expects his staff to undergo, so that he can test out their effectiveness at first hand, together with his staff. In the last few years, a significant number of European company chairmen and chief executives have announced that they were adopting the EQA model, but little evidence can be seen of the changes in management style on which this model is based. Why is this so? In not a few cases, the adoption of the EQA model has not generated the corresponding corporate values; in other cases, the values declared by the company are inconsistent with the model. Training on the model – and on leadership in particular – should begin at the highest level and work its way down the corporate pyramid, with the necessary adjustments. Moreover, it should be supplemented by practical experience of the new management concepts and, as soon as possible, by self-assessment and the integration of self-assessment into the company planning cycle. The steering committee should draw up a top-down training programme.

## 6.9 IMPLEMENTING SELF-ASSESSMENT

This section assumes that the self-assessment cycle is fully established, that each unit is able to assess itself and that the role of the central team is simply to promote, supervise and audit. Each team will conduct interviews, collect the necessary documentation, distribute and process the effectiveness questionnaires. The main purpose of the interviews is to find out directly from managers and their senior staff what they consider to be the unit's strengths and weaknesses in relation to its goals, following the procedures laid out in the self-assessment guide. During the assessment, the model and the guide will be the team's frame of reference (as well as experience, which is vitally important). The team will build up an overall picture by analysing the three areas of the model. At the level of *results*, it will collect all the data required and together with the relevant managers identify the largest gaps in relation to goals (of the previous year and/or those set by the business plan) and in relation to competitors, recording its findings for the subsequent assessment of processes and factors (see Chapter 4 and Appendix A) and for scoring. Moving on to *processes*, the team will identify the most important and/or critical processes in relation to its analysis of results and to any other indications (see Chapter 4 and

Appendix A). With the support of the process owners, it will then map out the relevant critical areas and, if necessary, conduct cross-diagnoses. At the level of *factors*, the area most lacking in objective data and cross-references, the team should assume the role of a *listener*, but a critical listener. In other words, it will base its assessments on the *evidence collected* by listening, watching, asking, discussing and asking for inconsistencies to be clarified. The formal tools used by the team to make its assessment are the documentation provided by the unit, the interviews, the effectiveness questionnaires, the carry-forwards and notes recorded during assessment of results and processes. All preconceptions must be eliminated. On the other hand, the personal opinions that will necessarily be formed through listening and dialogue – and the greater the experience of the assessors, the greater the range of opinions – must be openly expressed and discussed with the people being interviewed, until agreement is reached on what the true situation is (if this is not possible, the question will remain open, and, if important, recorded as such). A good assessment is an assessment where full transparency is achieved between assessors and interviewees, not only as regards strengths and weaknesses, but also in the area of scoring.

Once the interviews and critical analysis of the documentation have been completed, the team will draw up its self-assessment report, which should provide a synthesis of the findings of the self-assessment. The main part of the report will be a description of strengths and weaknesses in factors and processes found during the assessment, which began with the gaps between results and goals or between the new goals in the business plan and current goals. In the second part of the report, which will provide important data for comparative analyses and assessment of trends, scores are allotted. At this stage, a preliminary score should be given, which will be checked during the final phase when the external representatives join the team.

In the meantime, the unit will have distributed, collected and processed the effectiveness questionnaires (the processed results must in fact be available before the interviews begin, since they will provide valuable points for discussion). The results of the questionnaires will be, first, compared with the results of the interviews (as we said earlier, the degree of correspondence between the views of managers and their senior staff and those of other office staff and workers is an important indicator), and, second, combined with the results of the interviews (approach and deployment) as described in Chapter 3, to produce an overall score for each element.

This completes the first stage. The team now moves on to the second and final stage, in which scores are reviewed and finalized together with assessors from outside the unit (if, as highly recommended, provision has been made for external assessors). During this phase, the team reviews the entire PDCA cycle in relation to the previous year's planning. It examines what the unit has done (D) in relation to the improvement plan (P) drawn up after the previous year's assessment and on this basis analyses in depth the current assessment (C). Although the head of the unit may not attend the scoring discussion, he should be present when the team examines improvements achieved in relation to the previous plan, identifies the critical areas that emerge in the self-assessment and discusses the action to be taken. These measures, which will be presented by the unit director and the team leader, will be designed to consolidate and extend the improvements that have been achieved (the A stage of the previous PDCA cycle) and to plan improvements for the coming year (P phase of the new cycle). The final improvement plan will be drawn up once the necessary interactions with higher levels and with the unit's suppliers and customers have been completed (Chapter 7).

When self-assessment becomes part of the company planning cycle, the timetable must take account of the company's main short- and mid-term goals (Chapter 7). It should permit analysis of capabilities (strengths and weaknesses) in relation not only to current goals but also to future targets (this concept has been stressed repeatedly: it is essential to ensure that the right–left diagnostic self-assessment does not simply focus on problems but is a proactive process geared to the future). In this way, once the bottom-up self-assessment sequence has been completed, top management will have a full picture of the situation, and will be able to confirm or even raise goals in areas where the company is strong. In areas where weaknesses have emerged and where the company is unlikely to achieve its goals, top management will decide whether to lower its goals or to take specific action (improvements or re-engineering) to eliminate these weaknesses. This is discussed in Chapter 7.

## 6.10 POST-SELF-ASSESSMENT ACTIVITIES

Improvement planning is obviously the main activity once the self-assessment has been completed. This is such an important area, however, that it merits discussion in a separate chapter (see Chapter 7). This section examines other post-self-assessment activities, some of which are preliminaries for improvement planning.

After the Check phase (self-assessment), the PDCA cycle ends with the Act phase; the next cycle then begins with a new Plan phase. During the Act phase the company will: (a) consolidate and extend the positive findings of the self-assessment; (b) analyse weaknesses so as to plan suitable corrective action.

With regard to point (a), the company should analyse the mechanisms that have brought significant improvements, in order to consolidate them. It should also make sure that everyone is informed about the successful improvement initiatives introduced in the various sectors. These activities should be handled by the function delegated to the self-assessment, which will also be responsible for organizing benchmarking among similar units. Interesting benchmarking opportunities arise when one sector is found to be strong in a systemic factor or process in which comparable sectors are weak. Process benchmarking (and possibly also system benchmarking) with external companies is more difficult, but should be attempted. External benchmarking should be coordinated at central level, even if it concerns a specific division or department.

With regard to point (b), the company should not immediately assume that it has understood the root causes of its weaknesses. It should always avoid the superficial approach of moving straight from a problem to a remedy, without adequate diagnosis. Cross-diagnosis (Chapter 5) is a valuable tool here. If problems whose root cause is unclear still exist at the end of the self-assessment, a cross-diagnosis should be conducted before improvement planning begins.

Comparative analysis of the findings of the effectiveness questionnaires and interviews is another useful tool to help identify weaknesses and their causes. The company should pay particular attention to elements where questionnaire results are significantly worse than interview results. In these cases, it should organize meetings with groups of people in the second category of the company population (Section 6.6), from which the questionnaire respondents were selected (although the meetings should not be limited to the people who took part in the survey). The meetings should be presented as the promised feedback sessions designed to bring the self-assessment process full circle. After a brief presentation of the results of the self-assessment and a detailed presentation of the results of the questionnaires, the people attending the meeting will be asked to help the company identify the reasons for negative answers, so that corrective action can be planned. Care must be taken to avoid creating the impression that the company intends to dispute the data or wants to find out who gave negative answers, or that it implicitly attributes the findings to negative attitudes among the respondents. The correct approach is that having asked people to help identify areas of weakness, the company now requires their assistance to establish the underlying causes.

In short, the company should 'grill' the data it has collected, analyse the final self-assessment report in depth and hold meetings to discuss points that are still unclear. In this way it will obtain as much information as possible to plan improvement.

Telling the company population about the results of the self-assessment is a particularly important area of post-assessment activity. Company and division conventions, followed by a cascade of special boss–staff meetings are particularly useful. The conventions can also be used as award presentation ceremonies, but they should not be limited to this 'showcase' aspect; they should illustrate results and explain the strategic improvement lines the company intends to follow in relation to its business goals. In other words, they are an important opportunity for communication.

Finally, the company should improve its PDCA cycle every year. Meetings should be organized with all the members of the self-assessment teams to discuss any problems that have emerged and examine suggestions for improvement. At these meetings, the internal team members, as staff of the unit that was assessed, will also act as spokesmen for their units, and not just as collectors of comments and suggestions.

| 7 | **Integrating self-assessment and improvement planning into the company planning cycle** |
|---|---|

If self-assessment and subsequent improvement planning were concerned solely with 'quality', like every other corporate activity they would certainly be covered by company planning, but at the operational level; there would be no need to treat them as essential components of the strategic and operational planning cycle, even less to assert that self-assessment should be a cornerstone of this cycle. But, as stressed repeatedly in the previous chapters, self-assessment can realize its full value only if it refers to the company's missions and goals as a whole, if it sets out to identify the weaknesses and problems that can prevent missions and goals from being achieved and if the subsequent improvement planning phase aims to resolve these weaknesses. Consequently, self-assessment and improvement planning are neither a purely operational phase nor a simple addition to the planning cycle. Their integration into the company planning cycle involves the introduction of the 'PDCA philosophy' (Section 3.3) in *planning* – which therefore becomes a process for the continuous improvement and adjustment of the company's capabilities in relation to strategic goals – in *execution* and in the *monitoring of results* with reference to plans.

## 7.1 LINKS AMONG STRATEGIC PLANNING, SELF-ASSESSMENT AND IMPROVEMENT PLANNING

Self-assessment is characterized by the goals that are used as the yardstick to measure results. If the company adopts an 'inert' approach to assessment, if it simply measures results and assesses them in relation to existing goals (where these exist), without reviewing missions and goals, then self-assessment will necessarily be a low-profile, non-challenging, non-proactive process. Self-assessment acquires a strategic value only if a prior link is established with strategic planning. In Fig. 7.1, this link is represented by the 'strategic goals and priorities' block. This means that *the kick-off to self-assessment is an activity that must be handled by top management*, which must draw up a list of strategic priorities for the self-assessment. Once this initial link has been put in place, everything that follows will have a strategic value: most notably, the self-assessment (Fig. 7.1), whose main input is the list of goals in order of priority for each category on the right side of the model. In large companies where self-assessment is a multiple bottom-up process, a preliminary phase of top-down goal deployment will be necessary. Only then will the individual units be able to assess themselves in relation to their goals. The self-assessment also has a second input: goals from the previous PDCA cycle, plus any other goals that acquire critical importance during the self-assessment itself (Fig. 7.1). The first stage in the self-assessment process (assessment of results, right side of the model) will focus in particular on the gaps between results and the priority goals set by top management as described above.

The self-assessment produces a report identifying the weaknesses and strengths in processes and systemic factors that lie behind the weaknesses and strengths in results. This is translated into a series of proposals designed to improve/adjust capabilities; or, if improvement is impossible over the short term or too expensive, into proposed changes in goals. Proposed improvements of strategic significance or with a significant effect on plans or resource utilization, and proposed changes in goals are submitted for examination by strategic planning (Fig. 7.1). The decisions taken with regard to these proposals provide input for strategic improvement planning.

The flow chart in Fig. 7.1 illustrates self-assessment at the highest company-wide level, but with the appropriate adjustments, it can also apply at lower levels (function, division). At these levels too, proposed improvements will fall into two categories: those within the decision-making power of the unit, for which the process can move straight on to the planning stage; and those that require approval (typically proposals related to cross-functional/cross-divisional processes). Proposals in the second category, and any proposed changes in goals, will be submitted for the approval of the next hierarchical level (this is the difference compared with company-wide self-assessment as illustrated in Fig. 7.1).

The two parallel outputs of strategic planning – performance goal planning and process/systemic capability improvement planning – are the starting point for goal deployment, which transmits goals and verifies their

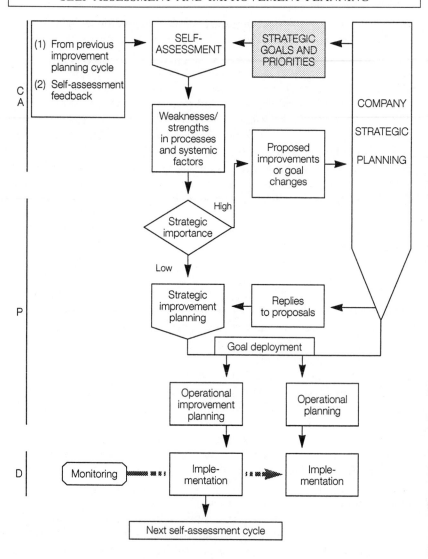

**Fig. 7.1** Links among company strategic planning, self-assessment and strategic improvement planning.

feasibility. Interactive by definition, goal deployment will have already taken place to a certain extent during the self-assessment (with reference to improvement), since this is when the feasibility of the capability improvements stemming from the proposed performance improvements is checked. The goal deployment process will produce a series of operational plans, in particular an operating improvement plan, which will include process improvement and/or re-engineering initiatives and systemic factor improvement and/or re-engineering initiatives.

The processes described above constitute the Check and Act phases of the previous cycle and the Plan phase of the new cycle. The Plan phase is followed by the Do phase, when all activities are monitored to ensure that they are in line with operating plans and produce the expected results (and if they are not, to make the necessary adjustments). The results on the left side of the flow chart in Fig. 7.1 (relating to improvement initiatives) will then converge with the secondary input of the next self-assessment phase.

## 7.2 THE TIME SEQUENCE

The timing of the flow described above must match the requirements of the planning cycle. Figure 7.2 illustrates the sequence of activities: in theory, self-assessment cannot begin until the list of strategic and operating macro-priorities (or targets, for which top management is responsible) is available on one hand, and the results of the period (normally the previous year) are available on the other. Self-assessment will be conducted as described in Chapters 4 and 5 and concludes with a description of strengths and weaknesses in the process and systemic factor areas and with proposals to be submitted to top management and the corporate planning function during self-assessment review sessions. Once these proposals have been examined and any necessary changes in the strategic plan have been

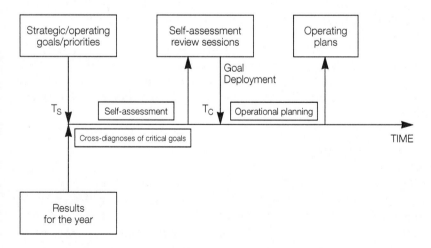

**Fig. 7.2** The time sequence for self-assessment activities in relation to the planning cycle.

approved, goal deployment can begin. If the self-assessment and cross-diagnoses have been sufficiently thorough, goal deployment should not find any significant incompatibilities between goals and capabilities. In Fig. 7.2, $T_s$ to $T_c$ represents the global timespan, that is, the time taken to validate the strategic goals established by planning as input for the self-assessment. A minimum period of time should, however, be provided for goal deployment after $T_c$, before goals are consolidated into operating plans.

We have assumed that the results of the previous year and strategic/operating macro-priorities are all available at the same time, $T_s$ in Fig.7.2. In practice, this is almost impossible, so a compromise is necessary. The best solution is to schedule the self-assessment to match the constraints of the planning cycle, especially those of the operational planning cycle which are the least easy to modify, bearing in mind that the results available are preliminary rather than final results. Moreover, both the strategic plan and the operating plan are subject to variations during the year, for a variety of exogenous and endogenous reasons. Clearly, then, the self-assessment process must be as simple and as flexible as possible (specifically, it should not be rigidly bound to the model in Fig. 7.2), so that it can be updated if necessary during the year and the relative modifications introduced to the operating plan.

The best conceptual tool to ensure the flexibility of the self-assessment process is cross-diagnosis. Whenever the unit is faced with a result that requires considerable improvement or a completely new goal, a cross-diagnosis can be rapidly conducted to identify the changes involved at the systemic and process levels. There is no need to repeat all the self-assessment phases; a specific cross-diagnosis will be sufficient. Since cross-diagnosis permits considerable flexibility, the unit can safely adopt the sequence illustrated in Fig. 7.2, with scheduling dictated by the company planning cycle (operating plan and annual strategic update). Generally speaking, results will not generally coincide with the financial year; depending on the type of result, they will be the results of the twelve-month period defined by the planning cycle, or the company's preliminary results.

## 7.3 GRADUAL INTEGRATION

Since integration of self-assessment into the planning cycle is a lengthy procedure, companies may find it best to adopt a gradual step-by-step approach. This is a decision that will be taken by management (in particular, by the steering committee, Section 6.1), on the basis of the presumed level of resistance to the changes proposed. The following gradual approach is recommended.

During the first year, the aim is to integrate self-assessment into the current operating plan. Results are therefore assessed in relation to current operating goals (and/or to the equivalent results of the company's competitors). Since achieving planned goals is in everyone's interests, a process designed to identify and remove the causes of gaps between results and goals, or the causes that prevent improvement of operating results, will generally be favourably received. This is already an important step forward: if the self-assessment is based on a business model of the type described in this book, people will begin to realize that it is not a 'quality planning programme' (related to product or service defects), but an improvement planning programme related to any and every result on the right side of the model (in other words, a programme with an impact on business, customers and stakeholders).

The next step – which should be implemented in the second year if possible – is to incorporate self-assessment into annual operating planning. Some of the performance goals set by the plan will certainly be higher than current goals. Self-assessment can be used to identify the capabilities that need to be improved if these goals are to be reached. At a more general level, it can be a tool to raise the plan's probabilities of success. At this second level, the self-assessment timetable should be based on the operating planning cycle, so that the findings of the feasibility checks are available prior to formalization of operating plans (Fig. 7.2).

During the third phase, self-assessment is integrated in full into the strategic planning cycle. When this third stage begins depends on the success of the two previous stages; if they have overcome suspicion and opposition, it is best to proceed immediately with full integration. The difference in relation to the second step is that since strategic planning covers the medium/long term, the relevant goals often require substantial improvements in existing capabilities or the creation of new competencies/capabilities (for this reason, the term 'improvement' should be flanked by the term 'expansion'). Creation of new capabilities (technological or marketing capabilities) usually requires long-term operational planning, and the level of uncertainty will be directly proportional to the extent to which the competencies are new to the company or, in the case of leader companies making a breakthrough, new in absolute terms. The essential purpose of self-assessment is to furnish managers with a series of tools (the control panel of Section 3.2) to help them make their way when visibility is low and when progress needs to be periodically checked, so that the next stretch can be planned on the basis of the experience gained and the information collected to date. Self-assessment enables the company to:

- perform critical analyses of progress since the previous check;
- identify the causes of deviations from the original plan;
- introduce any variations in goals;

- verify the state of capabilities in relation to the new set of goals;
- verify whether the toolset at management's disposal is sufficient to permit control of the system;
- plan the next stretch;
- plan expansion of capabilities (systemic factors and processes) in line with the requirements of the new stretch.

The curve in Fig. 7.3 represents the role of self-assessment and improvement planning in a continuous performance improvement/expansion strategy.

Obviously, the third stage, in which self-assessment is fully integrated with the strategic planning cycle, can bring significant improvements in the methods used by the company to monitor the long-term growth, in situations of uncertainty, of the competencies/capabilities needed to achieve its strategic goals.

Another point highlights the importance of integrating self-assessment into strategic planning, especially in innovative companies. When a company decides to improve the capabilities required by strategic planning, it often concentrates solely on specific (hard) capabilities, especially in technology and marketing. By linking systemic factors and processes to goals, self-assessment encourages the company to extend its investigation to soft characteristics such as leadership and motivation/involvement of human resources. Even if the company has improved its hard capabilities, it may still fail to achieve the planned performance improvements if its soft factors are inadequate. In addition to leadership

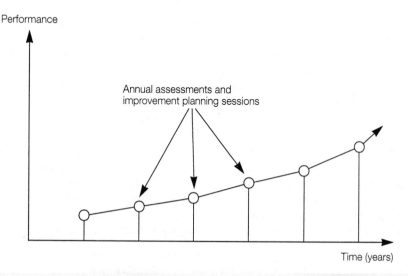

**Fig. 7.3** Self-assessment and annual improvement planning can be key moments in the company's pursuit of excellence.

and human resources, another critical systemic factors category that is often neglected when significant technological and market changes are introduced is organizational architectures. Very often, the changes that the company intends to pursue – especially those involving market innovations – require changes in the *ways* human, material, financial and information resources are organized. And innovation can often be introduced in these 'ways', in organizational architectures.

## 7.4 PERFORMANCE GAPS AND CAPABILITY GAPS

The three phases in the process of integration of self-assessment into the company planning cycle are represented in Fig. 7.4. The right-hand block represents assessment of 'results'. Since diagnostic self-assessment begins with results (right–left approach), the right-hand block also represents the nucleus and the starting point – and also the driver – of self-assessment. It consists of three components: the bottom component is the starting point for the first stage of integration; similarly the middle and top components are the starting points for the second and third stages respectively.

In all three cases, the self-assessment starting point and driver is a $\Delta$ (delta), a difference, a gap. In the first stage of integration, the delta is a performance gap, between current results and current goals: $\Delta = (cR - cG)$, or between results and those of a reference competitor: $\Delta = (cR - rR)$, or between results and those of a non-competitor best-in-class: $\Delta = (cR - bR)$. In the second stage of integration, further performance gaps are added: the deltas between current goals (or current results) and

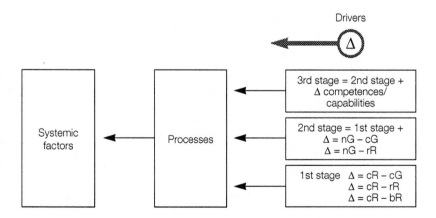

**Fig. 7.4** Performance gaps or competence/capability gaps ($\Delta$) are the drivers of self-assessment. cR = current Results; bR = Results of best-in class; cG = current Goals; rR = reference competitor Results; nG = new Goals.

the new goals of the operating plan being drawn up: $\Delta = (nG - cG)$ or $\Delta = (nG - cR)$ or $\Delta = (nG - rR)$.

In the third stage, the deltas between future goals and the current situation are added. They may still be performance gaps, but often they are competence gaps where no current reference or no significant current reference exists (e.g., new products and services for the market). In these cases, the factor that drives the company to develop new competencies/capabilities is its knowledge base and not, as in the first two stages, measurement of performance gaps. The first two stages of integration begin with performance gaps (drivers) and work back to the capability gaps in processes and systemic factors. The third stage begins, as far as goal innovation is concerned, with competence gaps (or gaps in macro-capabilities), which often emerge in technological and market areas, and works back to gaps in micro-capabilities at process or system level.

Figure 7.4 illustrates the concept that in all three cases the starting point for self-assessment is the gaps in performance and/or competencies. From there, the process moves from right to left, to identify capability gaps in processes and systemic factors.

Obviously, the self-assessment process becomes increasingly complex as it moves from one stage to the next. In the first stage, the first $\Delta$ considered is between results and goals. If goals have been carefully set, the system should have the capabilities to achieve them and the diagnosis will be geared to identification of 'special causes' (uncontrolled variations that may have entered the system). This is the simplest level of diagnosis. Diagnosis of the other $\Delta$s that may arise (between results and the equivalent results of competitors and/or non-competitor best-in-class) may involve greater complexities, similar to those encountered during the second phase, when the new goals set by the operating plan are more ambitious than current goals. In both cases, the problem is to identify the causes that prevent intrinsic system and process capabilities from being improved (and the levers that can be activated to facilitate improvement), so that higher performance levels can be attained than those for which that system and those processes were designed. Depending on the size of the $\Delta$, improvements will be incremental or discontinuous (re-engineering).

The third stage obviously poses the greatest challenge for the diagnostic capabilities of the self-assessment process, since the planned performance improvements will generally be greater than those set during operational planning and large competence gaps may need to be bridged. Increasingly, the company will find itself on unknown territory, particularly if it is a market leader. The diagnosis focuses on the existing system and on the (usually long-term) developments planned by the company to fuel the growth of new competencies. Compared with normal corporate practice, the added value of self-assessment is the systematic nature of the analysis, which extends to processes and systemic factors. Self-assessment should help the company improve its process capabilities, but it should also assist identification of the frequently neglected 'intangible' systemic capabilities that, together with hard capabilities (in technology and marketing), can hinder adequate development of process capabilities. For example, consider the capabilities – 'flexibility' and 'receptiveness of the corporate system of market and competition sensors' – which are often crucial to successful market innovation (together with the key ability to innovate). When the company operates in a rapidly changing external environment and is exploring new territory, each new area of knowledge, every move by the competition, can undermine the work performed to date and make a rapid change of direction necessary. It cannot be taken for granted that the above capabilities are present in direct proportion to the company's ability to innovate; self-diagnosis of soft factors can help reveal any shortcomings that could limit the effectiveness of the company's creative potential.

## 7.5 SELF-ASSESSMENT REVIEW AND STRATEGIC IMPROVEMENT PLANNING

The output of the self-assessment (the 'weaknesses and strengths in processes and systemic factors' block in Fig. 7.1) provides the input for the self-assessment review and strategic improvement planning, which consist of three processes: 'proposed improvements or goal changes', 'strategic planning' and 'strategic improvement planning' (Fig. 7.1). In Fig. 7.2 these activities are represented by the 'self-assessment review' block. This discussion looks at the global self-assessment review, but the same approach can be used for reviews at lower levels, provided the necessary adjustments are made (see above).

The company function delegated to handle the self-assessment will usually be responsible for processing the results and preparing the information needed to give top management (chief executive and first line) a clear picture of the current situation in relation to goals and, where possible, competitors. The purpose of the review sessions is to produce a rapid consensus with regard to strategic improvement goals.

The preliminary requirement for self-assessment review sessions is that results must be *accepted*. Not infrequently, the top management team is presented with unexpected and at times unpleasant results, which contradict its image of itself and the company. For example, a decline in customer support, lack of motivation, employees who observe a deterioration in the company values and inadequate leadership or discontented partners. The review sessions must not dispute the self-assessment. Results should be accepted as a matter of course; naturally, supplementary investigations may be necessary to verify incomprehensible or contradictory results, but the chief executive must not allow the findings to be impugned simply because they do not coincide with the opinion of top management.

This is vitally important; if results are not accepted, the company's conception of power (the opinion of those with the greatest weight is more important than measurements) is evidently incompatible with the idea of results-based continuous improvement and, in particular, with the self-assessment approach described in this book. Assessment of systemic factors in terms not only of 'approach' and 'deployment', which mainly reflect the view of management, but also of 'effectiveness' (Section 3.5) implies that although the viewpoint of management is fundamental, it is not the only one nor is it necessarily the best reflection of the real situation. A company that decides to survey its customers, employees and stakeholders does so because it believes that these groups can provide important indications. Questioning the views they express would undermine the entire self-assessment. The chief executive should therefore make sure that none of the voices in the assessment are challenged, with the proviso that any incomprehensible or contradictory information must be verified, even if its source is management. The details of the self-assessment review sessions can now be discussed.

Self-assessments provide large quantities of information, but most of it should be used at the level at which it is collected. Only significant aggregate data, and problem areas that have not been solved at lower levels, should filter up to top management. Consequently, the company-wide synthesis will simply provide information about weaknesses/strengths to be addressed by the improvement plans of the individual sectors whereas it will outline the problems that require the attention of top management (weaknesses in cross-functional/cross-divisional processes and in corporate systemic factors).

Presentation of syntheses will be more effective if the company uses the concept of the management 'control panel', that is, the measurement system covering 'results' as well as 'processes' and 'systemic factors' described in Section 3.2. The presentation to top management will use high-level aggregate indicators. In the 'results' area, performances will be aggregated into the various categories; in each category, they will follow the goal priorities set by top management as input for the self-assessment. Each performance will be compared with the relevant goal and where appropriate with the equivalent performance of reference competitors or non-competitor best-in-class. Historical data and trends must be presented for each performance. Where critical performance gaps exist at company level, the corresponding process and/or systemic weaknesses will be identified and the degree to which the planned improvement initiative intends to reduce these gaps will be specified. Assisted by strategic planning, the top management team will verify the overall consistency of the syntheses presented by the various divisions/functions and give its opinion on proposed changes in goals. These review sessions should produce a clear set of macro-goals approved by top management, which will be transmitted to the divisions/functions during the subsequent deployment phase. Top management will usually approve performance goals, since responsibility for correctly translating performance goals into process or systemic factor goals must lie with the relevant division/ function. It must have full visibility on the main improvement goals, and above all on the key process or systemic re-engineering goals; but this is part of the TQM philosophy, which holds that when goals are set, the 'way' they are to be achieved must also be established. In the case of innovative strategic goals, which require creation of new competencies/capabilities, the goals approved by top management will generally relate to those competencies/capabilities rather than to performance.

With regard to weaknesses in cross-divisional/cross-functional processes or in the company system, the top management team must take an active part in improvement, instead of simply receiving information. These weaknesses can only be resolved at the very highest level. In this area, therefore, top management becomes a company-wide self-assessment team. Normally, the function delegated to the self-assessment process will accompany its presentation of weaknesses with possible solutions based on feasibility and cost/benefit analyses. But responsibility for planning improvement lies with top management, supported by the function delegated to the self-assessment and by strategic planning. The result will be a series of goals; some will be functional/divisional goals, but the majority will be cross-functional/cross-divisional goals.

Figure 7.5 illustrates the self-assessment review and improvement planning sessions at top management level.

## 7.6 DEPLOYMENT OF IMPROVEMENT GOALS

This phase follows the corporate strategic planning stage. The aim is to ensure that goals are transmitted and accepted throughout the organization. To maximize goal feasibility, deployment is normally an interactive process. However, if improvement planning is based on input from a self-assessment process of the type described in this book, and in particular on cross-diagnosis, the participation of all sectors and levels in proposing improvements that stem from the diagnoses will already be guaranteed. In other words, the feasibility of improvement initiatives will already have been largely verified. So the confirmation of goals normally obtained through the interactive phases of goal deployment can be eliminated or cut down to a minimum. Figure 7.2 prudently provides for goal deployment; and it will of course be necessary if top management modifies the improvement goals proposed by the self-assessment teams or introduces new improvement goals during strategic planning.

As we saw in the previous section, the improvement goals that top

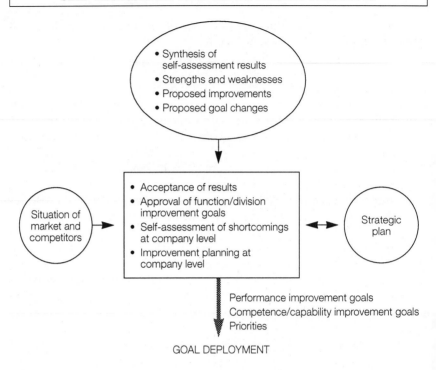

**Fig. 7.5** The self-assessment review and approval of strategic improvement goals at top management level.

management sets for the functions/divisions will normally refer to the right side of the model: 'what' the company must achieve rather than 'how' (the centre and left side of the model). Furthermore, they will be strategic goals, and will not deal with operational details (corporate staff should be so limited in number that the temptation to go into details does not arise). These details and the 'how' will gradually emerge as goals are deployed downwards through the corporate structure. The reader is referred to other literature for a full discussion of goal deployment [3, 17]; this section offers a description of the basic concepts of a correct goal deployment process (Fig. 7.6), with the emphasis on high interactivity among the various organizational levels.

The macro-goals are provided by top management; at operating level, they are translated into goals for the relevant processes. Feasibility is checked through cross-diagnosis. This is only a basic guideline, however. Figure 7.7 provides further details, with reference to a customer satisfaction goal. The customer satisfaction tree is shown on the right of the figure, with the trunk at the top and the branches below. This means that Result 1 (R1) represents overall satisfaction for a specific set of products/

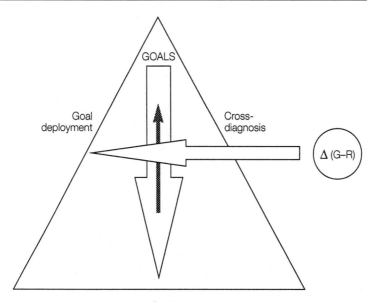

**Fig. 7.6** The goal deployment process intersects with the cross-diagnosis conducted to check goal feasibility.

services and a specific market segment. R2.1, R2.2, R2.3 and R2.4 are second-level components of customer satisfaction, for example, satisfaction with pre-sales service, with the product, with post-sales service, with supplier relations.

Let us assume that during the self-assessment review, top management decides that not only R1 but also the improvement goal proposed by operating managers are incompatible with the company's market share and profitability goals, and sets a high improvement goal, G1. This goal is transmitted to the lower levels, which begin to analyse customer satisfaction results from the second-level branches of the tree downwards, in order to identify the reasons for the weakness. By far the most significant cause of dissatisfaction lies in R2.3, the post-sales service. Goal G1 will have been sub-divided into component parts, including G2.3. The G2.3 − R2.3 performance gap will be the starting point for a cross-diagnosis designed to identify improvements/re-engineerings that may be necessary in the (mainly cross-functional) processes that generate R2.3 and any improvements needed in systemic factors. This is an example of rapid verification of the feasibility of a goal modified by top management after the self-assessment. Interaction across the various levels and cross-diagnosis enable the new goals to be rapidly endorsed.

Strategic improvement planning and goal deployment is followed by operational improvement planning. These processes proceed in parallel

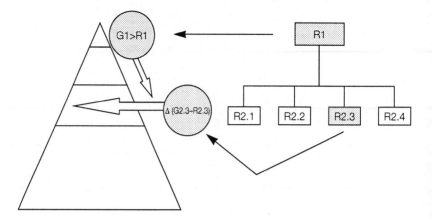

**Fig. 7.7** Deployment of a global performance goal in the area of customer satisfaction and cross-diagnosis starting from the 'new goal–current result' gap to identify the process and system capabilities that need to be improved in order to reach the new goal.

(left-hand flow in Fig. 7.1) with the corresponding strategic planning, deployment and operating planning processes (right-hand flow in Fig. 7.1). If the processes in the left-hand flow are conducted well, the success of those in the right-hand flow is guaranteed. This is because the left-hand process flow is designed to match process and systemic factor capabilities to activities. The greater the success of the company in integrating improvement planning into its business planning cycle, the better this match will be.

## 7.7 CONCLUSIONS

The self-assessment approach discussed in this book makes 'management by policies' geared to continuous improvement a feasible option. Top management is responsible for setting strategic macro-goals (right side of the model); the various organizational levels of the company structure are equipped with the tools they need to measure any performance gaps and subsequently identify capability gaps in processes and systemic factors (central and left sides of the model), and then plan action to bring capabilities into line with goals. Capability gaps are identified through self-assessment and, in particular, through cross-diagnosis. In other words, diagnostic self-assessment is an organizational tool that can be used to verify the feasibility of the goals set by strategic and operational planning and thus enhance the reliability of plans. If diagnostic self-assessment is to function correctly, however, a high degree of horizontal integration is

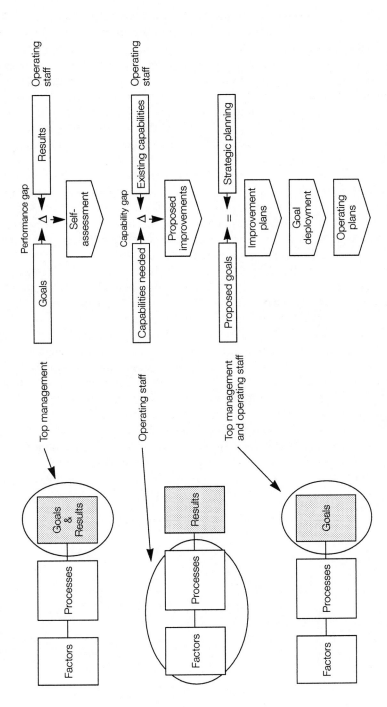

**Fig. 7.8** The activity flow shows how the activities for which top management is responsible make 'management by policies' possible.

necessary, since the processes (and certainly the company's key processes) that play a critical role as far as results are concerned are usually cross-functional. Figure 7.8 charts the activity flow through which self-assessment and improvement planning are integrated into strategic planning, to enable policies to be translated into operating plans.

Diagnostic self-assessment is a key factor in improving corporate competitiveness: once the company has a clear understanding of its means (process and system capabilities), its possibilities and the obstacles it must remove to achieve its goals, it will be encouraged to set itself greater challenges.

Too many large companies still have centralized planning systems, which, on the one hand, spend too much time on operating details, thus disempowering operating staff, and, on the other, are not in touch with the state of processes and critical systemic factors, and therefore have only a vague idea of the company's true capabilities and relative improvement potential. If challenging goals are set, the low level of involvement of operating staff, particularly front-end personnel, and the absence of appropriate methodologies mean that in the unlikely event that the company successfully reaches its goals, this will be at the expense of other parts of the system. This is the risk for companies operating on markets that force players to set challenging goals. At the other extreme, in protected market environments (a dwindling number), the danger is that the company will be content with low-profile goals it already knows it can achieve. In both cases, the risks are often aggravated by incentive systems based on faulty interpretations of management by objectives.

For companies that want to be successful players on today's increasingly competitive markets – but also for companies that are struggling to survive – a self-diagnosis and planning system that requires the involvement of the entire company and is based on the concept of continuous improvement and driven by missions and strategic goals is now an essential tool.

# Appendices

# Appendix A
# Guide to the self-assessment process

This guide is intended for people who wish to apply the basic concepts of diagnostic self-assessment illustrated in this book in a real corporate environment. Assuming the reader to be familiar with the first part of the book, the guide gives a step-by-step example of a 'right–left' assessment path, which begins from the goals/results area, moves back into the processes area and terminates with the systemic factors area. For full understanding, the reader should already have assimilated the contents of Chapters 3 and 4.

For assessment of the first two areas, goals/results and processes, the guide uses a series of 'standard forms'. Where necessary, to aid comprehension, these forms are filled in with examples. Naturally, each company will draw up the forms that best respond to its particular requirements.

For assessment of the third area, systemic factors, the guide illustrates the categories of the model one by one. Each category is sub-divided into 'factors', which are in turn sub-divided into 'assessment elements' (see Fig. 3.9). Examples are provided of the areas that could be investigated for each factor and each assessment element.

The guide does not examine 'cross-diagnosis'; the description provided in Chapter 5 provides the maximum level of detail possible in a written text. Any further details would make the discussion unnecessarily complex. Beyond this level, specific software tools of the type mentioned in the notes to Chapter 5 are required.

## AREA 1: GOALS AND RESULTS

Assessment of the goals/results area can be sub-divided into three phases. The first phase is *identification of priority goals*, those that constitute the main focus of attention during collection and assessment of results. Priority goals are not an exclusive frame of reference, however: as Chapter 4 explains, the self-assessment should highlight all important problems, including those outside the priority areas selected by management. Form GR.0 (and GR.0-Example) is used to collect and aggregate the priority goals selected by management.

The second phase is collection and assessment of results, in particular the results that correspond to the company's priority goals. Results are used to:

- identify areas of weakness for the purposes of diagnosis and correction, and areas of strengths for the purpose of scoring and to enable the company to exploit its advantages in full;
- give a score to each category in the area.

GR.1/2/3/4/5/6 provide guidelines for assessment of results in the six categories of the goals/results area. They are not form facsimiles (as GR.0, GR.7, GR.8 and GR.9 are), but assessment guides.

Once critical results have been identified in each category, the assessors will move on to the third phase, identification of 'priority action areas'. This is achieved by combining goal importance ranking and performance gap to create a 'priorities index'. The procedures performed in this phase are exemplified in forms GR.8 and GR.9.

The data obtained from the procedures in GR.8 and GR.9 will be used to identify 'priority processes', as described in the section on the processes area.

GR.0 is the first form to be filled in. It provides the main input for the self-assessment process, that is, input (1) in Fig. 4.1. Similar forms can be created for inputs (2) and (3) in Fig. 4.1, although for simplicity they are not considered here. GR.0 shows *goals given priority ranking by management*, in accordance with the company's strategic and operating plans. The goals are divided among the six categories of the model (one category for customers, one for business, four for the stakeholders). Management gives each goal an importance coefficient, from 5 to 1. The highest ranking – 5 – is given to strategic goals of the utmost importance, which must be included in the self-assessment. A priority ranking of 5 ensures that the relevant goals will be considered when deciding which processes require priority control. Values 4 to 1 indicate the importance of the remaining goals, in decreasing order. The 1 to 5 classification is the type recommended, but obviously each company will choose the criterion it considers most appropriate.

Form GR.0 is followed by a completed form (GR.0-Example). Since this is an example, only categories 'C' (customer preference) and 'P' (personnel contributions/personnel satisfaction) have been filled in.

GR.1/2/3/4/5/6 are used for assessment of the six results categories. Conceptually speaking, their contents are similar to the checklists used by the EQA and the Malcolm Baldrige awards for assessment of 'results' categories. Each assessment ends with a list of strengths and weaknesses in relation to goals, to reference competitors or to best-in-class, and a percentage score for the category.

This completes the actual assessment of the six categories in the results area. Since the main purpose of this stage is not so much to obtain a score, as to provide the starting point for an improvement planning process, the next step is to begin the diagnostic path, with two aids: form GR.7 on the one hand, and forms GR.8 and GR.9 on the other.

GR.7 is used to record observations and comments about symptoms found during assessment of results that suggest the possible presence of weaknesses in the processes and systemic factors areas. These notes are then carried forward to the assessments of these two areas. Symptoms of possible weaknesses in leadership, personnel, organization and resources will emerge during assessment of results and should be investigated when the corresponding categories are assessed. A GR.7 form should be used for each factors category and for the processes area. If necessary, forms will also be allotted for the six results categories, since links among them are far from uncommon.

Forms GR.8 and GR.9 are used to identify priority action areas, in preparation for the assessment of processes. Their input is goal importance ranking (GR.0) and performance gaps (GR.1/2/3/4/5/6). Form GR.8 provides the framework for the identification of priority action areas – PAA – while form GR.9 breaks down the results of the PAAs identified in GR.8 into their main components to permit identification of priority processes.

Specifically, GR.8 (upper part) shows the goals of form GR.0 for a specific category. For each goal, it shows the assessment result and the performance gap between that result and the goal (or between the company's result and that of the reference competitor or of the non-competitor best-in-class). In the lower part of the form, goal importance is combined with performance gaps on a graph to obtain a priority index: PI = Importance × Performance Gap. The priority action areas can therefore be identified. Two GR.8-Example sheets are provided, for the two goals/results categories shown in form GR.0-Example.

Form GR.9 is used to break down the critical results of the PAAs identified in form GR.8 into their individual components. Apart from the value of pinpointing specific weaknesses and strengths in results, this breakdown is important in diagnostic terms, since it assists identification of processes that generate weak or strong results. This provides the starting point for the subsequent analysis of processes. A GR.9 form is filled in for every PAA identified in form GR.8 that the company decides is significant (Pareto's Law is applied wherever possible, to exclude components whose effect on results is negligible). The use of form GR.9 will be even clearer when form P1 of the processes area is discussed.

Goals/results area                                        GR.0

### Identification of priority goals

Category: Customer preference
Priority goals:                                          Importance
                                                              (1–5)
GC.1 ...........................................................................................
GC.2 ...........................................................................................
GC.3 ...........................................................................................
GC.4 ...........................................................................................

Category: Business goals
Priority goals:
GB.1 ...........................................................................................
GB.2 ...........................................................................................
GB.3 ...........................................................................................
GB.4 ...........................................................................................
GB.5 ...........................................................................................
GB.6 ...........................................................................................

Category: Personnel satisfaction/contributions from personnel
Priority goals:
GP.1 ...........................................................................................
GP.2 ...........................................................................................
GP.3 ...........................................................................................
GP.4 ...........................................................................................

Category: Shareholder satisfaction/contributions from shareholders
Priority goals:
GSh.1 .........................................................................................
GSh.2 .........................................................................................
GSh.3 .........................................................................................
GSh.4 .........................................................................................

Category: Partners satisfaction/contributions from partners
Priority goals:
GPa.1 .........................................................................................
GPa.2 .........................................................................................
GPa.3 .........................................................................................

Category: Impact on society/contributions from society
Priority goals:
GS.1 ...........................................................................................
GS.2 ...........................................................................................
GS.3 ...........................................................................................

(Note on 'Importance': 5 = Absolute priority; 4 to 1, goals in descending order of priority.)

Goals/results area

GR.0
EXAMPLE

### Identification of priority goals

Category: Customer preference
Priority goals:                                        Importance
(1–5)

| | Importance (1–5) |
|---|---|
| GC.1 – Customer retention market segment S, customers class A: 90% | 5 |
| GC.2 – Customer satisfaction products/services X: level competitor Y | 5 |
| GC.3 – Customer satisfaction customers class A, market Z: 85% | 4 |
| GC.4 – Complaints rate: 50% reduction | 2 |

Category: Business goals
Priority goals:
GB.1 .............................................................................................................
GB.2 .............................................................................................................
GB.3 .............................................................................................................
GB.4 .............................................................................................................
GB.5 .............................................................................................................
GB.6 .............................................................................................................

Category: Personnel satisfaction/contributions from personnel
Priority goals:

| | |
|---|---|
| GP.1 – 65% personnel satisfaction (ref. best-in-class) | 5 |
| GP.2 – R&D personnel punctuality rate for new product releases: 50% improvement and simultaneous 50% reduction in modifications | 5 |

GP.3 .............................................................................................................

Category: Shareholder satisfaction/contributions from shareholders
Priority goals:
GSh.1 ...........................................................................................................
GSh.2 ...........................................................................................................
GSh.3 ...........................................................................................................
GSh.4 ...........................................................................................................

Category: Partners satisfaction/contributions from partners
Priority goals:
GPa.1 ...........................................................................................................
GPa.2 ...........................................................................................................
GPa.3 ...........................................................................................................

Category: Impact on society/contributions from society
Priority goals:
GS.1 .............................................................................................................
GS.2 .............................................................................................................
GS.3 .............................................................................................................

(Note on 'Importance': 5 = Absolute priority; 4 to 1, goals in decreasing order of priority.)

Goals/results area                                           GR.1

### Category GR.1: Customer preference

At this stage, this category is assessed in terms of results: for
customer satisfaction, customer retention, variations in the composi-
tion of the customer base, etc.
Results for goals to which top management has given priority should
be examined first (see form GR.0). However, the assessment should
cover all significant results, so as to build up a complete picture of
the company's situation in relation to plans and to competitors. See
Section 4.1.1 in the text.
Measurement of customer satisfaction is described in Sections 3.5.1
and 4.1.1.

There are two types of measurement: (a) direct customer perceptions; (b)
company measurements and indirect customer satisfaction indicators.

### (a) Direct customer perceptions

Direct customer perceptions are surveyed with reference to a customer
satisfaction 'tree' (Section 4.1.1), which must be designed to represent
customers' real perceptions in terms of both typology and importance
(weighting of the branches). Surveys can be conducted with questionnaires, telephone interviews (sometimes personal interviews) and listening
panels, depending on the type of relationship between the company and
the specific customer (large accounts, medium-size customers, consumers
in general). The customer satisfaction tree will usually cover the following
areas:

- appreciation of the company's products/services offer;
- pre-sales service quality;
- delivery services;
- documentation;
- new product training;
- quality and reliability of purchased products and services;
- warranty period;
- quality of after-sales technical support;
- quality of after-sales commercial support;
- personnel accessibility and helpfulness in relation to customer needs;
- quality of the relationship;
- administrative and contractual aspects;
- management of complaints;

- responsiveness and flexibility in relation to customer needs;
- overall judgement of value for money.

A score is given to each branch of the customer satisfaction tree and to the tree as a whole. The overall score will be based on answers to the last question on value for money, and should be more or less in line with the weighted average of the satisfaction scores for the individual branches (if the branch weights are correct).

A global value and an indication of customer satisfaction will therefore be obtained for every product/service area and key market segment. These values, together with the corresponding values of competitors, which will be measured in a similar fashion whenever necessary, will be used to identify weaknesses and strengths (see below). They will be combined with the measurements obtained at point (b) below and used to calculate the category score.

### (b) Company measurements and indirect customer satisfaction indicators

- variations in the customer base: new customers and lost customers by types of purchase;
- customer retention rates;
- complaints and correction trend;
- positive customer recognition;
- delivery speed and punctuality rates;
- product quality and reliability data collected by the field support service;
- customer returns, product recalls, significant field problems;
- call-out rate during warranty period;
- discounts to encourage purchases;
- public tributes, awards from customers;
- image surveys among non-customers.

Type (b) data will highlight weaknesses that should be diagnosed or considered for improvement. As far as scoring of this category is concerned, type (b) data should be used only as a corrective coefficient for the values obtained from type (a) measurements.

The assessment of the category ends by identifying 'weak' results and 'strong' results as input for subsequent diagnoses, and by allotting customer satisfaction scores for the various market segments in which the company operates. A global score will also be calculated, although significance decreases as the level of aggregation rises.

Note: Measurement of internal customer satisfaction is discussed in Section 4.1.1. The survey can be conducted with interviews and/or questionnaires focusing on two-way satisfaction. Questions will cover both service quality and partnership quality. The indications provided in Section 4.1.3.3 regarding business partner satisfaction questionnaires apply to internal customer satisfaction questionnaires, too.

Goals/results area | GR.2

## Category GR.2: Business goals/results

For this category, the assessment examines, first, results in relation to the goals of the company's operating plan and, second, the means deployed or to be deployed in order to achieve the goals set by the strategic plan, usually over a long-term period. Specifically, the first analysis will identify performance gaps between results and goals (or between the company's results and competitors' results); the second analysis will identify the goals for which an analysis of processes will probably be necessary. The priority goals set by top management for this category (form GR.0) will provide the main, though not exclusive basis of reference. See Section 4.1.2 of the text.

A variety of criteria can be used to classify business results for the purposes of assessment. The European Quality Award sub-divides them into financial and non-financial results. This guide advises sub-division into: (a) results of operations; (b) financial results (obviously the former will affect the latter). The items listed below are examples; they should not be regarded as exhaustive checklists.

### (a) Results of operations:

- improvements in human resources productivity;
- improvements in time-to-market;
- average improvement in product defect rate;
- improvements in significant cycle times;
- market share trends in main sectors of operation;
- significant improvements in key process efficiency.

### (b) Financial results:

- productivity of investments (ROE, ROA, ROI);
- operating cash flow;
- trend of income statement items such as sales, gross operating margin, net income;
- trend of balance-sheet items such as total assets, working capital, debt/equity ratio;
- capital turnover.

The assessment of the category ends by identifying 'weak' results and 'strong' results as input for the subsequent assessment of processes and systemic factors, and by allotting a global score as described in Section 4.1.2.

Goals/results area                                          GR.3
Grouping: Stakeholders

### Category GR.3: Satisfaction/contribution of shareholders

Few companies will consider themselves capable of making an exhaustive analysis of this category, but the self-assessment would be incomplete without it. At this stage, this category, too, is examined in terms of results: shareholder satisfaction with the company's performance and management satisfaction with the support received from shareholders and from the financial community. See Section 4.1.3.1 in the text. Interviews are the only way to survey satisfaction in this category: with the reference shareholder (or with a carefully selected financial analyst) on one hand, with top management on the other. Obviously, the interviews must be conducted by people of suitable seniority and experience.

The interviews should cover issues of the kind listed below.

**(a) Interview with the reference shareholder:**

- satisfaction with the company's competitive growth;
- satisfaction with the company image;
- opinion about short- and mid-term profitability;
- opinion about growth potential;
- top management's relations with reference shareholders and with the financial community;
- willingness to maintain current level of investment and, if necessary, to increase investment;
- acceptability of a possible review of the profit distribution policy to ensure equal involvement of all stakeholders.

**(b) Interview with top management:**

- financial support from reference shareholders;
- support for management from reference shareholders;
- relationship with reference shareholders, in particular extent of delegated powers;
- 'friendliness' of relationship with the financial community.

The assessment of the category ends with a list of strengths and weaknesses to be used as input for subsequent diagnoses of processes and factors, and with an overall percentage score.

Goals/results area                                                    GR.4
Grouping: Stakeholders

### Category GR.4: Satisfaction/contribution of personnel

At this stage, assessment of this category focuses on collection of results. Results for goals to which top management has given priority should be examined first (see form GR.0). However, all significant results should be considered, in order to identify weaknesses in areas that have not been selected but are nevertheless important. Unlike the European Award, this approach considers both sides of the relationship: personnel satisfaction with the company, but also the company's satisfaction with the quality and productivity of its human resources. See Section 4.1.3.2 in the text.

Employee satisfaction results are obtained mainly through questionnaires (a), but also through indirect indicators (b). Company satisfaction is assessed through interviews with management (c).

#### (a) Direct employee satisfaction surveys (or climate surveys)

The questionnaires will cover the following areas:

- **physical workplace:** safety, suitability of space, comfort, hygiene;
- **social environment:** quality of interpersonal relations; typology of relations among different hierarchical levels; formality in peer relations; stressful or relaxed atmosphere; presence of 'fear' as a behaviour-conditioning factor; cooperation and team work;
- **relations with the company:** sense of belonging; relationship with immediate boss and with corporate hierarchy; perception of equity in people management as regards career growth and remuneration; perception of sensitivity to people's needs; perception that jobs are guaranteed as far as possible; involvement, delegation, empowerment; social benefits provided for employees;
- **work satisfaction:** job gratification; self-realization; usefulness of work in relation to expected future developments; availability of support tools; difficulties in reaching workplace; facilities for female employees;
- **growth and career prospects:** opportunities for cultural growth; training; exposure to external environment; internal debate; perception of the company as an equal opportunities environment; perception that talent and dedication lead to greater responsibilities.

**(b) Indirect employee satisfaction indicators:**

- absenteeism;
- turnover;
- arriving late and leaving as soon as possible;
- workplace accidents;
- complaints;
- suggestions and proposed improvements;
- active participation in improvement groups;
- ease in attracting people who have many job opportunities;
- participation in social initiatives.

**(c) Company satisfaction with employees**

Interviews with management should produce judgements about:

- the match between current skills and the company's missions and goals:
  - in R&D
  - in marketing
  - in sales
  - in production, etc.;
- productivity of current resources;
- motivation;
- participation;
- ability and desire to work as a team.

Specifically, the interviews should investigate the suitability of current skills and personnel recruitment criteria in relation to the challenges of the future. Again, the above items are examples and should not be regarded as complete lists.

The assessment of the category ends with a list of weaknesses and strengths to be used as input for subsequent diagnosis and improvement planning. As far as scoring is concerned, objective quantitative data can be extracted from the employee satisfaction questionnaires only. Scoring in the other areas will refer to the usual percentage scale, applying common sense and experience and referring to the general criteria discussed in Chapters 3 and 4.

Goals/results area                                                                                          GR.5
Grouping: Stakeholders.


## Category GR.5: Contribution/satisfaction of business partners

Every company has key business partners: major suppliers, distributors, large accounts. In addition, many companies interact with a
wide range of business partners through a complex series of
arrangements. Results can be collected through interviews, but a
more effective approach is to draw up a questionnaire to be filled in
separately by the company and the partner. A critical analysis is then
performed on the two sets of results in order to produce a combined
assessment. See Section 4.1.3.3 of the text.

Use of a three-part questionnaire is recommended: the first two sections
cover the company's expectations of its business partner and the business
partner's expectations of the company. Both partners will state what they
should give and what they expect to receive with regard to 'product'
exchanges, specifications and feedback. The third section considers
interpersonal relations. Sections 1 and 2 can be completed at meetings
among the managers responsible for the partner relationship on either
side, the third section should be distributed to a significant sample of
people who operate at the interface. With regard to 'product' exchanges
(the term 'product' refers to everything that passes between the two
parties, both tangible and intangible), the partners should judge both
importance and performance, on a 1 to 5 scale. The quality of the
relationship can be judged on a similar scale. The 1 to 5 scale is equivalent
to a percentage scale using the levels 0–25–50–75–100. The result can thus
be easily translated into a percentage score.

A score should be obtained for each significant company–partner
interface. This will produce a map of poor relationships, which need
to be improved, and positive relationships, where ties could be made
even closer if desired. A detailed list of weaknesses (and strengths)
should be drawn up and a global score given to the category.

Goals/results area                                        GR.6
Grouping: Stakeholders

### Category GR.6: Impact on/contributions from society

As with all the other stakeholder categories, the assessment should ascertain the reciprocal level of satisfaction. In practice, management usually has continuous visibility on the company's satisfaction with the territory and society. Nevertheless, the assessment is an opportunity for management to review the positive and negative aspects of its relations with society and allot a global score. On the other hand, the company does not normally assess the satisfaction of society (in its various forms: national boards responsible for the welfare of people, property, the environment; local authorities; consumer associations, etc.). It must do so for the self-assessment, collecting results and judgements from various points of view (see Section 4.1.3.4). The assessment will produce a list of weaknesses and strengths, a score for company satisfaction and for society satisfaction, and a final average.

The Guide to the European Quality Award [18] is the most complete guide today (1996) and has been used as a reference in drawing up the lists of assessment elements that refer to the company's impact on society (b, c). With regard to the company's satisfaction with society (a), which is not covered by the EQA, a few key assessment criteria are offered as examples.

### (a) Company's satisfaction with its relations with society and the territory:

- favourable social environment;
- adequacy of education system;
- adequacy of local skills and educational levels;
- adequacy of infrastructures and services (especially housing and transport);
- legislative and union regulations and constraints;
- appeal of physical environment;
- potential of local industrial sub-structure.

### (b) Minimization of negative impact on the social and physical environment:

- respect for national and local water, soil and air pollution regulations;
- minimization of acoustic pollution;

- respect for legislation governing safety of people and property;
- respect for workplace legislation;
- in the above areas, the degree to which the company has moved from non-violation of laws to a policy of active prevention.

The assessments in group (b) should be formally requested from the company's public interlocutors. But since these parties are not always able to provide adequate information, additional data will be needed, based on objective documentation in the company's possession. First, any negative information: charges brought against the company, inspections by authorities that have had negative results, fires, electric shocks, legal action with regard to product responsibility, accusations in the media. Then positive information: conformity certificates, positive inspections, praise in the media, reductions in accident rates inside the company and from use of products in the field.

### (c)   Positive impact on the social and physical environment:

- support for local education structures (at financial and teaching levels);
- extension to the local community of social initiatives for employees;
- support for and cooperation with healthcare structures;
- contributions to territorial development;
- support for and participation in sports and social events;
- unsolicited donations to key social bodies;
- energy-saving policy;
- a materials consumption and recycling policy geared to environment-friendliness and the long-term good of the community.

The assessment will terminate with a list of weaknesses, which will be quantified in some way to enable an order of priority to be established; and with two scores, one for the company's satisfaction with the social environment, the second for the balance between positive and negative impact on society. An overall average will also be calculated, although it will not be of great significance.

Goals/results area                                                    GR.7


Carry-forwards to category: ...........................................................

This form is used during assessment of the results categories, to record notes assessors believe will be useful when assessing other categories. The main carry-forwards will be to processes and will be supplementary notes concerning the quantitative data in GR.8 and GR.9. Carry-forwards to factors will also be important, since analysis of results will certainly highlight symptoms that suggest the presence of weaknesses in factors. Assessment of the 'customer preference' category, for example, will frequently reveal symptoms that suggest a lack of focus on the customer and inadequacies in market sensors. Similarly, assessment of 'impact on society' may well indicate that although the company has set itself a series of goals, its approach to this issue is episodic rather than structured. In these cases, assessors will note the need for further investigation on the carry-forward sheet for the 'organizational architectures' category. Other examples: customer satisfaction surveys may indicate inadequacies in values and in personnel training; these will be recorded on the carry-forward sheets for 'leadership' and 'human resources'; as will problems that emerge in relations with public bodies, in ethical matters and possibly also in legal matters. Links may also emerge between the category being examined and other categories in the results area, especially among the 'business goals/results' category and the other categories. Before assessment of the various goals/results categories begins, therefore, a carry-forward sheet should be prepared for each category in each of the three areas. These sheets can also be used for carry-forwards from the other categories in the same area.

Goals/results area GR.8

Category ...................................

Identification of critical results in relation to priority goals and identification of related priority action areas

| Priority goals | Importance | Results | Performance gaps[1] |
|---|---|---|---|
| ................... | ............ | ................... | ................... |
| ................... | ............ | ................... | ................... |
| ................... | ............ | ................... | ................... |
| ................... | ............ | ................... | ................... |
| ................... | ............ | ................... | ................... |
| ................... | ............ | ................... | ................... |
| ................... | ............ | ................... | ................... |
| ................... | ............ | ................... | ................... |
| ................... | ............ | ................... | ................... |
| ................... | ............ | ................... | ................... |
| ................... | ............ | ................... | ................... |
| ................... | ............ | ................... | ................... |
| ................... | ............ | ................... | ................... |
| ................... | ............ | ................... | ................... |
| ................... | ............ | ................... | ................... |
| ................... | ............ | ................... | ................... |
| ................... | ............ | ................... | ................... |
| ................... | ............ | ................... | ................... |

[1]Gap in relation to goal or gap in relation to similar result of reference competitor (in this case add a note, e.g., Rkx) or of non-competitor best-in-class (Rbx).

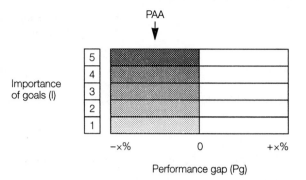

The priority action areas (PAA) are identified by multiplying importance of goals with performance gaps. This produces a priority index $PI = I \times Pg$.

Priority action areas and priority indices

PAA.1 ...............................................PI.1 = ..................
PAA.2 ...............................................PI.2 = ..................
PAA.3 ...............................................PI.3 = ..................
PAA.4 ...............................................PI.4 = ..................
PAA.5 ...............................................PI.5 = ..................
................................................................................................
................................................................................................

Goals/results area

GR.8
EXAMPLE 1

Category: Customer preference

Identification of critical results in relation to priority goals and identification of related priority action areas

| Priority goals | Import-ance | Results | Performance gaps[1] |
|---|---|---|---|
| GC.1) Retention rate market segment S, customers class A equal to or more than 90% | 5 | RC.1 = 75% | $-15/90 \times 100 = -16.7\%$ |
| GC.2) Customer satisfaction prod./service line X: reach at least the level of competitor Y (85%) | 5 | RC.2 = 78% | $-7/85 \times 100 = -8.2\%$ (Rki) |
| GC.3) Customer satisfaction customers class A, market Z: 85% | 4 | RC.3 = 75% | $-10/85 \times 100 = -11.8\%$ |
| GC.4) Complaints rate: −30% | 2 | – | −30% |

[1]Gap in relation to goal or gap in relation to similar result of reference competitor (in this case add a note, e.g., Rkx) or of non-competitor best-in-class (Rbx).

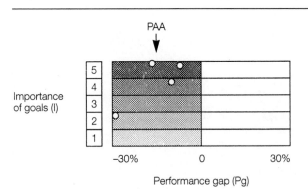

The priority action areas (PAA) are identified by multiplying importance of goals with performance gaps. This produces a priority index $PI = I \times Pg$.

## Priority action areas and priority indices

PAA.RC.1: Retention rate, Goal GC.1 ....................PI.RC.1 $= -5 \times 16.7 = -83$
PAA.RC.2: Customer satisfaction, Goal GC.2 ..........PI.RC.2 $= -5 \times 8.2 = -41$
PAA.RC.4: Complaints, Goal GC.4 ......................PI.RC.4 $= -2 \times 30 = -60$
PAA.RC.3: Customer satisfaction, Goal GC.3 ..........PI.RC.3 $= -4 \times 11.8 = -47$

Note: PAA.RC.2 has priority over PAA.RC.4 and PAA.RC.3, even though its $I \times Pg$ product is lower, since the related goal (GC.2) has a weighting of 5 and therefore belongs to the group of absolute priorities.

Goals/results area

GR.8<br>EXAMPLE 2

Category: Human resources (satisfaction of/contribution from)

Identification of critical results in relation to priority goals and identification of related priority action areas

| Priority goals | Importance | Results | Performance gaps[1] |
|---|---|---|---|
| GP.1) Satisfaction of personnel at level 65% (best-in-class) | 5 | RP.1 = 55 % | $-10/65 = -15$ % ($R_{BJ}$) |
| GP.2) R&D punctuality in new product releases (50% impr.) and reduction in changes after release (50% impr.) | 5 | RP.2–1: average: 15 days 3σ: 10 days RP.2–2 20% | $-50\%$ $-50\%$ |

[1]Gap in relation to goal or gap in relation to similar result of reference competitor (in this case add a note, e.g., Rkx) or of non-competitor best-in-class (Rbx).

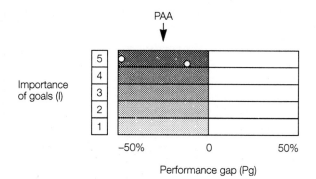

The priority action areas (PAA) are identified by multiplying importance of goals with performance gaps. This produces a priority index $PI = I \times Pg$.

## Priority action areas and priority indices

PAA.RP.2: R&D personnel performance, Goal GP.2 ...........PI.RP.2 = $-5 \times 50 = -250$
PAA.RP.1: Personnel satisfaction, Goal GP.1 ......................PI.RP.1 = $-5 \times 15 = -75$

Goals/results area                                          GR.9

Category: ...................................

*Priority action area (PAA):* ...................................

Breakdown of the result of the PAA into its main components and identification of critical components.

Note: By breaking down results and identifying critical components, form GR.9 provides the basis of reference for identification of processes requiring priority attention, when the self-assessment moves on from the 'results area' to the 'processes area' (form P1).

Goals/results area

GR.9<br>EXAMPLE 1

Category: Customer preference

*Priority action area (PAA)*: PAA.RC.2, result RC.2 (Ref. GR.8, Example 1)

Breakdown of result RC.2 into its main components and identification of critical components.

The customer satisfaction tree for RC.2 is assumed to sub-divide into the following branches: RC.2–1 = pre-sales service; RC.2–2 = product/service sold; RC.2–3 = after-sales service; RC.2–4 = administration; RC.2–5 = customer relations. The customer satisfaction results for each branch or component are shown in the figure below. In the Pg column, the component performance gap is the difference between the customer satisfaction result for the component and the global RC.2 value of the reference competitor (it is assumed that de-aggregated data, for the individual components, is not available for the competitor):

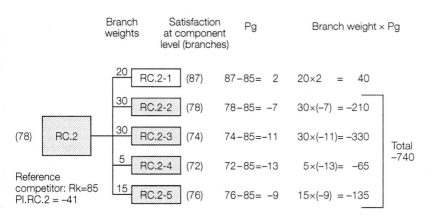

| Branch weights | Satisfaction at component level (branches) | Pg | | Branch weight × Pg | |
|---|---|---|---|---|---|
| 20 | RC.2-1 (87) | 87−85= | 2 | 20×2 | = 40 |
| 30 | RC.2-2 (78) | 78−85= | −7 | 30×(−7) | = −210 |
| 30 | RC.2-3 (74) | 74−85= | −11 | 30×(−11)= | −330 |
| 5 | RC.2-4 (72) | 72−85= | −13 | 5×(−13)= | −65 |
| 15 | RC.2-5 (76) | 76−85= | −9 | 15×(−9) | = −135 |

(78) RC.2

Reference competitor: Rk=85
Pl.RC.2 = −41

Total −740

The importance × performance gap priority index for RC.2 (PI.RC.2) is −41. It is distributed among the various components (PI.RC.2–i) as follows:

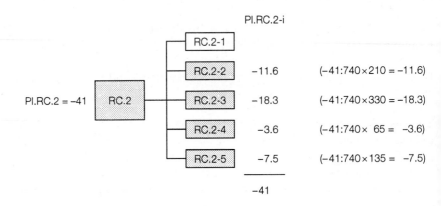

$$PI.RC.2 = -41$$

PI.RC.2-i

| RC.2-1 | | |
| RC.2-2 | −11.6 | $(-41:740\times210 = -11.6)$ |
| RC.2-3 | −18.3 | $(-41:740\times330 = -18.3)$ |
| RC.2-4 | −3.6 | $(-41:740\times 65 = -3.6)$ |
| RC.2-5 | −7.5 | $(-41:740\times135 = -7.5)$ |

−41

Goals/results area

GR.9
EXAMPLE 2

Category: Personnel satisfaction

*Priority action area (PAA)*: PAA.RP.1, Result RP.1 (Ref. GR.8, Example 2).

Breakdown of Result RP.1 into its main components and identification of critical components.

The employee satisfaction tree is assumed to sub-divide into five main branches representing satisfaction with: work; social environment; physical environment; company; advantages and personal gratification as a whole. For simplicity, the branches have the same weight. Analysis of the questionnaires shows that the main performance gaps refer to social environment and to relations with the company/sense of belonging (components RP.1–2 and RP.1–4).

| Branch weights | Satisfaction at component level (branches) | Pg | Branch weight × Pg |
|---|---|---|---|
| 20 · RP.1-1 | (62) | –3 | 20×(–3) = –60 |
| 20 · RP.1-2 | (40) | –25 | 20×(–25) = –500 |
| 20 · RP.1-3 | (67) | 2 | 20×2 = +40 |
| 20 · RP.1-4 | (43) | –22 | 20×(–22) = –440 |
| 20 · RP.1-5 | (63) | –2 | 20×(–2) = –40 |

(55) RP.1

Best-in-class = 65
Pl.RP.1 = –75

For simplicity, components RP.1–1 and RP.1–5, which contribute less than 5% each to the result, are ignored (and so of course is RP.1–3, which is positive). As a first approximation, the critical area (PI.RP.1) stems equally (50%) from RP.1–2 and RP.1–4. For greater precision, 48% from RP.1–2 and 42% from RP.1–4.

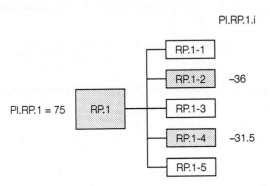

# AREA 2: PROCESSES

The following pages, marked with the letter P and a progressive number, refer to the processes area. Forms P.1 and P.2 are used to identify the processes that require priority attention, with reference to the importance of goals and critical results (forms GR.8 and GR.9). Process priority must be taken into account when selecting the processes to be assessed (and those that need to be monitored and improved).

Some priority processes will have to be monitored and assessed in any case, irrespective of the results found (in some cases results may not be available, for example when new goals are set). These are processes that relate to the company's strategic goals, i.e., those goals that were classified as 'absolute priorities' and given a class 5 ranking (form GR.0). Such processes can therefore be described as 'strategic'.

Strategic processes automatically emerge from the definition of strategic goals. In addition, a number of critical processes will be identified through the combination of goal importance and critical result. Since it is more difficult to establish priorities for critical processes, this section presents a diagnostic procedure, which begins with forms GR.0/8/9 in the previous section and continues with forms P.1 and P.2 in this section, to produce a list of critical processes for each goals/results category.

In the case of strategic goals for which no results exist as yet, form P.1 can be used to identify the processes that contribute to these goals (see alternative 1 of form P.1). These processes may be completely new, re-engineered or existing processes without results. For priority goals – strategic or not – for which results are available, the diagnostic procedure based on the combination of importance with critical result will be used (alternative 2 of form P.1).

Once processes have been selected, they can be assessed using the criteria described in Section 4.2 of the text, which are summarized, with fuller details as regards application, in form P.3.

Form P.4 (the equivalent of form GR.7) is used for carry forward notes from the processes area to the systemic factors area. The explanation provided for form GR.7 applies.

Processes area P.1

Identification of priority processes for the category: ...........................

1) for strategic goal (absolute priority) (from GR.0): .........................
2) for the priority action area (from GR.8 and GR.9): .......................
   which corresponds to critical result: ...........................................

A P.1 form is completed for every strategic goal and for every PAA identified in GR.8, with breakdown of the relevant result in GR.9 where applicable.

Processes Area                                          P.1
                                                   EXAMPLE 1

Identification of priority processes for the category: *Customer preference*

specifically, for the priority action area (from GR.8 and GR.9): *PAA.RC.2, corresponding to critical result: RC.2.*

This example refers to critical result RC.2 for the 'customer preference' category (see GR.8, Example 1), which represents satisfaction of a certain class of customers compared with a specific competitor (Goal GC.2 on form GR.0). The critical result has been broken down into first-level components in form GR.9, Example 1. The customer satisfaction tree from GR.9 is reproduced here with priority indicators shown for each component.

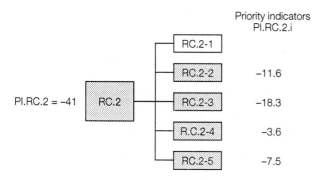

At this point, the assessors may decide to apply Pareto's Law and ignore the last two components, which together contribute less than 30% to the result, or RC.2–4, which contributes less than 10%. In a real assessment, this point would be investigated further; for the sake of simplicity, only RC.2–2 and RC.2–3 are considered here.

The next step is to identify the main processes that generate RC.2–2 and RC.2–3. The figures below represent these processes: the weight given to each process represents its estimated influence on the result. The sum of the weights may be less than 100; this means that processes with a less significant influence have been ignored.

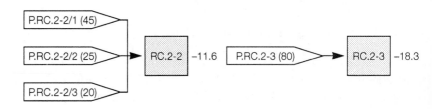

The priority coefficients for the processes are obtained by sub-dividing the priority coefficient of the relevant result in proportion to the weights of the processes. The following list of priorities is obtained:

1) P.RC.2–3 = 18.3:100 × 80 = 14.6     3) P.RC.2–2/2 = 11.6:100 × 25 = 2.9
2) P.RC.2–2/1 = 11.6:100 × 45 = 5.2     4) P.RC.2–2/3 = 11.6:100 × 20 = 2.3

These process priorities refer to one priority goal (GC.2 in this case). They must be combined with the priorities found for the other goals of the category (P.2, Example 1).

Processes area

P.1
EXAMPLE 2

Identification of priority processes for the category:
*Personnel satisfaction/contribution*

specifically, for the priority action area (from GR.8 and GR.9):
*PAA.RP.1, corresponding to critical result: RP.1.*

This example refers to critical result RP.1 for the 'personnel satisfaction/ contribution' category (GR.8, Example 2), which represents personnel satisfaction as specified by Goal GP.1 (form GR.0, Example). The critical result has been broken down into first-level components in form GR.9, Example 2. The customer satisfaction tree from GR.9 is reproduced here, with global priority indicator PI.RP.1 divided between the two components considered, RP.1–2 and RP.1–4 (in this case, Pareto's Law was applied when filling in form GR.9).

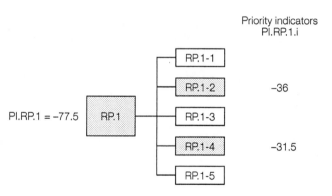

The next step is to identify the main processes that generate RP.1–2 and RP.1–4. The figures below represent these processes: the weight given to each process (figure in brackets) represents its estimated influence on the result. The sum of the weights may be less than 100; this means that processes with a less significant influence have been ignored.

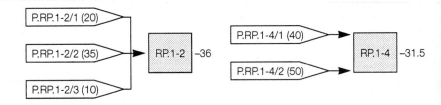

The priority coefficients for the processes are obtained by sub-dividing the priority coefficient of the relevant result in proportion to the weights of the processes. The following list of priorities is obtained:

1) P.RP.1–4/2 = 31.5:100 × 50 = 15.7     4) P.RP.1–2/1 = 36:100 × 20 = 7.2
2) P.RP.1–4/1 = 31.5:100 × 40 = 12.6     5) P.RP.1–2/3 = 36:100 × 10 = 3.6
3) P.RP.1–2/2 = 36:100 × 35 = 12.6

These process priorities refer to one priority goal (GP.1 in this case). They must be combined with the priorities found for the other goals of the category.

Processes area                                                          P.2

Identification of priority processes for the category:  ...........................

Aggregation of all P.1 forms for this goals/results category. With reference to forms GR.8, GR.9 and P.1, this form identifies the chains that lead back from the priority action areas for this category to processes.

Processes area

P.2
EXAMPLE 1

Identification of priority processes for the category: *Customer preference*

Aggregation of all P.1 forms for this goals/results category. With reference to forms GR.8, GR.9 and P.1, this form identifies the chains that lead back from the priority action areas for this category to processes.

This form reproduces the data in GR.8, GR.9 and P.1, 'Example 1', relating to priority action area RC.2. The data for RC.1, RC.3 and RC.4 has been invented, in order to provide a complete example. The priority indicators for processes relating to strategic goals (an importance ranking of '5' on GR.0) are shown with an asterisk.

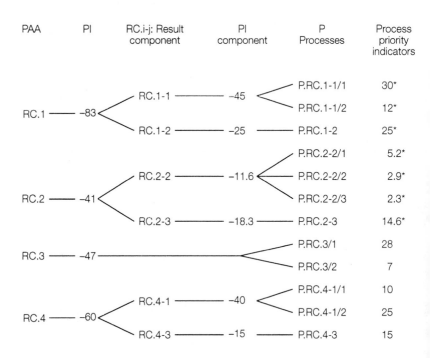

| PAA | PI | RC.i-j: Result component | PI component | P Processes | Process priority indicators |
|-----|-----|-----|-----|-----|-----|
| RC.1 | −83 | RC.1-1 | −45 | P.RC.1-1/1 | 30* |
| | | | | P.RC.1-1/2 | 12* |
| | | RC.1-2 | −25 | P.RC.1-2 | 25* |
| RC.2 | −41 | RC.2-2 | −11.6 | P.RC.2-2/1 | 5.2* |
| | | | | P.RC.2-2/2 | 2.9* |
| | | | | P.RC.2-2/3 | 2.3* |
| | | RC.2-3 | −18.3 | P.RC.2-3 | 14.6* |
| RC.3 | −47 | | | P.RC.3/1 | 28 |
| | | | | P.RC.3/2 | 7 |
| RC.4 | −60 | RC.4-1 | −40 | P.RC.4-1/1 | 10 |
| | | | | P.RC.4-1/2 | 25 |
| | | RC.4-3 | −15 | P.RC.4-3 | 15 |

Since the goals to which results RC.1 and RC.2 refer – GC.1 and GC.2 – are strategic goals, the relevant processes will have high priority, even though their priority indicators are lower than those of many processes for

RC.3 and RC.4. Of the twelve processes listed above for the 'customer preference' category, only two can be ignored at this preliminary stage (P.RC.3/2 and P.RC.4-1/1). In practice, closer analysis of the strategic processes could lead to the exclusion of processes P.RC.2-2/2 and P.RC.2-2/3.

Processes area                                                    P.3

Assessment of process: ...............................................................

The text reference is Section 4.2, specifically Fig. 4.8. The factors listed below are used to assess processes. They enable strengths and weaknesses to be identified and provide the starting point for any cross-diagnoses that may need to be performed. They also provide the input for calculation of the overall score.

*Current measurements* (output 1 of Fig. 4.8):

*Conformity* (output 2 of Fig. 4.8, labelled 'process audit'):

*Effectiveness* (output 3 of Fig. 4.8):

*Alignment* (output 4 of Fig. 4.8):

*Improvement trend* (output 5 of Fig. 4.8):

*Benchmarking with similar processes* (output 6 of Fig. 4.8):

*Overall assessment of the state of the process, showing weaknesses:*

*Final score:*

Processes area

P.3<br>EXAMPLE

Assessment of process: P.RC.2-3, Corrective maintenance process

This example refers to the following process (see P.1 and P.2, Example 1)

Process assessment factors:

*Current measurements* (output 1 of Fig. 4.8):
The assessors collect all process indicator data and the corresponding customer satisfaction data. The information will be used mainly to assess the factors below, but an initial assessment will be made of the availability, organization and current use of data: this is essential for identification of weaknesses. A quantitative assessment (percentage) should also be made, as input for the overall score.

*Conformity* (output 2 of Fig. 4.8, labelled 'process audit'):
This covers all the information provided by a conformity audit of the process: conformity with established company procedures, in particular process management organization, existence of indicators, state of control. See the 'organizational architectures' category, 'process organization' factor for a complete list of audit criteria. This formal check provides useful information for assessment of the other elements and receives information from them. The judgement of the audit will be used to calculate a score.

*Effectiveness* (output 3 of Fig. 4.8):
This measures the ability to satisfy customers' expectations.
GR.9, Example 1, shows that customer satisfaction is 78%. The causes of this weak result will be investigated with a cross-diagnosis based on deeper analysis of customer satisfaction data and possibly also on specific diagnostic surveys. An effectiveness score can be calculated by using a criterion similar to that used to score customer satisfaction (Section 3.5, Fig. 4.7 in the text). More simply, the customer satisfaction measurement itself can be used: in this case, 78%.

*Alignment* (output 4 of Fig. 4.8):
This measures the consistency between internal measurements (final process indicators) and the satisfaction of the customers of the process. This indicator is of fundamental importance: if alignment exists, it means the company's measurements are reliable. In the example, satisfaction with corrective maintenance, measured by RC.2-3, can be sub-divided into its main components (speed, punctuality, effectiveness, etc.), each of which should have an internal process indicator. A quantitative correspondence should be established between the internal indicators and the relevant survey indicators (for example, between the measured percentage of cases in which maintenance was provided within the guaranteed time and the percentage of customers found to be satisfied or very satisfied with the speed of the operation). The alignment between every measured component with a corresponding component in the surveys is measured. The choice of scoring method is up to the assessors: for example, a 'physiological misalignment' of, say, +/– 5% can be set, for errors in measurements and acceptable variations. All measurements that come within this range will be given a score of 100. Zero can be set at the maximum allowed (e.g., +/– 30%). This scale will be used to calculate a score for each process indicator whose alignment has been measured. The average score will then be calculated, taking account of any essential process indicators that are missing, given that identification of weaknesses is the ultimate objective. Missing indicators will be given a score of 0, and their absence will be recorded in the process conformity audit.

*Improvement trend* (output 5 of Fig. 4.8):
Self-assessment geared to improvement must above all assess the unit's structural capabilities: the commitment of management, full participation, an organization focused on improvement and widespread use of improvement tools. These elements will be assessed for the unit as a whole when the 'systemic factors' area is examined; here, they are assessed in relation to the specific process. Historical trends and current improvement capabilities are analysed, with reference to data and improvement plans (PDCA cycles for the last few years). A percentage score is given.

*Benchmarking with similar processes* (output 6 of Fig. 4.8):
If the unit has benchmarked the process against similar processes in other units or in another company regarded as the best-in-class, a comparative judgement will be made for all the factors considered above (or those which were benchmarked). A global score will be calculated: if improvement is the sole purpose of the assessment, the best-in-class can be set at 100, to simplify the calculation. If the assessment is for comparative purposes, for example with the winners of an award, the average score of the winners can be given to the best-in-class.

*Overall assessment of the state of the process, showing weaknesses*:
An overall assessment is made of the state of the process, based on the findings of the analysis of the above factors and on any notes carried forward from the goals/results area (form GR.7). For the purposes of improvement planning, the assessment will focus in particular on weaknesses.

*Final score*:
The assessors will adopt a conventional criterion to combine the scores of the factors described above and produce a final score. They may decide simply to give equal weights to all the factors, or to give greater weights to what, objectively speaking, are the two most significant factors: effectiveness (factor 3) and alignment (factor 4). Weights of 25 can be given to each of these two factors, 20 to conformity audit and improvement trend and 10 to current measurements. These weights will depend on the unit's situation and goals.

The unit can obtain a final score for the process – by calculating the weighted average of the five individual scores – and then obtain a global score for the processes category by calculating the average for all the priority processes that have been assessed. Alternatively, it can obtain a 'cross' average for each factor (e.g., alignment), by combining the relevant scores for all the processes considered (and then calculating the weighted average of the factors to produce a final score).

This emphasis on scores is due solely to the relatively greater difficulty of defining assessment criteria. It does not detract from the main purpose of the procedure, which is to identify specific weaknesses and strengths in priority processes.

Processes area                                                               P.4

Carry-forwards to Category: ..................................................

This sheet is used during assessment of the processes area, to record notes assessors believe will be useful when assessing the specific category in the systemic factors area. Analysis of processes will frequently highlight symptoms that suggest probable weaknesses in factors. A typical example is the recurrence of the same type of problem in all processes, for example, shortcomings in monitoring (organizational problem) and in control (technical problem). Before beginning assessment of the processes area, a carry-forward sheet should be prepared for every systemic factors category.

## AREA 3: SYSTEMIC FACTORS

In the text, Sections 3.5.2, 4.3 and 6.6 are the main references for assessment of the systemic factors area. The assessment of the various categories is based chiefly on personal and group interviews and on effectiveness questionnaires. The guide therefore provides a set of 'assessment elements' for each factor of every category in the area (see Fig. 3.9). The assessment elements provide the basic framework for the interviews and also for the formulation of the effectiveness questionnaires, which are discussed at the end of this section, after the description of the assessment elements. When examining these elements, assessors should be careful not to lose sight of the category as a whole. During the interviews, therefore, they are advised to adopt a top-down and then a bottom-up procedure for each category. The analysis begins at the top with the general situation, based on the improvement plan drawn up after the previous assessment and a review of the results achieved. Notes carried forward from assessment of the results area and the processes area are introduced (Fig. 4.9). The assessment then moves on to make a detailed analysis, at the level of factors and elements, and finally aggregates its findings into a global assessment of the category. Section 3.5.2 explains how elements should be assessed in order to produce a list of strengths and weaknesses and a score for *approach* and for *deployment*. Although each element will have its own list and score, the information should be recorded on a form for the relevant factor, to avoid a proliferation of forms and maintain a global perspective. Form SF.1/1 below is an example of an aggregate factor assessment form: weaknesses and strengths are noted in the main area, at element level if possible, while the scores of the various elements are recorded in the table at the bottom of the form. The process can be simplified by calculating scores directly at factor level; the result will be less precise, but this approach is preferable when assessing a small unit or company. In this case, the table at the bottom of the form will have just one line (SF.1/2). The upper part of the form does not change, since the assessment always refers to the assessment element checklist.

Employees' responses to the effectiveness questionnaire should be analysed before the interviews take place. In this way, the effectiveness column will have already been filled in, and can provide a useful point of reference during the interviews. The interviews will provide the information that the assessors need to fill in the 'approach' and 'extension' columns.

The table is useful not only for scoring, but also for direct comparison of 'approach × deployment' on one side and 'effectiveness' on the other; in other words, of the situation 'as seen from the right' and 'as seen from the left', to use the expression employed in Section 6.6 (effectiveness is measured only for less tangible, less objective factors, which concern the entire company population: see Section 3.5.3 and, below, the introduction to the section on the effectiveness questionnaire).

The data from all the SF.1/1 forms (or SF.1/2 forms) concerning the various factors of a particular category is aggregated into a single form illustrating the weaknesses and strengths of that category. This form will also show the overall score for the category: the weighted average of the scores of the factors. Weights will have already been given to the factors, when the model is constructed.

The guide provides an example of a completed SF.1/1 form. It then describes the categories – beginning with leadership – and their sub-division into factors and assessment elements.

In addition to a brief explanatory comment on the relevant factors and elements, the introduction to each category discusses similarities and differences with the corresponding categories of the Malcolm Baldrige Award (MBA) and the European Quality Award (EQA), where such categories exist. Hopefully, readers who are familiar with the awards will find these notes helpful. A qualification is necessary, however. The award assessment guides are necessarily non-prescriptive: it is up to the individual company to describe 'how' it achieves the 'what' described by the model. Indeed, the 'how' is the key source of added value as far as the awards are concerned. Self-assessment, on the other hand, takes a more prescriptive approach, since the company cannot allow the various sectors complete freedom as to 'how' they achieve the 'what'. The company has certain values, rules and procedures, which must be taken into account during the assessment, to the extent to which they can be regarded as positive achievements. Values are a case in point: they should constitute a reference for everyone, even if any inconsistencies or incompatibilities can be expected to emerge during the self-assessment. Another example concerns the organization structure: if the model assumes that the company has a process-based organization, the assessment will investigate if and how this organization is implemented, although naturally it will also analyse its effectiveness and the degree to which it is accepted.

Individual company models – and the 'assessment guides' that interpret these models – must therefore be more prescriptive (because they are less neutral) than the award models. They must reflect any 'personalizations', that is, the company's key decisions with regard to 'how' it approaches the main systemic issues. Since this is a general guide, it offers examples or, sometimes, suggestions rather than actual prescriptions. Each company will then decide whether to follow or ignore these suggestions, or tailor them to its own needs. Typical examples can be found in the description of leadership, specifically in factor F1.b: 'leadership and corporate values', which assumes a series of specific values (which have already been discussed in Section 4.3.1).

All this is to do with the *personalization of the model*, which, as we have already seen, is essential if self-assessment is to have an impact on the real situation of the company. Once management has constructed the basic framework and assigned weights, the company model will take shape through the details provided in the guide to the self-assessment process.

SF.1/1

Category: ...................................

Systemic Factor:..........................

| Assessment Element | Weaknesses |
|---|---|
| | |
| Assessment Element | Strengths |
| | |

| A Element | B Approach (%) | C Deployment (0 - 1) | D Approach x Deployment (BxC) | E Effective- ness (%) | F Global Score GS (Average D-E) |
|---|---|---|---|---|---|
| 1 | a1 | d1 | a1 x d1 | Eff1 | GS 1 |
| 2 | a2 | d2 | a2 x d2 | Eff2 | GS 2 |
| 3 | a3 | d3 | a3 x d3 | Eff3 | GS 3 |
| 4 | a4 | d4 | a4 x d4 | Eff4 | GS 4 |
| | | | Average (ai x di) | Average (Effi) | Average GSi |

SF.1/2

Category: ....................................

Systemic Factor:..........................

| Assessment element | Weaknesses |
|---|---|
| Assessment element | Strengths |

| A<br>Factor | B<br>Average<br>Approach | C<br>Deployment | D<br>Approach x<br>Deployment<br>(B x C) | E<br>Effectiveness | F<br>Global<br>Score GS<br>(Average<br>D-E) |
|---|---|---|---|---|---|
| F | a | d | a x d | Eff | GS |

SF.1/1-Example

Category : *F3: Human Resources*

Systemic Factor: *F3.c: Involvement and Empowerment*

| Assessment Element | Weaknesses |
|---|---|
| *F3.c.1* | —Involvement with values is low because values are not clearly defined and communicated.<br>—Improvement groups are still not widespread.<br>—Existing improvement groups were not set up as initiatives stemming from process management but as personal initiatives of individual bosses. |
| *F3.c.2* | —No awareness of the importance of stakeholder relations as yet. Relations with suppliers is the only relationship that is considered. |
| *F3.c.3* | —Decision-making is still restricted to a small group of managers. Process owners are rarely consulted.<br>—A timid move towards empowerment can be observed, but there is no clear empowerment policy. |

| Assessment Element | Strengths |
|---|---|
| *F3.c.2* | —New recruit orientation courses, management courses, quarterly management meetings followed by cascade manager-staff meetings, the annual managers convention all focus heavily on involving all personnel with vision, missions and goals (which are clearly defined).<br>—The company has a well-structured form of Policy Deployment, but interaction is still low.<br>—Strong focus on business goals and customer satisfaction. |

| A<br>Element | B<br>Approach<br>(%) | C<br>Deployment<br>(0 - 1) | D<br>Approach x<br>Deployment<br>(B x C) | E<br>Effective-<br>ness<br>(%) | F<br>Global<br>Score GS<br>(Average<br>D-E) |
|---|---|---|---|---|---|
| *F3.c.1* | 25 | 0.6 | 15 | 35 | 25 |
| *F3.c.2* | 60 | 1 | 60 | 65 | 62.5 |
| *F3.c.3* | 20 | – | 0 | 25 | 12.5 |
| | | | | | |
| | | | 37.5 | 62.5 | 33.3 |

**Category F1: Leadership**

Reference can be made to the assessment criteria of either the EQA model or the MBA when defining factors and elements for the leadership category. Both offer an excellent selection. The following comments are necessary, however.

In defining the category (*criterion*) and relevant factors (*criterion parts* or *sub-criteria*, to use the official terminology), the EQA model (1996) states repeatedly that the purpose of leadership is 'to guide the organization towards Total Quality' (or towards continuous improvement). Since Total Quality is not the ultimate goal of a company, but an albeit essential means to reach that goal – an approach, a secondary goal – the EQA's conception of leadership is restrictive; at the very least, it can give rise to limited interpretations. Leadership should be considered in its own right, as both the cause and the effect of growth in excellence, without placing any limits on its range and purposes. Another point is that the EQA model does not make a clear distinction between the interpersonal aspects of leadership (the leader of people) and the entrepreneurial aspects (the leader as the head of the company, the figure responsible for the pursuit of its goals). With the MBA (1996), less confusion surrounds the conceptual approach to leadership, since Total Quality is not mentioned and the definitions of the category, factors (*items*) and elements (*areas to address*) make it quite clear that leadership is considered in relation to all the company's main goals. As far as qualification of leadership is concerned, the MBA places very heavy emphasis on entrepreneurial characteristics; some attention is given to establishing values, very little to interpersonal relations.

This guide offers another approach, stemming from a different type of interpretation – and therefore assessment – of leadership. The text (Section 4.3.1) builds up a profile of leadership from three perspectives: 'interpersonal leadership', that is, relations with individuals and groups (another description would be 'leadership style'); 'corporate values', the way leadership characterizes the social corpus through a shared system of values; 'entrepreneurial leadership', the way leadership guides the company towards its missions. The first two perspectives are not dissimilar; the second could even be merged with the first. However, they are kept separate to give assessors the opportunity to make a specific analysis of the important question of corporate values. The third perspective must be stressed because it has a precise counterpart in the business model: leadership as a force that 'propels' systemic factors and processes (left and central blocks of the model) in order to guide the company towards its missions (right block).

The leadership category is therefore sub-divided into three factors: interpersonal leadership, leadership and corporate values, entrepreneurial leadership.

Category F1: Leadership

## Factor F1.a: Interpersonal leadership

Managers' ability to create a common vision and lead people (as individuals and as a group) towards achievement of the company's purposes.

### Elements:

**F1.a.1: Managers as creators of a common vision and as integration factors**
How senior executives inspire a common vision of the future of the company among their staff; how they chart a course and give a 'sense of direction' to employees; how they integrate the human and social system with the key corporate values and common goals.

**F1.a.2: Managers as role models**
How senior managers are aware of their responsibilities as role models and provide leadership through example rather than through words.

**F1.a.3: The manager–staff relationship**
How managers relate to their staff: communicate, listen, help, encourage, reward results and the effort involved in achieving such results (simile with the coach–team relationship).

**F1.a.4: Empowerment**
How managers delegate and encourage involvement and empowerment.

**F1.a.5: Decision-making**
How broad participation in decision-making is conceived and implemented.

**F1.a.6: Control**
How managers maintain effective control of the behaviour and results of their staff, in a context of trust and empowerment.

Category F1: Leadership

**Factor F1.b: Leadership and corporate values**

Top management's demonstrated ability to instil key values so that the company can successfully achieve its missions.

The values described here are those normally regarded as important for success. As the introduction to the systemic factors area explains, every company that uses a self-assessment guide will have to make its own 'ideological' choice of values; it should not adopt a neutral position. The following is a typical selection, which can be tailored to meet individual needs. See Section 4.3.1.2.

**Elements:**

**F1.b.1: Managers as the source and guarantor of corporate values**
How senior executives create and transmit a corporate value system that can produce positive changes in individual and collective behaviour.

**F1.b.2: Positive human and social environment**
If and how leadership focuses on the development and transmission of values such as respect for the individual, correct interpersonal relations, cooperation; the extent to which these values already exist within the company.

**F1.b.2: Focus on the customer**
How leadership promotes a genuine customer culture, which regards the needs of the customer (external and internal) as the starting point for every activity and customer satisfaction as the final goal; the extent to which this culture exists within the company.

**F1.b.3: Continuous improvement and innovation**
How leadership ensures that continuous improvement and widespread innovation are perceived as corporate values and as the way to boost market competitiveness; the extent to which these values exist within the company.

**F1.b.4: Integrity**
The extent to which relations with customers and stakeholders are based on correctness, transparency and honesty.

**F1.b.5: A factual, diagnostic attitude, geared to continuous learning**
How leadership fosters a diagnostic culture that verifies hypotheses against

facts and measurements; how this culture generates a problem-solving approach.

### F1.b.6: Flexibility, elimination of bureaucracy

How rapid responsiveness is encouraged and how flexibility is stressed and recognized. The extent to which the fight against bureaucracy is a common value.

### F1.b.7: Curiosity, open-minded approach to change, willingness to question assumptions

How leadership promotes an attitude of continuous learning, based on the belief that curiosity, an open-minded approach to change, a willingness to question assumptions are values that should be cultivated; the extent to which such an attitude already exists.

### F1.b.8: Teamwork

The extent of team spirit, the extent of cooperation on cross-functional/ cross-divisional issues.

Category F1: Leadership

## Factor F1.c: Entrepreneurial leadership

Management's behaviour in leading the company towards successful achievement of its missions.

Assessment of this factor covers the degree of leadership provided by management – above all by top management – as regards the company's missions; that is, leadership in achieving competitive success. Key characteristics therefore include the importance attached to analysing the market and competition; to building an ambitious vision of the company's market position and setting challenging missions and goals; to driving the company to achieve these goals by taking competent, decisive action to bring capabilities into line with these challenges. For a complete, methodical assessment, reference to the model – a personalized model – is useful here, because it provides a clear description of the company's missions and goals. The analysis will look first at leadership provided in relation to the right side of the model (missions and goals) and then at leadership in relation to the left and central blocks (the way goals are achieved). See Section 4.3.1.3.

**Elements:**

### F1.c.1: Leadership and personalization of the business model
Whether top management has constructed a personalized business model that helps people focus on the company's market and competitors and on its missions and goals in general.

### F1.c.2: Leadership in relation to definition of missions and goals
How top management stimulates and participates personally in the definition of the missions and strategic goals on the right side of the model. How it encourages development of market 'sensors' capable of detecting even the weakest signal of interest for competitive purposes. How it promotes analysis of competition. How it approaches the issue of competitive customer satisfaction. How it approaches the issue of stakeholder expectations/satisfaction in relation to the company's expectations of its stakeholders, and satisfaction of such expectations.

### F1.c.3: Leadership and development of the capabilities needed to ensure competitive growth
How leadership ensures that the left side (systemic factors) and the central block (processes) of the model are geared to the company's missions and goals in order to develop the necessary capabilities and competences.

Assessment of this element analyses the basic attitude of management – especially top management – which should set the lead in establishing the company's approach and style. The following elements refer to the specific type of leadership provided in relation to each category in the left and central blocks of the model.

### F1.c.4: Leadership and strategic planning

How management structures the goal and strategy planning process and what its role is. How it ensures the widest possible participation, especially front-end participation, in strategic planning. How it maintains a strong focus on innovation and improvement to guarantee competitiveness. The extent to which self-assessment is an integral part of the corporate planning cycle.

### F1.c.5: Leadership and human resources

How leadership ensures the development of the company's human resources. How it ensures strategic personnel management, geared to the company's missions and its future.

### F1.c.6: Leadership and financial, technological, material and information resources

How top management sets guidelines for strategic management of these resources, to ensure that they are used effectively and efficiently in the interests of the company's declared goals, rather than in the interests of its bureaucratic procedures.

### F1.c.7: Leadership and organizational architectures

How leadership emerges in critical reviews of traditional structures and development of new organizational architectures that match the new competitive scenarios. This is a key element for assessment of leadership. If a full range of Total Quality Management tools exists at formal level, but the company still has a traditional, bureaucratic, pyramid structure, leadership is inadequate.

### F1.c.8: Leadership and processes

Whether top management puts strong emphasis on process management, on identification of the links between processes and strategic goals and critical results, on process control, on reporting, control and administrative systems that are consistent with a process-based approach.

**Category F2: Strategies and plans**

This category is very clearly defined by both the MBA and the EQA. The US award takes a more 'secular' approach: it makes no mention of total quality but leaves it up to the 'areas to address' to set guidelines that actually incorporate total quality principles; and it makes a sharper distinction between 'strategy development' and 'strategy deployment'. The EQA provides greater detail with its five factors, the first of which is specifically intended to ensure that the concepts and principles of total quality are reflected in the formulation of strategies and plans.

Therefore, no conceptual difference exists between the approach suggested here and the approaches of the two awards. From a formal point of view, the approach described here is closer to the MBA with the sub-division into just two factors, but it goes into greater detail at the elements level. The reason for this is that diagnostic self-assessment requires deeper introspection as well as a certain dose of 'prescriptiveness', which the awards naturally avoid (see introduction to the systemic factors area).

Assessment of every category in the systemic factors area should highlight the links with the categories in the goals/results area, and this is particularly important when assessing strategies and plans. Strategic planning should take account not only of the external scenario, but also of the company's missions as described on the right side of the model; it should also consider the information provided by results and, finally, ensure that the new goals set in the plan are clear to everyone. The strategic plan involves all the company sub-systems and therefore all the other systemic factors, categories and processes, indicating what each one should contribute to the achievement of goals. Consequently, it will also define the relationship between each category with the goals/results categories.

For all these reasons, strategies and plans occupies a central position as regards the links between systemic factors, processes and results, and this must be taken into account by the assessment.

Category F2: Strategies and plans

**Factor F2.a: Formulation of strategies**

The methods used to define vision and missions; to formulate competitive strategies and operating plans that are consistent with vision and missions and with the company's analysis of the external scenario. The methods used to identify stakeholders and formulate an appropriate stakeholder policy.

**Elements:**

**F2.a.1: Vision and missions**
If and how management has defined a company vision and related missions, and the degree of participation in this.

**F2.a.2: Stakeholder policy**
How management defines a consistent global stakeholder policy that highlights stakeholder expectations together with the company's expectations as regards each group. How the company intends to ensure a balance between the satisfaction of its expectations and those of its stakeholders, and thus optimize the effectiveness and productivity of relations with stakeholders (win–win relationship).

**F2.a.3: Strategies and plans in relation to the company's key missions**
How management formulates strategy in relation to its missions. The method used (Fig. 4.10) and the people involved (Sections 4.3.1.3 and 4.3.2). Specifically, if a correct balance exists between strategic vision and the missions on the right side of the model. How plans are developed from strategies.

**F2.a.4: Information about expectations and results**
Whether formulation of strategies and plans is based on:

a) adequate information about the expectations of each group on the right side of the model (the company for business goals, customers for products/services, stakeholders and the company for goals that concern their relationship);
b) business results with reference to previous plans and to competitors;
c) the company's customer satisfaction results and those of its reference competitors;
d) results as regards relations with stakeholders, especially suppliers and partners;
e) information about the market, competition, technology;

and takes account of financial, technological and market risks.

**F2.a.5: Information about company capabilities**
Whether formulation of strategies and plans is based on adequate information about the capabilities of the company's processes and systemic factors (central and left blocks of the model); this is also useful for exploration of new market opportunities.

**F2.a.6: Introduction of the self-assessment process into the company planning cycle**
Whether self-assessment has become an annual corporate process and whether it provides systematic and adequate information for elements F2.a.4 and F2.a.5. Whether self-assessment and the resulting improvement plan have become an integral part of the company planning cycle.

**F2.a.7: Review of strategies and plans**
How strategies and plans are reviewed to take account of changes in external scenarios and in the internal situation.

**F2.a.8: Improvement of planning processes**
How the company's strategic and operating planning processes are improved on the basis of quality measurements of processes and results.

Category F2: Strategies and plans

## Factor F2.b: Deployment of strategies and plans

The methods used by the company to ensure that feasibility is verified by all levels and sectors involved before plans are formalized. The methods used to communicate strategies and plans.

**Elements:**

### F2.b.1: Goal deployment and formalization
How the goals and strategies on which strategic plans are based are deployed in order to check feasibility, and then formalized, from the top down to operating staff. How formalized strategic goals and related plans are communicated to everyone in the company.

### F2.b.2: Formalization of cross-functional goals
How cross-functional goals are formalized and how responsibilities for reaching these goals are assigned. Specifically, how global cost-reduction targets and global cycle-time reduction targets are handled.

### F2.b.3: Formulation of operating plans
The degree to which operating plans take account of strategic plans and related goal deployment, of results on the right side of the model, of analyses of process and systemic factor capabilities. How self-assessment contributes to the formulation of sound operating plans.

**Category F3: Human resources**

The human resources category covers the methods used by the company to recruit suitable personnel, develop their skills, make full use of their potential to achieve the missions and goals described on the right side of the model and, at the same time, ensure the greatest possible satisfaction of their expectations (Section 4.3.3).

Once again, reference can be made to the criteria and sub-criteria of the EQA and the items and areas to address of the MBA. In this case, the EQA model probably offers a fuller basis of reference, since it ranges from resource planning, selection and development to management by objectives and involvement in continuous improvement. Here, the emphasis is on empowerment in general rather than on continuous improvement alone, although this is naturally a very significant consideration. The final factor identified by the EQA concerns communication, but this is a question of organization rather than of human resources management.

In the MBA, the first and third items approximate the first three sub-criteria of the EQA; the second item (high performance work systems) is an organizational issue, while the fourth (employee satisfaction) belongs to the right side of the model in terms of the logic adopted by this model and the EQA. The sub-division into factors and assessment elements used here is therefore conceptually closer to the EQA; the EQA criteria that are not considered pertinent to human resources are covered here by the organizational architectures category. The human resources category is thus sub-divided into four factors: human resources planning; human resources management and development; involvement and empowerment; personal and group performance objectives.

We noted earlier that self-assessment of the systemic factors area should analyse relations between each category and the goals/results categories. Since verification of consistency between the left and right sides of the model is one of the main aims of the strategies and plans assessment, assessment of all the other systemic factors categories should begin by checking consistency between planning for the individual category and the company's master plan.

Nevertheless, a direct examination of the relationship between the individual category and those on the right side of the model should not be omitted. The human resources category will be checked principally with satisfaction of personnel, although, to some extent, the other goals/results categories too are affected by the planning, management and development of human resources: specifically, business results and customer satisfaction, but also satisfaction of stakeholders, for example, business partners.

Category F3: Human resources

**Factor F3.a: Human resources planning**

The way the company ensures that its human resources are consistent, over the long term, with its vision, missions and strategies.

**Elements:**

**F3.a.1: Consistency with strategic planning and operating plans**
How the human resources plan is developed and reviewed to ensure consistency with the general strategic plan and relative operating plans and, at a more general level, with the needs expressed on the right side of the model as a whole.

**F3.a.2: Use of feedback information**
How planning takes account of information from:

a) employee satisfaction surveys (or climate surveys);
b) interviews or other periodic surveys of management;
c) customer satisfaction surveys;
d) the other stakeholders;
e) effectiveness questionnaires.

**F3.a.3: Use of projections regarding changes of scenario**
How planning takes account of possible changes in the labour market, in technology, in labour organization.

Category F3: Human resources

## Factor F3.b: Human resources management and development

Approach to personnel selection, insertion, utilization, development, reward system and career development in relation to the need to optimize utilization and satisfy employees' expectations.

**Elements:**

### F3.b.1: Selection of new personnel

The degree to which personnel selection criteria are based not only on contingent needs but also on the company's values, vision and missions, and take account of possible changes of scenario.

### F3.b.2: Insertion of new personnel

How insertion ensures that new personnel acquire sufficient knowledge about the company and its values, vision, missions and goals.

### F3.b.3: Personnel management to optimize use and growth

Whether personnel management optimizes use of resources and development of potential. For example: management of skills maps in relation to company requirements; training criteria in relation to long- and short-term needs; internal mobility criteria; salary and career development criteria; identification and development of special talents; criteria for cooptation of new managers.

### F3.b.4: Attention to interpersonal relations and company 'atmosphere'

How the company encourages good interpersonal relations and teamwork. If and how it fosters a sense of belonging and social contacts in and outside the workplace.

Category F3: Human resources

## Factor F3.c: Involvement and empowerment

How the company involves personnel in its vision, missions and goals and ensures that employees support corporate values, especially the principle of continuous improvement. How empowerment, delegation and participation in decision-making is encouraged.

### Elements:

### F3.c.1: Involvement in values
Whether corporate values inspire personnel selection, training, management, recognition and promotion. Specifically, how involvement in continuous improvement is ensured at individual and group level.

### F3.c.2: Involvement in missions and goals
If and how all members of the company are strongly involved with and therefore support the company's vision, missions and goals: first as regards business and customer satisfaction, but also as regards stakeholders.

### F3.c.3: Delegation and empowerment
How employees are encouraged to take on greater responsibility. What is done to ensure that employees have the necessary knowledge and information to assume responsibility. How greater participation in decision-making is achieved. If and how delegation is practised.

Category F3: Human resources

## Factor F3.d: Personal and group performance objectives

Management of personal and group objectives

## Elements:

### F3.d.1: Basic criteria
The basic criteria of the company's objectives system: assignment of objectives left entirely up to managers; analysis of objectives by managers and staff to decide how objectives are to be reached; links to an interactive goal deployment system, which ensures that feasibility is checked before objectives are assigned. Whether objectives are personal only, or whether group objectives are also assigned, especially as regards cross-functional processes.

### F3.d.2: Assignment of objectives, monitoring, results achieved
In relation to the system used by the company, how objectives are actually assigned, the checks performed during the year, how results are analysed.

### F3.d.3: Link between personal and group objectives and operating plans
The extent to which personal and group objectives are the terminal elements of the goal deployment process, whether they enable such goals to be achieved and whether they are based on decentralization and empowerment. Specifically, if and how a link exists between cross-functional process goals and group performance objectives.

**Category F4: Other resources**

The other resources category refers to four main types of resource: financial, technological, material and information resources. The assessment examines how the company equips itself with the resources it needs to achieve its missions and goals, and how it ensures that resource utilization is as cost-effective as possible. Resource productivity is a fundamental concept. The reference here is to the EQA, since the MBA does not have a resource category. The sub-division into factors reproduces the rational and effective sub-division adopted by the EQA. Once again, assessors are advised always to keep missions and goals in mind when conducting interviews. In assessing financial resources, for example, they should investigate whether resources have been invested efficiently and effectively, rather than the type of investments made in relation to business goals, customer satisfaction goals or employee satisfaction goals (this aspect is covered by the assessment of strategies and plans). Consequently, they will refer to the business results category to assess investment returns on major initiatives; to the increase in value of the customer base due to financial resources invested in the customer preference category (or the financial resources forgone by the company in favour of the customer). Similarly, assessment of information resources will verify the impact of IT investments on business results, but also on personnel efficiency, personnel satisfaction and customer satisfaction. Vice versa, competitive disadvantages arising from inadequate investment in these areas will also be assessed, so that specific recovery action can be planned.

This category is sub-divided into four factors: financial resources; information resources; material resources (fixed and non-fixed assets); technological resources.

Category F4: Other resources

## F4.a: Financial resources

How the company ensures that financial resources are utilized in the most effective, efficient manner, at minimum risk, to achieve the long- and short-term goals of its strategic and operating plans, and, more generally, of its vision and missions.

## Elements:

### F4.a.1: Financial strategies and company strategies
How consistency is achieved between short/mid-term financial strategies in relation to plans on one side and the long-term interests of the company and stakeholders on the other. Specifically, what strategy if any is adopted to ensure a fair balance among the various stakeholders, in relation to the company's mid/long-term interests.

### F4.a.2: Financial performance parameters
What parameters are used to measure financial performance, whether these parameters permit comparison with competitors and whether they are subject to continuous improvement.

### F4.a.3: Investments
How investment decisions are reached. The role of short/mid/long-term financial considerations and of the company's foresight in forecasting market, technology and industry trends.

### F4.a.4: Financial risk
How the financial risk associated with specific initiatives – entry into new markets, acquisition of new technologies, company acquisitions, major investments, etc. – is calculated and contained.

### F4.a.5: Operating parameters with a significant financial impact
What operating parameters with a significant financial impact (e.g., working capital) are taken into account for the purposes of improvement.

Category F4: Other resources

**Factor F4.b: Information resources**

How the company uses information to achieve its mission and goals. Specifically, the attitude towards the capabilities of information technology.

**Elements:**

**F4.b.1: Information strategies and company strategy**
Whether the company has a strategy to maximize the productivity of information resources and how this is related to the company strategy as expressed in the master plan.

**F4.b.2: Corporate information systems**
Whether the company adopts an integrated approach to its corporate IT systems architecture, so as to provide an infrastructure that enables information to be accessed wherever it is needed, irrespective of its source. Whether the necessary safeguards and security measures have been implemented.

**F4.b.3: Information and processes**
Whether process information follows the process flow from start to finish unimpeded by organizational barriers. Whether it also flows freely along value chains that extend outside the company (to suppliers, distributors, partners in general).

**F4.b.4: Information systems and company missions**
If and to what extent information systems focus on the company's missions: business goals; acquisition and retention of customers; mutual satisfaction of company stakeholders (employees, shareholders, partners, society). Specifically, the level of employee access to information technology tools.

Category F4: Other resources

**Factor F4.c: Material resources**

The way the company manages its materials, fixed and non-fixed assets in order to maximize effectiveness (as regards attainment of the purposes for which such resources were acquired or produced) and minimize costs.

**Elements:**

**F4.c.1: Management of material resources and company strategies**
Whether the company has a general material resources management policy that ensures consistency with company strategies (e.g., purchasing, inventories management, control and improvement of working capital).

**F4.c.2: Management of suppliers**
How suppliers are managed to optimize the effectiveness and efficiency of the company value chains that originate from suppliers (vendor ratings, partnership with best suppliers, comakership).

**F4.c.3: Management of inventories and logistics**
How inventory and logistics management minimizes global costs and times.

**F4.c.4: Management of property and plant**
How maintenance of property and plant minimizes global costs for the company and safeguards against a loss of value in fixed assets.

**F4.c.5: Minimization of waste**
Whether the company has a policy to minimize waste (energy, materials, services) and maximize recycling of resources. If so, how it is formulated and applied.

Category F4: Other resources

**Factor F4.d: Technological resources**

What the company does to develop and safeguard its technological resources, and make sure they are used in the most cost-effective manner in relation to its strategic needs

**Elements:**

**F4.d.1: Technology and competitive advantage**
How technology is made – or bought – and utilized in order to achieve and/or maintain a competitive advantage. How the company maintains an observatory on new technology and competitor trends. How alternative or new technologies are assessed.

**F4.d.2: Technology and personnel development**
How technology development is linked to personnel planning and development to provide the company with the skills it needs.

**F4.d.3: Intellectual property**
How intellectual property is used and protected.

**F4.d.4: Internal technology applications**
The degree to which new technologies are applied to the company's processes and its information and telecommunication systems.

## Category F5: Organizational architectures

This category, which does not exist in the EQA and MBA, refers to the *ways* the company organizes its resources and processes in order to reach its goals (Sections 2.2, 2.3 and 4.3.5). A major justification for its inclusion is the fact that many Total Quality Management projects are unsuccessful because companies fail to understand the enormous organizational implications. They comprehend the importance of processes; in many cases, they even formally adopt the solutions suggested for cross-functional/cross-divisional process management (control teams, process owners). Yet they fail to consider the systemic issue of how traditional hierarchical-functional structures (which are often never questioned, but regarded as untouchable) can be reconciled with the new horizontal process responsibilities (and if indeed they are reconcilable). As a result, they produce an organizational monster in which continual conflicts and/or frustrations are inevitable, and the TQM project is brought to a rapid close. Companies that give much serious thought to this problem find that the process-based approach calls for an organizational rethinking, for new organizational architectures.

Even if a model includes a processes category, this does not necessarily mean that the company will make a sufficient critical appraisal of its vision of processes. Many companies have adopted the EQA model for self-assessment, but their functional structure has survived assessment of the processes category intact. A category is therefore needed that compels the company to question the value of traditional structures and to analyse critically the architectural solutions it adopts to meet the competitive challenge.

We have already seen that the notes carried forward from the assessments of goals/results and processes provide essential input for assessment of systemic factors (Fig. 4.9). This is particularly true for assessment of organizational architectures, above all as regards the carry-forwards from processes. Assessment of these notes and the findings of any cross-diagnoses often indicate the presence of organizational problems.

The organizational architectures category is sub-divided into five factors. The first factor (basic organizational structure) considers whether the company has a predominantly functional structure or whether this is offset by unified management of cross-functional/cross-divisional processes; or even whether a process-based approach prevails. The second factor assesses the company's approach to process management. The third factor assesses the organization's focus on missions, especially business goals, customer acquisition and retention, positive relations with society, and a win–win relationship with business partners. The fourth factor focuses on the most important set of processes: those that cover the development and market introduction of new products. The fifth factor deals with organization of communication.

Category F5: Organizational architectures

### Factor F5.a: Basic organizational structure

Assessment of the basic organizational structure adopted by the company to meet its competitive challenges. Specifically, whether the organization is centralized or decentralized, sub-divided into small or large units, based on processes or functions or a combination of both, rigid or flexible, reactive to external stimuli.

N.B. Assessment of this factor will give absolute priority to the interview with the company's chief executive.

### Elements:

### F5.a.1: Organizational vision
How top management justifies its basic organizational approach in relation to the market, competition, and the company's competitive position, technology, the socio-environmental context and the company's particular characteristics. The main stages in the company's organizational development and the reasons for changes. Organizational comparison with key competitors.

### F5.a.2: Relationship between processes and functions
The organizational solution adopted by top management as regards the relationship between functions and cross-functional processes. Whether responsibilities are shared among cross-functional teams, and if so, how.

### F5.a.3: Line responsibilities, staff responsibilities, decision-making
How responsibilities are organized in relation to key processes. How the process flow moves from one area of responsibility to another (from division to division, from function to function, from line to staff) and, within a specific area of responsibility, from one level to another (e.g., to a higher level for approval). How decisions are made (average number of people involved in a decision). Specifically, how staff participate in line decision-making processes.

Assessment of this element should refer to significant specific processes (e.g., purchasing, product development, investment decisions). These processes should be followed through from beginning to end, where necessary with the support of maps showing the flow from one area of responsibility to another.

Category F5: Organizational architectures

**Factor F5.b: Organization of processes**

The company's approach to process management.

Assessment of organizational architectures must take account of the result of the assessment of the state of the company's main processes (processes area), which will have been performed at an earlier stage. This will provide the interviews with a concrete basis of reference, since correspondences will always be found in the processes (by definition highly significant) that have been assessed.

**Elements:**

**F5.b.1: Identification of priority processes**
How the company identifies priority processes, i.e., processes that require priority monitoring for the purposes of control and improvement. Whether they are identified as suggested in forms P1, P2, or in other ways and if so how.

**F5.b.2: Organization of process monitoring**
How regulations and responsibilities regarding process management are established. Specifically, what regulations are used and how responsibility for unified monitoring of cross-functional/cross-divisional processes is assigned (control teams, process owners, etc.).

**F5.b.3: Technical methods used to manage processes**
The methods used to:

- map processes;
- identify output indicators and goals;
- set efficiency goals;
- construct process indicators;
- define input indicators and goals;
- define the control system (reference standards and feedbacks);
- achieve and maintain a state of control.

For cross-functional processes, how organizational integration among the various functional segments is monitored.

**F5.b.4: Process improvement and re-engineering**
How the organization identifies opportunities to improve processes or the need for re-engineering; how it organizes itself to improve or re-engineer; how it improves and re-engineers.

Improvement:

- improvement organization (links with monitoring organization, improvement groups);
- collection of internal data and information, and of data and information from customers and suppliers;
- benchmarking;
- diagnostic path;
- application of remedies and stabilization of result.

Re-engineering:

- involvement of appropriate levels;
- criteria adopted in the formation of the re-engineering team;
- methodology.

Category F5: Organizational architectures

**Factor F5.c: Organization and focus on missions and goals**

The organizational solutions adopted to ensure that resources (human resources and other resources) and processes focus on the company's missions and goals.

This factor is important because it covers the company's organizational responses to the questions raised by the right side of the model: what organization solution should be adopted to achieve business goals, customer loyalty, good relations with society and the environment, etc.

**Elements:**

**F5.c.1: Focus on business goals**
How the company uses organizational tools to improve the focus of human, technological and financial resources and of processes on its key business goals. Typical examples include cross-functional groups, task forces, assignment of global responsibility for specific product lines, concurrent engineering to reduce time-to-market and improve quality and costs.

**F5.c.2: Focus on the customer**
If and how the company uses specific organizational solutions to address customer retention in specific market sectors, to acquire new customers or, at a more general level, to improve the value of the customer base.

**F5.c.3: Development of positive relations with the social environment**
If and how the company adopts organizational solutions in relations with public institutions, schools, local communities and consumer protection associations. What regulatory, operational, control and supervisory responsibilities are assigned in relation to the issues of personal health and safety and respect for the environment. Whether the company has a reactive attitude (non-violation of the law) or a proactive approach (contribution to the collective good). Attention to minimizing negative impact and creating a positive impact. This element corresponds to the 'society' stakeholder category on the right side of the model.

**F5.c.4: Development of positive relations with business partners**
Positive relations with business partners, an issue of increasing importance for many companies today, depend on careful control. Relations with suppliers and with distributors are cases in point. The assessment will look at the way the company organizes its relations with the main business partner categories to maximize mutual satisfaction.

Category F5: Organizational architectures

**Factor F5.d: The products organizational sub-system**

The company sub-system for the development, production, distribution, maintenance and withdrawal of products – in the broad sense of manufactured goods and services. This factor covers all the activities performed during the corporate product life cycle. The assessment examines whether activities are consistent with the company's competitive goals. It will refer specifically to the notes carried forward from assessment of customer satisfaction results. The ISO 9000 standards in general and ISO 9004 in particular provide a useful point of reference; but assessors should bear in mind that although ISO 9000 represents a good basis for product quality assurance, it does not guarantee product competitiveness or time-to-market. In addition to a comparison of the company's customer satisfaction results with those of its competitors, a detailed assessment will generally require system and process benchmarking data (especially for time-to-market).

**Elements:**

**F5.d.1: Definition of product specifications**
How product specifications (or offer specifications) are drawn up in relation to the company's analysis of market expectations, its competences and its knowledge of competitors. The company's positioning as leader or follower in terms of product performance.

**F5.d.2: Product development**
The company's approach to product development at the systemic and process levels, compared with the approaches of market leaders and best-in-class in comparable sectors.

**F5.d.3: Production**
The company's distinguishing characteristics in terms of production, for software or hardware manufacturers. In terms of ability to plan and implement services and optimize costs, for service providers.

**F5.d.4: Product purchasing, warehousing and logistics**
How the company optimizes handling of materials, semi-finished and finished products at the functional and financial levels.

**F5.d.5: Order fulfilment**
How the company organizes processes from placement of orders to delivery and billing, to ensure customer satisfaction.

**F5.d.6: Customer support**

How the company organizes its preventive and corrective maintenance processes and its technical assistance and commercial support processes, to maximize the satisfaction of customers once they have purchased products and services.

Category F5: Organizational architectures

**Factor F5.e: Organization and communication**

How the company guarantees that information about its activities reaches the relevant people and sectors as directly as possible, without encountering hierarchical/bureaucratic or functional constraints or obstacles.

NB. This factor assesses global communication (top-down, bottom-up and cross communication), from a formal point of view (organizationally structured communication). It is not concerned with interpersonal communications between managers and staff, which are examined in the leadership category.

**Elements:**

**F5.e.1: Information policy**
Whether the company has an information policy that sets rules for employees to follow. Whether this policy endorses the principle of maximum communication, taking account of areas where confidentiality is necessary.

**F5.e.2: Communication channels**
Whether the company has set guidelines for its communication channels: specifically, whether it has established the principle that communication channels should be as direct as possible, top-down, bottom-up and cross channels; whether it has moved beyond the hierarchical–bureaucratic notion that all communications to other sectors must necessarily have management approval.

**F5.e.3: Computer networks and communication**
How the company uses computer and telecommunication equipment to implement networks that give every employee real-time access to all the information he or she needs for his or her work.

## THE EFFECTIVENESS QUESTIONNAIRE

This questionnaire refers to the assessment elements of the 'soft' systemic factors – those whose assessment relies chiefly on the opinions expressed by the company's employees in personal or group interviews (managers at the various levels) and questionnaire surveys (operating staff, employees and workers); see Section 6.6. These soft factors are Category F1, 'leadership', factor F2.b in the strategies and plans category, factors F3.b/c/d in the human resources category, factor F5.e in the organizational architectures category. The remaining systemic factors (F2.a, F3.a, Categories F4 and F5 with the exception of factor F5.e) are either technical factors or of strategic relevance, and therefore cannot be covered by questionnaires. Their effectiveness can be assessed in part through reference to business results (e.g., effectiveness of financial investments); and, at a more global, rational – but also most costly – level, through audits commissioned especially for this purpose.

The effectiveness questionnaire therefore refers to those soft issues (leadership, human resources, communication and involvement in strategies and plans) where a significant perception gap may exist between the 'internal supplier' and the 'internal customer' and will therefore require attention (for this reason, interviews must be supplemented by questionnaires).

Each company will organize the questionnaire to meet its particular needs. The model illustrated here is simply a guideline, to be personalized by the individual company.

The questionnaire makes a series of statements, positive and negative, and asks the respondent to give his or her opinion. The respondent should do his best to ensure that his opinion relates to his role in the company, rather than to his personal view, and (unless otherwise specified) to his sector. Since the questionnaire is distributed to a significant sample of the population, but not to everyone, those who do receive it should do their best to express a pondered, shared opinion rather than strictly personal impressions. The communication activity that precedes the distribution of the questionnaire is essential (Section 6.6) to create a climate of participation and stimulate a desire to make a contribution.

The statements require a very brief agree/disagree (true/false) response, on a 1 to 5 scale:

| 1 | 2 | 3 | 4 | 5 |
|---|---|---|---|---|
| TOTALLY DISAGREE | DISAGREE | HALF AGREE HALF DISAGREE | AGREE | FULLY AGREE |

Each statement is shown with its corresponding assessment element ('reference to element' column). Obviously, this reference will not be shown on the questionnaire, since it is needed only to process the answers and make the correlation between the 'approach × deployment' and 'effectiveness' parameters possible (tables in forms SF.1/1 and 1/2).

When the questionnaire is drawn up, the statements should appear in a different order to their logical sequence. Similarly, the distribution of positive statements and negative statements will depend on the company's preference. For reasons of space, the column headings in this example show just the numbers from 1 to 5. In practice, the column headings should also include the relevant opinion, as shown above.

| Statements | Reference to element | 1 | 2 | 3 | 4 | 5 |
|---|---|---|---|---|---|---|
| 1 Our company's top management provides a strong sense of guidance and sense of direction, which has a significant impact on achievement of a common vision | F1.a.1 | | | | | |
| 2 The people who work in this company share its missions and goals and regard themselves as members of a team committed to achieving them | F1.a.1 | | | | | |
| 3 In our company managers are the first to practise what they preach | F1.a.2 | | | | | |
| 4 The managers in our sector are open to dialogue with staff and listen to them | F1.a.3 | | | | | |
| 5 Fear of making a mistake does not affect us: our bosses help and encourage us when necessary | F1.a.3 | | | | | |
| 6 Our bosses are only interested in results. How we obtain them and the effort involved isn't their concern | F1.a.3 | | | | | |
| 7 We work well together as a team and our boss is our coach | F1.a.3 | | | | | |
| 8 We are always encouraged to take on greater responsibility and are given the tools to do so | F1.a.4 | | | | | |
| 9 When our bosses have to make decisions, they want the facts and involve everyone who has relevant information, regardless of their hierarchical level | F1.a.5 | | | | | |
| 10 In our sector, there is a climate of trust between boss and staff | F1.a.6 | | | | | |
| 11 Our boss checks every detail of our work | F1.a.6 | | | | | |

| Statements | Reference to element | 1 | 2 | 3 | 4 | 5 |
|---|---|---|---|---|---|---|
| 12 Our boss is always well informed about our work | F1.a.6 | | | | | |
| 13 The company's top management has a clear and absolutely binding set of values | F1.b.1 | | | | | |
| 14 Respect for the individual, whatever his level, is a firm rule in our company | F1.b.2 | | | | | |
| 15 Individualists who attract attention to themselves get further ahead here than people who collaborate with colleagues | F1.b.2 | | | | | |
| 16 Our company differs from many others because it always puts the interests of the customer first | F1.b.3 | | | | | |
| 17 In assessing behaviour, one of the first things managers examine is relations between internal suppliers and customers | F1.b.3 | | | | | |
| 18 Continuous improvement is a slogan that may last for a few years | F1.b.4 | | | | | |
| 19 Morals and ethics have nothing to do with achievement of the results the company wants from us | F1.b.5 | | | | | |
| 20 Problem-solving is a job for the specialists or for those appointed to the task by managers | F1.b.6 | | | | | |
| 21 Rapid decision-making when problems arise is of much greater value than time wasted in analyses, diagnosis and tests | F1.b.6 | | | | | |
| 22 In our company, lack of respect for roles, rules and hierarchy is dangerous | F1.b.7 | | | | | |

| Statements | Reference to element | 1 | 2 | 3 | 4 | 5 |
|---|---|---|---|---|---|---|
| 23 In our sector, the non-conformists who question the traditional way of doing things are clearly not appreciated | F1.b.8 | | | | | |
| 24 Here, there is a strong sense that we're all working for the same company. This makes it easy to deal with problems together, without any clannishness | F1.b.9 | | | | | |
| 25 A sure hand steers our company in the difficult sea of competition | F1.c | | | | | |
| 26 Our bosses want us to be aware of the ends to which our efforts are directed and spend time explaining them, using a model that helps us understand the direction in which we are going and the commitment we should be making | F1.c | | | | | |
| 27 Our bosses always stress the concept that success is never guaranteed and that all of us – beginning with them – must strive continually to improve and renew ourselves and the company, to meet the challenges of the future | F1.c | | | | | |
| 28 The external perception of our company is that it is well directed | F1.c | | | | | |
| 29 During the planning period, everyone is involved in seeing what we can change – and how – in order to achieve the company's goals | F2.b | | | | | |
| 30 The planning period is like being in training for a race. Goals are often challenging and we are encouraged to respond to the challenge | F2.b | | | | | |

| | Statements | Reference to element | 1 | 2 | 3 | 4 | 5 |
|---|---|---|---|---|---|---|---|
| 31 | We have to think carefully before accepting the goals that are proposed, because if we fail to achieve them we're in trouble | F2.b | | | | | |
| 32 | We have to accept goals even if we know they are unattainable, because that way they say we are constantly stimulated | F2.b | | | | | |
| 33 | Our bosses are inflexible as regards goals, but flexible as regards results | F2.b | | | | | |
| 34 | New personnel seem to be well matched to the company's declared growth targets | F3.b.1 | | | | | |
| 35 | New employees are given no opportunity to learn about the company other than the sector to which they have been assigned | F3.b.2 | | | | | |
| 36 | In our sector, training is not sufficiently well matched to our work requirements | F3.b.3 | | | | | |
| 37 | On average, we believe our bosses are selected well, according to their professional skills and leadership ability | F3.b.3 | | | | | |
| 38 | Creating good interpersonal relations and a harmonious climate on the factory floors and in the offices is a visible goal for the company and its managers | F3.b.4 | | | | | |
| 39 | The company has a set of values that it pursues with rigour and for which it demands respect. Everyone knows that assessment of behaviour is based on these values | F3.c.1 | | | | | |
| 40 | In our sector, everyone is expected to offer concrete suggestions for improvement, of any kind | F3.c.1 | | | | | |

| Statements | Reference to element | 1 | 2 | 3 | 4 | 5 |
|---|---|---|---|---|---|---|
| 41 We know what contributions are expected from our sector and we have been told how these contributions help the company achieve its goals | F3.c.2 | | | | | |
| 42 In our sector, people whose job is to obey, obey, people whose job is to decide, decide; everyone has to stick to their role. Precise orders are all that count | F3.c.3 | | | | | |
| 43 Our bosses explain how our personal goals stem from the sector's goals and exactly what is expected from each one of us | F3.d | | | | | |
| 44 Our boss doesn't just assign goals, he spends all the time needed with each of us to verify if and how we can achieve these goals and how we can resolve any difficulties that could arise on the way | F3.d | | | | | |
| 45 We have been told that information is not a private resource but a corporate resource and we have been given precise rules regarding the circulation of information | F5.e.1 | | | | | |
| 46 Information reaches interested parties quickly and directly, without any bureaucratic complications | F5.e.2 | | | | | |
| 47 Top-down communication works well | F5.e.2 | | | | | |
| 48 Bottom-up communication works well | F5.e.2 | | | | | |
| 49 Cross communication among different sectors is effective and follows the shortest route | F5.e.2 | | | | | |

| Statements | Reference to element | 1 | 2 | 3 | 4 | 5 |
|---|---|---|---|---|---|---|
| 50 Our boss prefers us not to communicate directly with our peers in other sectors | F5.e.2 | | | | | |
| 51 We have been given the tools to communicate effectively and rapidly with all internal and external operating interfaces | F5.e.3 | | | | | |

# Appendix B
# Integrating TQM concepts
# into business management

This appendix, which is referred to chiefly in Section 2.5 of the text, is a revised version of a paper presented by the author at the 39th EOQ Annual Congress in Lausanne from 13 to 15 June 1996. It examines the integration of TQM concepts into ordinary company management; above all, it presents a vision of the company in relation to its stakeholders and customers, which is the foundation for the business model described in Chapter 2. In the first part of the paper, readers will find repetitions of comments in Chapter 2; they have been allowed to remain so as not to alter the logical development of this paper.

## 1 INTRODUCTION

These are dark days for Total Quality Management. One hears more about failure than about success. Even mention of the name is forbidden in some companies.

Everyone who believes that the strategy known as Total Quality Management (TQM) was and still is a major opportunity for the corporate sector, the economy and our standard of living – and fears it may turn out to be a lost opportunity – is bound to feel a deep interest in an analysis of the reasons why so many TQM implementations have been unsuccessful. Correct diagnosis of the reasons for these failures is essential if appropriate remedies are to be formulated. Without doubt, the main reason is that, from lack of conviction, a misunderstanding of the nature of its own role or an inability to fulfil it, top management has not assumed leadership in the process of change. But this is itself the result of other causes. The first is incorrect representation of TQM concepts by business opinion-makers. Many descriptions fail to create a convincing picture of a global, competitive business strategy that requires the direct leadership of senior management. They also fail to indicate the extent of cultural and organizational change that a TQM strategy entails and the consequent need for top management to act as an 'organizational architect'. This paper examines ways of reaching an interpretation of TQM that has strategic significance for companies and therefore stimulates the active interest and commitment of top management.

The second reason for the lack of top management leadership stems from cultural attitudes. Executives may find it difficult – in extreme cases impossible – to understand fully the need for change and the significance of the change involved. There is little to say on this point: the only way forward is for senior posts to be occupied by people who accept the need for change.

The third reason is what is referred to in a previous paper [19] as 'the fox and grapes syndrome': since management is not capable of implementing the changes involved in TQM, it concludes that the strategy does not work (the grapes are sour, in other words) and decides to look for another vine. After attempting unsuccessfully to introduce a TQM approach, many major companies have turned to the lower, more accessible 'bunches of grapes' on the ISO 9000 vine, disguising their retreat behind a flourish of promotional fanfares designed to suggest that, in fact, this is a move towards goals of a more concrete nature.

## 2 THE COMPANY FROM THE CUSTOMER/STAKEHOLDER PERSPECTIVE

No-one would dispute the statement that the company's institutional objective is to remunerate the risk capital invested in it – in other words, to make a profit. On the other hand, the view that this is the company's sole aim, and that its shareholders are therefore the only beneficiaries of its results, is outmoded. It is also counter-productive: *exclusive* focus on financial results would inevitably neglect other critical variables such as customer satisfaction and employee satisfaction, with negative repercussions for the company's profit-making capacity.

Over the last few years, companies have become increasingly aware that customer satisfaction and customer loyalty are essential to profitability and long-term survival. Similarly, the realization has spread that the company consists of people with rising expectations, in terms not only of salary but also of self-realization, who have to be satisfied; and that the company is a social entity whose dynamics and needs must be considered. At a wider level, the society in which the company operates also has requirements that must be met. Society today is more aware of the impact the company can have on both the physical and the social environment: a negative impact, to be contained and regulated, and a positive impact, which must be encouraged.

Customers, employees and society are therefore other groups, besides shareholders, that have expectations of the company and can be affected positively or adversely by its behaviour. Another category to be taken into consideration are business partners. The corporate monolith is an increasingly rare species, as more and more companies operate in complex customer–supplier networks, whose success depends directly on loyalty and fair sharing of advantages.

Companies that introduce some sort of TQM strategy think about customer satisfaction, they take employee satisfaction and empowerment into account, at times they even consider impact on society; but too often they lack a global, systemic view. Many companies take the quality award models as their guideline: the EQA model, for example, which in effect identifies a range of customers whose expectations must be satisfied. Nevertheless, these are essentially assessment models, used more to evaluate the current situation and correct any glaring imbalances, rather than redefine the corporate mission and, if necessary, re-engineer the company.

The first step in a truly strategic TQM implementation is a review of the company from the customer/stakeholder perspective, where the heading 'stakeholder' includes all the groups that legitimately expect benefits from the company in return for specific contributions: financial support, labour, services and goods. The logic behind this review is that the company's success in achieving its missions depends both on winning and retaining customers and on the legitimate satisfaction of the expectations of the various stakeholders that constitute the 'company system'. This reasoning stems in part from awareness of a common historical distortion, when relations between the company and its customers and stakeholders were unfairly weighted in the company's favour. This was not deliberate policy, but the consequence of insufficient understanding of the complex ties between global results on the one hand and customer satisfaction and stakeholder satisfaction/motivation/loyalty/sense of belonging on the other. Today, the desire to remedy this distortion often results in the simplistic extrapolation of the customer satisfaction concepts that apply to the company's real customers (i.e., customers free to change supplier whenever they wish) to the groups to which the term 'customer' is extended, but which can be more accurately defined as stakeholders. Unlike its relationship with customers, the company's relationship with its stakeholders is two-way, and the best results are always obtained when both parties are satisfied. The nature of the company/stakeholder relationship means the legitimate expectations of the two sides can be established beforehand, after which it is up to each party to satisfy the other. In fact, dissatisfaction often occurs simply because the relationship has not been adequately defined. The first important effect of a focus on satisfaction of expectations is identification of the expectations of both parties. The satisfaction of one side does not always entail a cost for the other. Frequently, simple 'alignment' of the two parties raises the satisfaction of both and the efficiency of the 'company system', at zero cost.

Figure B.1 represents the company as a system geared to the optimization of results, in relation to the various customer/stakeholder categories.

The outer ring shows the recipients and the agents of the company's activities: customers, who expect maximum value for money, and stakeholders, who contribute to the company and expect benefits in return.

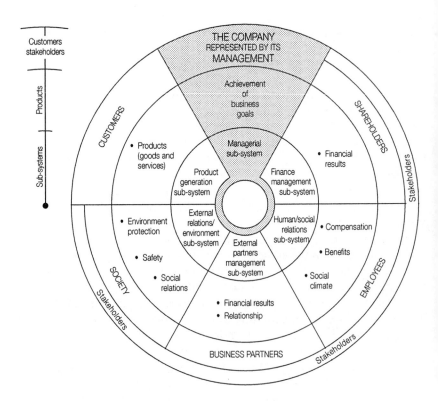

**Fig. B.1** The company as a system that generates 'products' to satisfy the needs of a variety of customers/stakeholders.

But the main agent is the company itself, personified by its top management, whose task is to define missions and goals and then achieve them, to the benefit of all stakeholders. The penultimate ring represents the 'products' the company provides for its customers/stakeholders, while the inner ring represents the corporate sub-systems that generate these products. The managerial sub-system obviously affects all the sub-systems; it is represented by the grey ring that extends through 360 degrees beneath the other sub-systems.

Representing the company and its customers/stakeholders in this way is not only useful for the purpose of this paper: an integrated view of the company as a basis for a consistent Total Quality Management philosophy. It is also, and primarily, a way to rediscover and redefine the company's missions. Top management can only draw up a balanced policy and set goals designed to optimize the company's relationships if it has a clear, comprehensive picture of its customers/stakeholders and their expectations. In figurative, if somewhat simplistic terms related to the figure, the company has to decide how to 'divide up the benefits pie' (simultaneously with the 'responsibilities pie') among its customers and stakeholders in the fairest and, as far as results are concerned, most effective way.

The typical paleo-industrial company could consider its owners the sole beneficiaries of results. Relations with all other groups would be geared to minimizing the return provided for the contribution received. In today's scenario, with its fragmented value chains, where demand is low, and individual and collective expectations are high, the company must achieve a fair balance of satisfaction across the full range of customers/stakeholders, or risk failure. In practical terms, the choices made in establishing this balance determine the real policy pursued by the company. The decisions the company takes (or does not take) in this area are a significant differentiating factor.

## 3 THE 'REACTIVE' VIEW OF CUSTOMER/STAKEHOLDER RELATIONS

Quality concepts and practice originated and evolved in relation to products (manufactured goods initially, then services). For a long time, therefore, quality was considered only in relation to the segment in Fig. B.1 that refers to customers and products. Quality developments passed through a number of stages, eventually reaching the *quality assurance* stage, based on *standards* (quality assurance inside the company, subsequently extended to suppliers). The ISO 9000 standards are the international consolidation of this stage.

The idea of Total Quality has led to the extrapolation to the whole of the company and therefore to all the segments in Fig. B.1 of the quality concepts that have gradually evolved in the products area (or, better, the products sub-system). Although, historically speaking, this generalization has taken place in the Total Quality age and is only complete within the context of a TQM approach, it is also meaningful and justifiable at the level of 'quality assurance'.

The ISO standards regarding environment quality are one example of the extrapolation of the quality assurance concept. Some commentators were surprised that product quality assurance concepts could be applied to environmental quality assurance. This type of generalization would not be surprising in a company-wide quality context: the environment, too, can be viewed in terms of a customer (society), products (whose negative impact must be reduced to a minimum), processes that generate the products; and a quality sub-system can be defined. The extrapolation not only applies to the second segment in Fig. B.1, society and the environment, it can also be extended to all the subsequent segments.

When this unified, integrated approach is adopted, there is no need to create the 'umbrella' anew for each sub-system; the concept of standards-based product quality management and assurance is gradually extended to all the various sub-systems (Fig. B.2), with the term 'product' representing what the company generates for each customer/stakeholder category.

Quality as conformity, as compliance with established standards or contractual conditions, is a 'reactive' approach: the customer requests, the supplier provides what is requested and, if possible, nothing else. The reactive culture fosters the attitude of trying to 'get away with' giving less when various considerations (for example, invoicing) induce a company to take the risk. When quality is seen as an external constraint rather than a corporate value, there is no guarantee that individuals will behave correctly. This applies not only to product quality and the company's relations with its real customers, but also to customers in general. As far as the company's legal obligations towards society are concerned – ensuring the safety of individuals, the environment and goods – the reactive approach is wholly inadequate. 'The law does not inspire excellence and distinction. It is not a guidebook for exemplary behaviour – or even for good practice. Managers who regard conformity with legal requirements as a code of ethics implicitly support a code of moral mediocrity for their organizations' [20].

Figure B.3 illustrates the 'reactive' interpretation of the quality mission (quality as conformity) applied through 360 degrees and extended to all customers/stakeholders.

Conceptually, this is the ISO 9000 approach extrapolated to all the sub-systems that generate 'products' for customers/stakeholders in the broad sense. This is what would happen if the quality management and assurance standards already extended to environmental products were applied

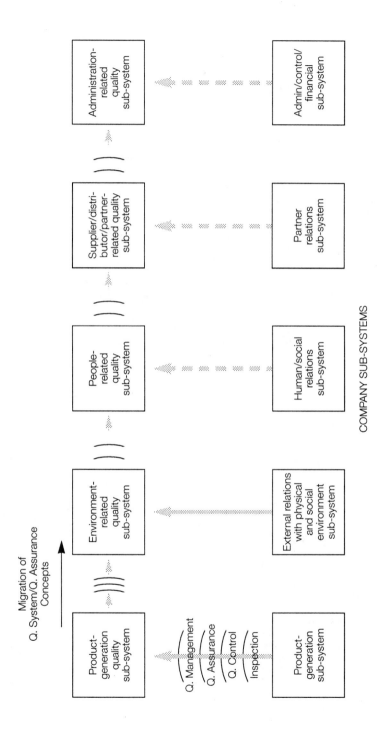

**Fig. B.2** Extension of the 'quality system' and 'quality assurance' concepts to all company sub-systems that generate 'products' for the various customer/stakeholder groups.

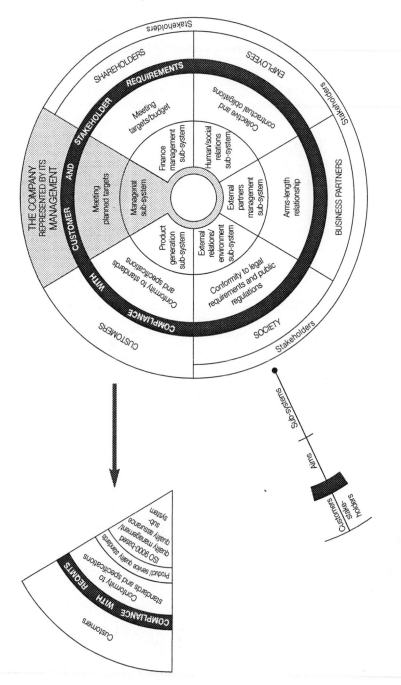

**Fig. B.3** A 'reactive' view of the company's relations with its customers/stakeholders.

throughout the company. Certainly, the company would be more certain of reaching its goals and results would be less variable: a not insignificant achievement. But it would still lack that competitive potential that can only be attained when a 'proactive' approach and the principle of continuous improvement are adopted.

It should be noted that even when the standards-based view of quality is adopted throughout the company, as in Fig. B.3 – the ISO 9000 philosophy extrapolated to the entire organization – the cultural and organizational changes involved are not on a scale requiring the direct leadership of top management. This only becomes necessary when the company moves into the competitive quality dimension.

## 4 THE 'PROACTIVE' VIEW OF CUSTOMER/STAKEHOLDER RELATIONS

The characteristics of a competitive view of quality supported by a TQM strategy are:

- competition at the level of *quality perceived by the customer* (provide greater value for money than competitors);
- competition at the level of efficiency, *through quality* (in processes, in organization).

This is a 'proactive' view of customer relations. It stems from the company's primary relationship with the market, and can be extended to relations with all customer/stakeholder groups shown in Fig. B.1. The *rationale*, behind this extension is as follows:

- all customers/stakeholders have expectations which the company legitimizes when it incorporates them into its policy (obviously after establishing how and to what degree these expectations can be met, during the strategic planning process). The methods used to identify the market's expectations, transform these expectations into process goals, and assess satisfaction (or loyalty when applicable, as in the case of employees, investors, business partners) can be applied to customers/ stakeholders in the broad sense;
- all the results the company produces for these customers are generated by processes. The valuable experience acquired in managing the processes that generate products/services for the market, and in achieving unprecedented levels of quality and efficiency, can be applied to all corporate activities;
- the principle of continuous improvement – incremental and large-scale – by which the company remains competitive can and must be transferred to all results and therefore to all company processes. Even when this is

not necessary in terms of commercial competitiveness, it is necessary for the purpose of improving efficiency. But due to the interconnection of satisfaction in the various customer/stakeholder categories, continuous improvement in all categories is also indispensable for global market competitiveness.

In Fig. B.4, which is a development of Fig. B.2, TQM is extended to the entire corporate system. The key phrases here are:

- *Company-wide Quality System*, in other words, not separate sub-systems but sub-systems unified by a global strategic approach to customers and stakeholders as a whole;
- *continuous improvement in relation to goals*, based on a strategic plan that *transforms the expectations of customers/stakeholders as a whole* into a harmonious, balanced set of goals;
- *continuous improvement in relation to implementation*, based on *processes*.

The result is an *integrated management strategy aimed at excellence*.

Figure B.5 illustrates the 'proactive' view of customer/stakeholder relations as opposed to the 'reactive' view represented in Fig. B.3 (conformity with requirements and standards).

A proactive strategy can be based only on common values that provide clear behavioural guidance (the innermost circle in the figure). The guiding values of a TQM strategy should incorporate the ethical values that underlie an integrity-based strategy. This applies to relations between the company and society, but also to relations with and among employees and with customers and stakeholders. The same guiding values should also inspire the development of an organizational structure capable of meeting market and customer/stakeholder needs and of adapting rapidly to change. This issue – culture and values – is obviously the most critical area of the integrity-based strategy and requires the direct intervention of top management, on a continuous basis.

The innermost circle together with the second ring illustrate the integrated view of the company quality system.

The next ring, when compared with the corresponding ring in Fig. B.3, highlights the main differences in attitude to customers/stakeholders entailed by a proactive view. The attitude to the market becomes exceeding customer expectations, providing greater value for money than competitors. In relation to society: adopting an integrity-based strategy. Unlike a compliance strategy, which aims to avoid legal sanctions, an integrity-based strategy attempts to define guiding values, to create an environment that fosters ethically correct behaviour, to augment responsibility. In relation to employees, the proactive view means, at individual level, growth, empowerment, leadership, a rewarding climate, future prospects; at collective level, it means social values, group empowerment,

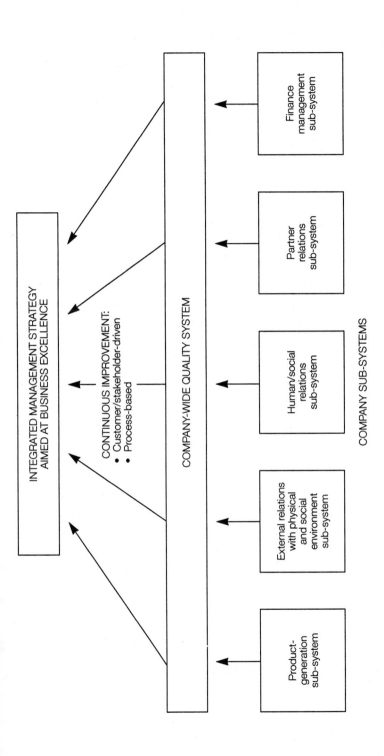

**Fig. B.4** A continuous improvement strategy aimed at business excellence, based on a company-wide quality system.

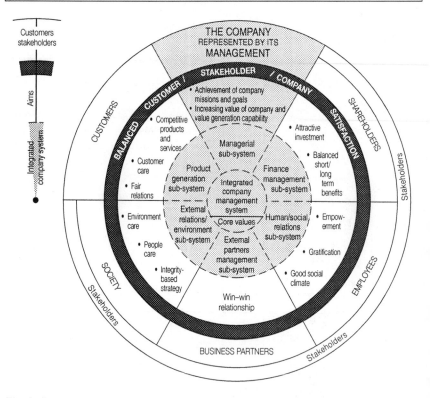

**Fig. B.5** A 'proactive' view of the company's relations with its customers/ stakeholders.

etc. In relation to business partners, it means fair sub-division of benefits in the interests of a win–win relationship. In relation to shareholders, it means enhancing the 'company system' and its long-term value-generation capability, as well as providing fair remuneration of capital.

The external rings represent the final goal: customer/company/stakeholder satisfaction, within a context of fair reciprocity.

The alignment, optimization and partnership logic that applies to the company's relations with the groups in the outer ring should also apply to the interfaces between the inner rings, in other words, to the internal supplier – customer relationships, or, better, internal partnerships. Only then will it be possible to optimize the company's global results in terms of efficiency and effectiveness.

This representation of company strategy through 360 degrees is based on:

- a systemic view of the company, which highlights the interrelations among the different generators/beneficiaries of results;

- a corresponding integrated customer/stakeholder-driven management approach to the various sub-systems;
- a proactive view that requires application of the continuous improvement principle throughout the company;
- integrated management of cross-functional processes.

It is not unreasonable to assert that this representational approach demonstrates the need for the direct involvement of top management. Management's main task is to introduce the cultural and organizational changes necessary for implementation of what can be conventionally termed a TQM strategy. This is not a one-off programme, but a journey in which strategic planning gives the company the opportunity to plot, check and adjust its route.

## 5 A BUSINESS MODEL BASED ON TQM CONCEPTS

The proactive vision of the company represented in Fig. B.5 is the starting point for constuction of a model representing the company in relation to its missions and to the ways those missions are achieved (Fig. B.6); conceptually speaking, this model is similar to that used by the European Quality Award.

A detailed description of the left side of the model – the 'systemic factors' block – is not provided here, since the focus is on the right side of the model, the company's missions and goals. It should be noted that processes form a separate category and are not part of the systemic factors area.

As a global, integrated representation of the company's aims, which permits a unified vision of its missions and goals, Fig. B.5 provides the conceptual basis for the model in Fig. B.6. The right side of the model corresponds exactly to the external rings of the circle diagram. The left and central parts of the model are a description, from the TQM perspective, of the inner circles of Fig. B.5: the integrated company management system.

The left side of the model shows critical systemic factors in relation to the missions and goals on the right side. There are no 'one-to-one' correspondences between the factors on the left and the customer or stakeholder categories on the right. In fact, the correspondence is of a 'one-for-all' type, since each factor on the left will have an impact on all the goals on the right. The central part of the model represents a process-based rather than functions-based view of the company. Regardless of the function to which they refer (or functions, in the case of cross-functional processes), the processes are of interest in terms of their link with the result they generate on the right.

The model in Fig. B.6 therefore represents both the company's purposes

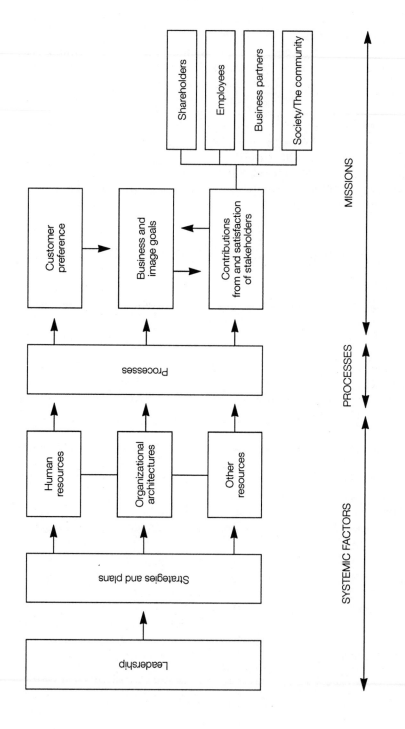

**Fig. B.6** The model.

and the ways in which the company pursues its goals. In short, it represents a *systemic, process-based* vision of the company.

This model is referred to as a 'business model' because it focuses on the company's fundamental purposes. A model showing results on the right can be used for awards and also for the executive phase of self-assessment. It is not appropriate during planning, however, nor is it sufficient when preparing for self-assessment, which has to focus on the plan's goals, especially its strategic goals.

The model in Fig. B.6 is a general model, with no weights. Each company will construct its own model, personalizing the block structure, alloting weights and analysing the contents of each block in detail. Specifically, it will:

- establish its own *specific* customer/stakeholder typologies;
- ensure that the weights of the various customer/stakeholders reflect the company's 'remuneration' policy in relation to the specific contribution each group makes to results.

If the model is not personalized, self-assessment remains an abstract exercise, detached from the reality of the company.

## 6 STRATEGIC IMPROVEMENT PLANNING

Improvement planning is the cornerstone of a TQM strategy. It must be an integral part of strategic business planning (Fig. B.7) because it has to address any limitations that might prevent the company from achieving its goals; and, even more important, it has to stimulate the company to set challenging goals. Only then will improvement planning acquire a strategic dimension.

Narrow interpretations of TQM still regard product quality and customer satisfaction as the main objects of improvement planning. Broader interpretations, informed by the awards, extend planning to include people satisfaction and society satisfaction. Figure B.7 represents a more global view. Strategic improvement planning is an appendix of the strategic business planning process, whose task is to identify and help remove the obstacles that could prevent the company from achiving its performance improvement targets, in any business area. It takes the improvement goals the company hopes to achieve and validates them. For this purpose, it uses the tools that were applied to market products/services in the old quality era: tools designed to identify weaknesses and analyse the underlying causes. As Fig. B.7 suggests, today these tools can be used together with more modern, sophisticated instruments for any sort of performance improvement formulated during business planning: higher market share, reduction of costs, reduction of time-to-market, etc. They

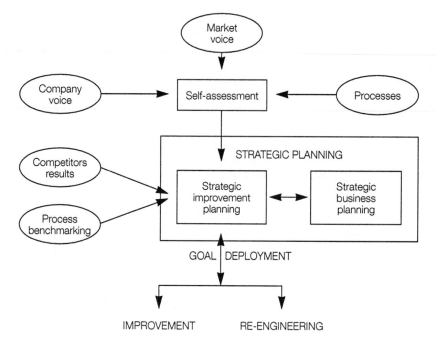

**Fig. B.7** Self-assessment and strategic improvement planning as integral parts of the company planning cycle.

are applied to the weaknesses the company wishes to overcome and to the strengths it wants to consolidate.

In short, business planning identifies the performance improvements needed to enable the company to pursue its strategic goals; improvement planning assesses their feasibility and validates them. Its main input is *self-assessment/self-diagnosis* (Fig. B.7), which verifies the current situation and current capabilities in the targeted improvement areas and identifies the causes of any weaknesses that represent a potential obstacle.

Self-assessment should highlight the weaknesses of the results in the various customer/stakeholder categories; if the self-assessment is diagnostic (i.e., a right–left procedure that moves back along the processes, Fig. B.8), then the causes of the problems should also emerge.

Self-assessment stimulates the company to clarify its global strategy in relation to its customers/stakeholders, if it has not already done so. In fact, it is impossible to assess results if goals have not been defined. As noted earlier, satisfaction targets are unilateral only in relation to customers in the strict sense of the word, who are free to change supplier if they are dissatisfied. For all other customer categories, and above all stakeholder categories, goals are two-way. Self-assessment should therefore investigate

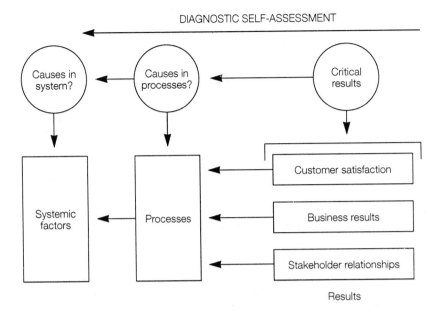

**Fig. B.8** Right–left diagnostic self-assessment.

the degree to which the expectations of both parties are satisfied, although the company will always bear the greater responsibility since it is globally responsible for the company system and its results.

During the planning phase that follows self-assessment (combined if necessary with benchmarking against other companies) the company will define – or review – its satisfaction goals for its customer/stakeholder expectations, in the context of its global corporate strategies. For example, the company may decide to redirect benefits towards specific customer groups whose loyalty it wishes to enhance; to examine new ways of motivating/gratifying its employees when change is particularly stressful; to invest in an integrity-based strategy so as to improve the company's image, and so on.

The output of the strategic improvement planning process is goal deployment. By transferring goals from the top of the company downwards, goal deployment completes the catch-ball process (not described here) that takes place among the various levels during the validation and goal-planning phase. Goal deployment transfers to the corporate processes the improvements the company intends to achieve in its results, and can generate process improvement or process re-engineering initiatives (Fig. B.7), depending on the state of current process capabilities in relation to the level of improvement planned.

## 7 CONCLUSION

Representing the company in relation to a multiplicity of missions for the complete range of customer/stakeholder categories is useful for the introduction of an effective TQM strategy: in other words, for the extension of the customer satisfaction and continuous improvement criteria to the company's activities as a whole. The proactive view of customer/stakeholder relations paves the way for a strategy geared to improving market competitiveness, enhancing customer retention and stakeholder loyalty and strengthening the ability to generate value. This strategy can be called TQM, or it can be given a name that makes no reference to quality; whatever the case, it is an extrapolation to the company system of the approaches and techniques successfully implemented in the 'sub-system' that generates satisfaction among customers in the strict sense of the word. By addressing the weaknesses that could prevent the company from achieving its strategic business objectives, improvement planning based on self-assessment constitutes the most crucial phase in this strategy, which is completed with a process-based view of the company and a process-based management approach.

# References

1. Arter, D.R. (1989) *Quality Audit for Improved Performance*, ASQC Quality Press, Milwaukee, WI.
2. Juran, J.M. (1982) *Management of Quality*, copyright J.M. Juran, New York.
3. Conti, T. (1983) *Building Total Quality*, Chapman & Hall, London.
4. Kast, F.E. and Rosenzweig, J.E. (1985) *Organization and Management. A System and Contingency Approach*, McGraw-Hill, Singapore.
5. Nadler, D.A., Gerstein, M.S., Shaw B.R. *et al.* (1992) *Organizational Architecture*, Jossey-Bass, San Francisco, CA.
6. Conti, T. (1994) Time for a critical review on quality self-assessment. *Proceedings of the First European Forum on Quality Self-Assessment*, EOQ, Bern.
7. Conti, T. (1995) Improving the model. *European Quality*, European Quality Award Special Issue.
8. Imai, M. (1986) *Keizen – The Key to Japan's Competitive Success*, ASQC Quality Press, Milwaukee, WI.
9. Hamel, G. and Prahalad C.K. (1994) *Competing for the Future*, Harvard Business School Press, Boston, MA.
10. Beer, M., Eisenstat, R.A. and Spector, B. (1990) *The Critical Path to Corporate Renewal*, Harvard Business School Press, Boston, MA.
11. Hersey, P. and Blanchard, K (1982) *Management of Organizational Behavior*, Prentice-Hall, Englewood Cliffs, NJ.
12. Juran, J.M. (1964) *Managerial Breakthrough*, McGraw-Hill, New York.
13. Goshal, S. and Bartlett, C.A. (1995) Changing the role of top management: beyond structure to processes. *Harvard Business Review*, January–February.
14. Ishikawa, K. (1976) *Guide to Quality Control*, Asian Productivity Organization, Tokyo.
15. Akao, Y. (1990) *Quality Function Deployment*, Productivity Press, Cambridge, MA.
16. Conti T. (1996) *GFP – Diagnosi Trasversale – Descrizione del programme e manuale d'utente* (in 1996, software and manuals available only in Italian).
17. King, B. (1989) *Hoshin Planning – The Developmental Approach*, GOAL/OQPC, Methuen, MA.
18. *The European Quality Award Application Brochure* (1995), European Foundation for Quality Management, Brussels.
19. Conti, T. (1994) Taking the Strategic View. *European Quality*, **1**(1).
20. Paine, L.S. (1994) Managing for Organizational Integrity. *Harvard Business Review*, March–April.

# Further reading

Bartlett, C.A. and Goshal, S. (1990) Matrix management: not a structure, a frame of mind. *Harvard Business Review*, July–August.

Bartlett, C.A. and Goshal, S. (1994) Changing the role of top management: beyond strategies to purposes. *Harvard Business Review*, November–December.

Bartlett, C.A. and Goshal, S. (1995) Changing the role of top management: beyond systems to people. *Harvard Business Review*, May–June.

Becker, S.W. and Golomski, W.A.J. (1995) The ethicism implicit in Total Quality Management. *39th EOQ Congress*, Lausanne.

Becker, S.W., Golomski, W.A.J. and Lory, D.C. (1994) TQM and organization of the firm: theoretical and empirical perspectives. *Quality Management Journal (ASQC)*, July.

Beer, M., Eisenstat, R.A. and Spector, B. (1990a) *The Critical Path to Corporate Renewal*, Harvard Business School Press, Boston, MA.

Beer, M., Eisenstat, R.A. and Spector, B. (1990b) Why change programs don't produce change. *Harvard Business Review*, November–December.

Bhide, A. (1994) How entrepreneurs craft strategies that work. *Harvard Business Review*, March–April.

Boaden, R.J. and Dale, B.G. (1994) A generic framework for managing quality improvement: theory and practice. *Quality Management Journal (ASQC)*, July.

Brassard, M. (1995) Creating required behaviors and skills for maximum creativity. *39th EOQ Congress*, Lausanne.

Brown, M.G. (1994) *Baldrige Award Winning Quality*, ASQC Quality Press, Milwaukee, WI.

Camp, R.C. (1989) *Benchmarking: The Search for Industry Best Practices that Lead to Superior Performance*, ASQC Quality Press, Milwaukee, WI.

Charan, R. (1991) How networks reshape organizations – for results. *Harvard Business Review*, September–October.

Cole, R. (1994) Reengineering the corporation: a review essay. *Quality Management Journal (ASQC)*, July.

Dahlgard, J.J., Kanji, G.K. and Kristensen, K. (1994) Aspects of leadership. *European Quality* 1 (2).

Davenport, T.H. (1993) *Process Innovation*, Harvard Business School Press, Boston, MA.

Farkas, C.M. and Wetlaufer, S. (1996) The way chief executive officers lead. *Harvard Business Review*, May–June.

Feigenbaum, A.V. (1983) *Total Quality Control*, McGraw-Hill, New York.

Feigenbaum, A.V. (1995) What total quality leadership means for a national economy. *The Best on Quality*, vol. 1, ASQC Quality Press, Milwaukee, WI.

Fuchs, E. and Wyndrum, R.W. Jr (1994) The quality metrics of the future. *38th EOQ Congress*, Lisbon.

Fuchs, E. and Wyndrum, R.W. Jr (1995) The role of leaders in TQM transformations. *39th EOQ Congress*, Lausanne.

Gallagher, W.M. (1994) Self-assessment using the European Quality Award model – lessons learned by assessors. *The First European Forum on Quality Self-Assessment*, Milan.

Garvin, D. (1993) Building a learning organization. *Harvard Business Review*, July–August.

Goshal, S. and Bartlett C.A. (1995) Changing the role of top management: beyond structures to processes. *Harvard Business Review*, January–February.

GOAL/QPC Research Committee (1989) *Hoshin Planning: A Planning System for Implementing Total Quality Management*, GOAL/QPC, Methuen, MA.

Godfrey, A.B. (1995) Beyond the basics revolutionary versus evolutionary rates of change. *39th EOQ Congress*, Lausanne.

Godfrey, A.B. and Myers, D.H. (1994) Self-assessment using the Malcolm Baldrige National Quality Award. *The First European Forum on Quality Self-Assessment*, Milan.

Golomski, W.A.J. (1995) What is Total Quality Management? *The Best on Quality*, vol. 6, ASQC Quality Press, Milwaukee, WI.

Hakes, C. (1994) *The Corporate Self-Assessment Handbook*, Chapman & Hall, London.

Harrington, H.J. (1995) *Total Improvement Management*, McGraw-Hill, New York.

Harris, T.G. (1993) The post-capitalist executive: an interview with Peter F. Drucker. *Harvard Business Review*, May–June.

Hayes, R.H. and Pisano, G.P. (1994) Beyond world class: the new manufacturing strategies. *Harvard Business Review*, January–February.

Hersey, P. and Blanchard, K. (1982) *Management of Organizational Behavior*, Prentice-Hall, Englewood Cliffs, NJ.

Hutchins, D. (1995) Hoshin Kanri – the force behind successful Total Quality programs. *39th EOQ Congress*, Lausanne.

Juran, J.M. (1989) *Juran on Leadership for Quality*, The Free Press, New York.

Juran, J.M. (1994) The upcoming century of quality. Address by J.M. Juran, *1994 ASQC Annual Quality Congress*, Las Vegas.

Juran, J.M. (1988) *Juran on Planning for Quality*, ASQC Quality Press, Milwaukee, WI.

Kano, N. (1995) ISO 9000, TQM and Quality Awards. *39th EOQ Congress*, Lausanne.

Kast, F.E. and Rosenzweig, J.E. (1985) *Organization and Management: A System and Contingency Approach*, McGraw-Hill, Singapore.

King, B. (1994) The future of quality: companywide creativity and innovation. *38th EOQ Congress*, Lisbon.

Kogure, M. (1995) Some fundamental problems on Hoshin Kanri in Japanese TQC. *The Best on Quality*, vol. 6, ASQC Quality Press, Milwaukee, WI.

Kondo, Y. (1993) Quality and human motivation. *European Quality Journal*, special showcase edition.

Kondo, Y. (1994) Creativity versus work standardization. *38th EOQ Congress*, Lisbon.

Kondo, Y. (1995a) *Companywide Quality Control*, 3A Corporation, Tokyo.

Kondo, Y. (1995b) Foster employees' ability. *39th EOQ Congress*, Lausanne.

Kotter, J.P. (1990) What leaders really do. *Harvard Business Review*, May–June.

Kotter, J.P. (1995) Leading change: why transformation efforts fail. *Harvard Business Review*, March–April.

Kume, H. (1995) TQM: the management improvement system. *39th EOQ Congress*, Lausanne.

Luther, D.B. (1995) Strategies for achieving Total Quality. *39th EOQ Congress*, Lausanne.

Mintzberg, H. (1979) *The Structuring of Organizations*, Prentice-Hall, Englewood Cliffs, NJ.

Mintzberg, H. (1994) The fall and rise of strategic planning. *Harvard Business Review*, January–February.

Nadler, D.A., Gerstein, M.S., Shaw, R.B. *et al.* (1992) *Organizational Architectures – Design for Changing Organizations*, Jossey-Bass, San Francisco, CA.

Naisbitt, J. (1982) *Megatrends*, Warner Books, New York.

Ohmae, K. (1988) Getting back to strategies. *Harvard Business Review*, November–December.

Pfeffer, J. (1996) *Competitive Advantage Through People*, Harvard Business School Press, Boston, MA.

Schaffer, R.H. (1992) Successful change programs begin with results. *Harvard Business Review*, January–February.

Seghezzi, H.D. (ed.) (1992) *Top Management and Quality*, Carl Hanser Verlag, Munich.

Seghezzi, H.D. (1995) The integration of quality into Total Management. *39th EOQ Congress*, Lausanne.

Senge, P.M. (1990) *The Fifth Discipline*, Doubleday

Shapiro, B.P. (1988) What the hell is 'market oriented'? *Harvard Business Review*, November–December.

Steeples, M.M. (1993) *The Corporate Guide to the Malcolm Baldrige National Quality Award*, revised edition, ASQC Quality Press, Milwaukee, WI.

Strebel, P. (1996) Why do employees resist change? *Harvard Business Review*, May–June.

Tichy, N.M. and Charan, R. (1995) The CEO as coach: an interview with Allied Signal's Lawrence A. Bossidy. *Harvard Business Review*, March–April.

Wheelwright, S.C. (1985) Competing through manufacturing. *Harvard Business Review*, January–February.

Womack, J.P., Jones, D.T. and Roos, D. (1990) *The Machine That Changed the World*, Rawson Ass., New York.

# Index

# Index to Appendix A